Using Moodle

Using Moodle

Teaching with the Popular Open Source
Course Management System

Jason Cole

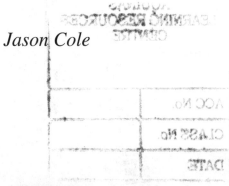

O'REILLY®
COMMUNITY PRESS

Beijing · Cambridge · Farnham · Köln · Paris · Sebastopol · Taipei · Tokyo

**Using Moodle: Teaching with the Popular
Open Source Course Management System**
by Jason Cole

Published by O'Reilly Media, Inc., 1005 Gravenstein Highway North, Sebastopol, CA 95472.

O'Reilly books may be purchased for educational, business, or sales promotional use. Online editions are also available for most titles (*safari.oreilly.com*). For more information, contact our corporate/institutional sales department: 800-998-9938 or *corporate@oreilly.com*.

Editor: Allen Noren

Production Editor: Matt Hutchinson

Cover Designer: Edie Freedman

Printing History:

July 2005:	First Edition.

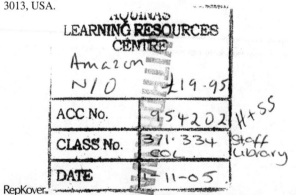

RepKover.
This book uses RepKover™, a durable and flexible lay-flat binding.

ISBN: 0-596-00863-5

[M]

Table of Contents

Preface

What Is Moodle?

Moodle is an open source course management system (CMS) used by universities, community colleges, K-12 schools, businesses, and even individual instructors to add web technology to their courses. Moodle is currently used by more than 2,000 educational organizations around the world to deliver online courses and to supplement traditional face-to-face courses. Moodle is available for free on the Web (*http://www.moodle.org*), so anyone can download and install it. More on that later in this chapter.

The name Moodle has two meanings. First, it's an acronym (what isn't these days) for Modular Object Oriented Developmental Learning Environment. Moodle is also a verb meaning "to let the mind or body wander and do something creative but without particular purpose."

Moodle was created by Martin Dougiamas, a computer scientist and educator, who spent time supporting a CMS at a University in Perth, Australia. He grew frustrated with the system and learned that engineers, not educators, had built it. He realized that a system built by someone who started with the educational process, rather than an engineering process, would be infinitely better than what he had to work with. He put his graduate degrees in education and computer science to work and started developing Moodle as an alternative. He now works on Moodle full-time. A community of dedicated open source developers from around the world works with him in a collaborative effort to make Moodle the best CMS available. He still lives in Australia with his wife, daughter, and son.

Who Is This Book For?

This book is for people who want to teach a course using Moodle. You can use Moodle to teach a course fully online or to supplement a face-to-face course taught in a traditional setting. It doesn't matter if you teach at a primary school, at a secondary school, in higher education, or in a corporate setting, the tools and features available in Moodle can be used to create an effective class.

Prerequisites – What Do You Need Before You Start?

To use this book, you will need the following before you start:

- Moodle installed and configured on a server

- A computer with Internet access

- A modern browser such as Internet Explorer 6, Netscape 7, Firefox 1

- Instructor access to a course on Moodle, or administrator access to the Moodle server.

Who Is This Guy?

Since we're going to be spending some time together, I'd better introduce myself. I've been working in the field of educational technology for 10 years. I've been a school district technology administrator, developed commercial web-based training, written supplemental CDs for inclusion with textbooks, and I even did a short stint at NASA. I'm currently an administrator/trainer/developer for a CMS at San Francisco State University. We're gradually converting our courses from Blackboard to Moodle.

I've spent a lot of time working with teachers to incorporate technology into their classes. I've seen what works, what doesn't, and some of the pitfalls to avoid.

I'm really an education geek. I love living at the intersection of technology and learning. There are so many new and exciting opportunities in this area that I can see myself doing this for at least another 10 years.

How to Use This Book

This book is written for instructors learning how to use Moodle. It's not just a how-to manual, however. Every chapter includes suggestions, case studies, and best practices for using Moodle effectively. Using Moodle won't make your course better by itself. Only by applying effective educational practices can you truly leverage the power of Moodle.

The Moodle interface is customizable by instructors and the system administrator. The descriptions and screenshots are of the default interface without any customization. If you have changed the order of the blocks in your course or the system administrator has changed the look and feel of the main interface, your system will look different from the screenshots here.

Chapter 1 discusses Moodle as a CMS and surveys its tools and features. We'll compare Moodle to the big commercial systems and see how it stacks up.

Chapter 2 gets us started using Moodle. We'll sign up for an account, review the basic interface, get used to some of the conventions, and start a course.

Chapters 3 through 12 cover individual tools in the basic Moodle package. We'll discuss how and why to upload content, use forums, give quizzes, peer review papers, give assignments, write journals, develop shared glossaries, create pathed lessons, collaboratively develop documents, and record student grades. Each chapter will cover how to add the tool to your course, discuss the options available, and give you some creative ideas for effectively using it in your class.

Chapter 13 delves into the management of your course, including adding and removing users, creating user groups, and backing up your course.

Chapter 14 covers Moodle's built-in survey functions for assessing your class.

Chapter 15 pools all the disparate tools into a comprehensive whole and will show some of the creative ways teachers have used Moodle.

Chapter 16 covers how to administer an entire Moodle site. A system administrator will usually handle these function, but if you're on your own, there's a lot of power behind the curtain.

You can use this book in a couple different ways. First, you can read it cover to cover. Hopefully, you'll find it so compelling that you won't be able to put it down until you've finished it. Or you can use it like a reference manual. The beginning of each tool chapter covers the how-to's and the options. If you get lost, flip to the appropriate chapter and take it from the beginning. If you're looking for inspiration, Chapters 3 and 14 and the end of each tool chapter should fuel the creative fire. Happy Moodling!

Acknowledgments

I am indebted to several people in the writing of this book: my wife Jeanne for her constant love and support; Allen Noren, my editor at O'Reilly, for suggesting I write a proposal on Moodle and for shepherding the book through from the beginning; Vicki Cassella for supporting my request for time off to write; Kevin Kelly and Albert Tong for filling in for me while I was gone; Josh Mindel, Sameer Verma, and the members of the Moodle Documentation project who provided feedback on drafts of the book.

Any remaining errors in the book are entirely mine.

1

Introduction

If you teach, you've probably heard for years about the revolution the Internet would bring to teaching and learning. As with so many promises of revolution, the changes haven't materialized. Instead, a new suite of tools, called course management systems (CMSs), can be used to enhance your teaching by taking advantage of the Internet without replacing the need for a teacher.

What Is a Course Management System?

CMSs are web applications, meaning they run on a server and are accessed by using a web browser. The server is usually located in your university or department, but it can be anywhere in the world. You and your students can access the system from anywhere with an Internet connection.

At their most basic, CMSs give educators tools to create a course web site and provide access control so only enrolled students can view it. Aside from access control, CMSs offer a wide variety of tools that can make your course more effective. They provide an easy way to upload and share materials, hold online discussions and chats, give quizzes and surveys, gather and review assignments, and record grades. Let's take a quick look at each of these features and how they might be useful:

Uploading and sharing materials

Most CMSs provide tools to easily publish content. Instead of using an HTML editor and then sending your documents to a server via FTP, you simply use a web form to store your syllabus on the server. Many instructors upload their syllabus, lecture notes, reading assignments, and articles for students to access whenever they want.

Forums and chats

Online forums and chats provide a means of communication outside of classroom meetings. Forums give your students more time to generate their responses and can lead to more thoughtful discussions. Chats, on the other hand, give you a way to quickly and easily communicate with remote students. They can be used for everything from course announcements to entire lectures. I know one professor who, unable to speak due to throat surgery, held his entire class using online chats and readings. Student workgroups can use online discussions for class projects.

Quizzes and surveys

Online quizzes and surveys can be graded instantaneously. They are a great tool for giving students rapid feedback on their performance and for gauging their comprehension of materials. Many publishers now provide banks of test questions tied to book chapters. A professor teaching a marketing class at San Francisco State uses weekly mini-tests to keep students engaged with the lectures and reading. He then uses proctored online testing to give the final exam using the same question banks.

Gathering and reviewing assignments

Tracking student assignments is an annoying and bulky task. Online assignment submissions are an easy way to track and grade student assignments. Also, research indicates that using an online environment for anonymous student peer reviews of each other's work increases student motivation and performance. One of my colleagues teaches a course where students review each other's written work at every stage of the writing process.

Recording grades

An online grade book can give your students up-to-date information about their performance in your course. Online grades can also help you comply with new privacy rules that prohibit posting grades with personal identifiers in public places. CMS grade books allow students to see only their own grades, never another student's. You can also download the grades into Excel for advanced calculations.

While you could find or write programs to do all of these things on your own site, a CMS combines all of these features into one integrated package. Once you've learned how to use a CMS, you'll be free to concentrate on teaching and learning instead of writing and maintaining your own software.

Over the past five years, CMS systems have matured rapidly and are now considered critical software for many colleges and universities. The CMS market is now a multimillion dollar market and is growing quickly. One of the biggest vendors, Blackboard, has recently gone public.

Why Should You Use a CMS?

Good question. After all, we've run classes for thousands of years without the use of computers and the Web. Chalk and talk is still the predominant method of delivering instruction. While traditional face-to-face meetings can still be effective, applying the tools listed above opens up new possibilities for learning that weren't possible just a few years ago. Currently, there is a lot of research into how to effectively combine online learning and face-to-face meetings in what are called "hybrid" courses.

Hybrid courses combine the best of both worlds. Imagine moving most of your content delivery to an online environment and saving your course time for discussion, questions, and problem solving. Many instructors have found they can save time and increase student learning by allowing students to engage the material outside of class. This allows them to use face-to-face time for troubleshooting.

Online discussions give many students the opportunity to express themselves in ways they couldn't in a regular class. Many students are reluctant to speak in class because of shyness, uncertainty, or language issues. The ability to take their time to compose questions and answers in an online discussion is a boon to many students, and instructors report much higher participation levels online than in class.

There are a number of other reasons to think about using a CMS in your courses:

Student demand.
> Students are becoming more technically savvy, and they want to get many of their course materials off the Web. Once online, they can access the latest information at any time and can make as many copies of the materials as they need. Having grown up with instant messaging and other Internet communication tools, online communication is second nature to many students.

Student schedules
> With rising tuitions, many students are working more hours to make ends meet while they are in school. About half of all students now work at least 20 hours a week to meet school expenses. With a CMS, they can communicate with you or their peers whenever their schedules permit. They can also take quizzes or read course material during their lunch break. Working students need flexible access to your course, and a CMS is a powerful way to give them what they need.

Better courses
> If used well, CMSs can make your classes more effective and efficient. By moving some parts of your course online, you can more effectively take advantage of scheduled face-to-face time to engage students' questions and ideas. For example, if you move your content delivery from an in-class lecture to an online document, you can then use lecture time to ask students about what they didn't understand. If you also use an online forum, you can bring the best ideas and questions from the forum

into your classroom. We'll discuss lots of strategies and case studies for effective practice throughout the book.

You probably heard all of this in the early 90s as well. So what's changed? Today, CMSs are more mature and easier to use than they've been at any time in the past. The underlying technology is becoming more robust, and programmers are writing good web applications. In the past, most systems were built as departmental or even personal projects and then commercialized. The two leading commercial packages, WebCT and Blackboard, both started out as small college projects and have since grown to be the market leaders.

However, market leadership does not automatically mean that a given application is the best, or most reliable, piece of software. In fact, the market leaders have struggled to manage their growth, and some would argue that product quality has suffered as a result.

What Makes Moodle Special?

Part of my day job is to administer a commercial CMS for a large university. I've been researching CMSs for a few years now, and I've become a huge fan of Moodle because it is open source, built on a sound educational philosophy, and has a huge community that supports and develops it. It can compete with the big commercial systems in terms of feature set and is easy to extend. Let's take a closer look at some of these advantages and why they are important to you and your institution.

Free and Open Source

The phrase "open source" has become a loaded term in some circles. For those who are outside of the techie culture, it's hard to understand what a weird and powerful idea this has become, and how it has forever changed the world of software development. The idea itself is simple; open-source simply means that users have access to the source code of the software. You can look under the hood, see how it works, tinker with it, or use parts of it in your own product.

So why is this important? For one, open source software is aligned with the academic community's values of freedom, peer review, and knowledge sharing. Just as anyone can download and use Moodle for free, users can also write new features, fix bugs, improve performance, or simply learn from looking at how other people solved a problem.

Secondly, unlike expensive proprietary CMSs that require hefty maintenance contracts, Moodle costs nothing to download and you can install it on as many servers as you want. No one can take it away from you, increase the license cost, or make you pay for upgrades. No one can force you to upgrade, adopt features you don't want, or tell you how many users you can have. They can't take the source code back from users, and if Martin decides to stop developing Moodle, there is a dedicated community of developers who will keep the project going.

Educational Philosophy

Martin's background in education led him to adopt social constructionism as a core theory behind Moodle. This is revolutionary, as most CMS systems have been built around tool sets, not pedagogy. I would call most commercial CMS systems tool-centered while Moodle is learning-centered.

Social constructionism is based on the idea that people learn best when they are engaged in a social process of constructing knowledge through the act of constructing an artifact for others. That's a packed sentence, so let's break it down a bit. The term "social process" indicates that learning is something we do in groups. From this point of view, learning is a process of negotiating meaning in a culture of shared artifacts and symbols. The process of negotiating meaning and utilizing shared artifacts is a process of constructing knowledge. We are not blank slates when we enter the learning process. We need to test new learning against our old beliefs and incorporate it into our existing knowledge structures. Part of the process of testing and negotiating involves creating artifacts and symbols for others to interact with. We create artifacts and in turn negotiate with others the meaning of those artifacts in terms of a shared culture of understanding.

So how does that relate to Moodle? The first indication is in the interface. While tool-centric CMS systems give you a list of tools as the interface, Moodle builds the tools into an interface that makes the learning task central. You can organize your Moodle course by week, by topic, or by a social arrangement. Additionally, while other CMSs support a content model that encourages instructors to upload a lot of static content, Moodle focuses on tools for discussion and sharing artifacts. So the focus isn't on delivering information, it's on sharing ideas and engaging in the construction of knowledge.

Moodle's design philosophy makes this a uniquely teacher-friendly package that represents the first generation of educational tools that are truly useful.

Community

Moodle has a very large, active community of people who are using the system and developing new features and enhancements. You can access this community at *http://www.moodle.org/* and enroll in the Using Moodle course. There you'll find people who are more than willing to help new users get up and running, troubleshoot, and effectively use Moodle. As of this writing, there are 4,000 people enrolled in the Moodle community and over 3,000 Moodle sites in 112 countries. The global community has also translated Moodle into 40 languages.

The Moodle community has been indispensable to the success of the system. With so many global users, there is always someone who can answer a question or give advice. At the same time, the Moodle developers and users work together to ensure quality, add new modules and features, and suggest new ideas for development. Martin and his core team are responsible for deciding what features are mature enough for official releases and where to go next. Because users are free to experiment, many people use and test new features, acting as a large quality control department.

These three advantages - open source, social constructivism, and community - make Moodle unique in the CMS space.

Feature Comparison

Moodle also stacks up well against the feature sets of the major commercial systems. I've been investigating alternatives to Blackboard and WebCT for over a year now, and I've been very concerned about feature compatibility between any alternative and the current systems. If instructors can't do what they've been able to do with their commercial system, they'll reject an open source alternative immediately. Moodle is the only open source system currently available that can compete with the big boys' features.

In fact, the educators in the developer community have given Moodle some features that the commercial vendors haven't even thought of. That's the advantage of an educator-driven, open source system versus a marketing-driven, for-profit system. In Table 1-1, I compare the features in the two leading commercial CMSs and Moodle.

Table 1-1. Feature comparison

Feature	Blackboard	WebCT	Moodle
Upload and share documents	Y	Y	Y
Create content online in HTML	N	Y	Y
Online Discussions	Y	Y	Y
Grade discussions / participation	N	Y	Y
Online Chat	Y	Y	Y
Student peer review	N	N	Y
Online Quizzes / Suveys	Y	Y	Y
Online Gradebook	Y	Y	Y
Student submission of documents	Y	Y	Y
Self-assessment of submission	N	N	Y
Student workgroups	Y	Y	Y
Lessons with paths	Y	Y	Y
Student Journals	N	N	Y
Embedded glossary	N	N	Y

You can see that Moodle already has all of the major features of the commercial systems, and a few that they don't. In the rest of the book, we'll discuss how you can use each of these features to enhance your teaching and provide your students with a powerful learning environment.

2

Moodle Basics

In this chapter, we'll cover the basics of the Moodle interface and some of the options you have when setting up your class. Then we'll start adding some content to your first Moodle class.

Getting Started

As I mentioned in Chapter 1, Moodle is a web-based tool you can access through a web browser. This means that in order to use Moodle you need a computer with a web browser installed and an Internet connection. You also need to have the web address (called a Uniform Resource Locator, or URL) of a server running Moodle. If your institution supports Moodle, it will have a server with Moodle up and running. You can

7

then get the server address from the system administrator. If you don't have access to a server with Moodle installed, and you'd like to set up your own, visit the Moodle website for instructions on setting up a Moodle server on any platform.

After you've gotten the URL, open your web browser and type the address in the address bar. You'll then be taken to the Moodle main screen.

The Moodle Interface

When you first visit your Moodle site, you'll see the main screen with the site news and the courses you are teaching or taking (see Figure 2-1).

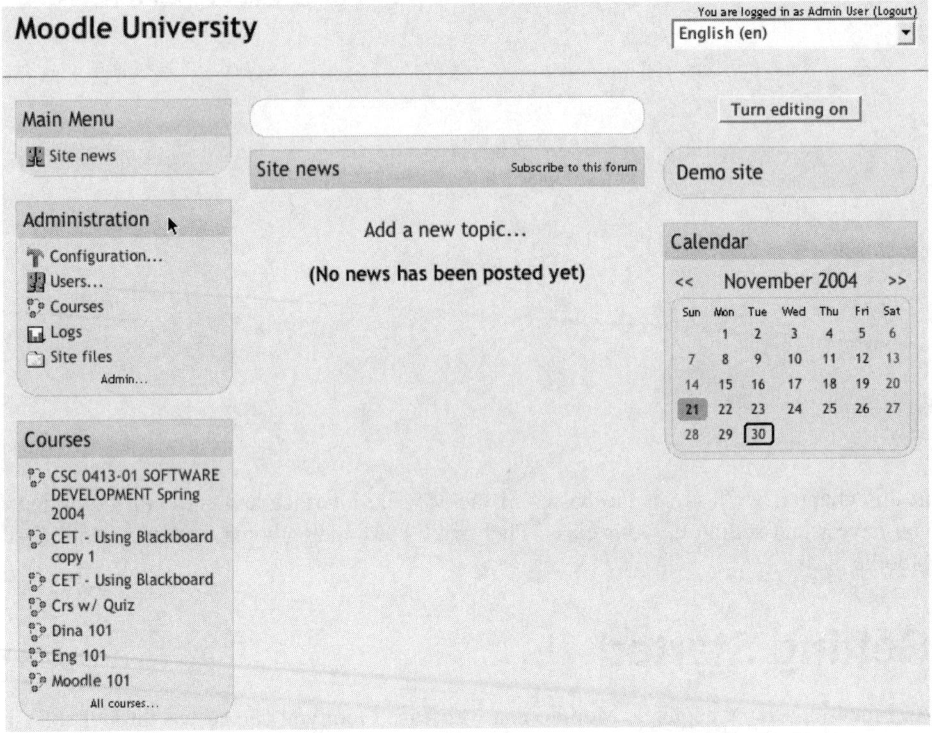

Figure 2-1. Moodle main screen

Take a moment and familiarize yourself with the interface. Moodle uses a number of interface conventions throughout the system. Frequently updated or important information is presented in the middle of the screen. On the lefthand side of the screen you'll see several "blocks" that list available courses and site news. Blocks are useful for holding all kinds of tools and content. I'll be using the block terminology throughout the rest of the book.

Languages

On the upper right, you'll see a dropdown menu with language options. As of August 2004, Moodle has been translated into 40 languages by the developer community. Anyone who uses Moodle, both students and teachers, can select the language in which Moodle's tabs and instructions will appear. For example, if I choose to view the site in Norwegian, the system labels will be translated into that language. However, Moodle does not translate user content. Any user-generated content remains in the language in which it was entered.

You can choose the language settings for the main site and for each course you visit. As an instructor, you can also force students to use a given language. This is a useful feature if you're teaching a language course and want the entire course to be in that language. Or you can simply confuse the heck out of your students by choosing some really obscure language and have them guess what everything means.

The system administrator can override this feature and force everyone to use the same language. If you cannot change the language for a course or for the Moodle main page, contact your system administrator and make sure he isn't forcing everyone to use one language.

Moodle's Help System

Throughout Moodle, you will see a question mark in a yellow circle. This is a link to Moodle's very extensive help system. Although you shouldn't need it very frequently after you read this book, the community has worked hard to provide you with a help system that is tied to what you are doing at that moment.

When you click the question mark icon, a new window pops up with the help entry for the item you are asking about (see Figure 2-2). After your read the help entry, you can close the window with the "Close this window" or look at other help files by clicking on the "Index of all help files" link. You can then select any help item from anywhere in the help system.

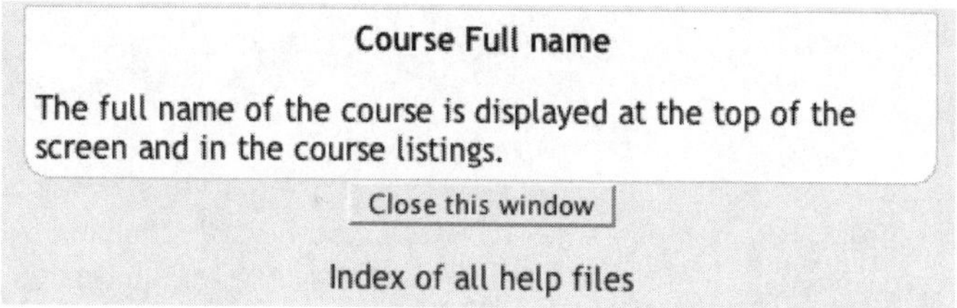

Course Full name

The full name of the course is displayed at the top of the screen and in the course listings.

Close this window

Index of all help files

Figure 2-2. A help screen

Creating an Account

Right above the language selection list, you'll find a hyperlink that says "Login." Click the link and Moodle will present you with the login screen, as shown in Figure 2-3. Your username and password will depend on how your system administrator set up the system. Moodle has a number of options for user authentication, including email authentication, or an LDAP (Lightweight Directory Access Protocol) server, or users can register their own accounts. Self-registration is the default method, and many sites use this.

If you need to create your own account:

1. Click the "Start now by creating a new account" button.

2. Fill in the new account form by creating a username and password for yourself (see Figure 2-4).

3. Enter a valid email address because the system will send you an email to confirm your account. You won't be able to log in again until you confirm your account.

4. Click "Create my new account."

5. Within a few minutes, you should receive an email at the account you specified on the form.

6. Click the link in the email (or copy and paste it into the address window in your browser) to confirm your account.

Returning to this web site?	Is this your first time here?

Login here using your username and password:
(Cookies must be enabled in your browser) (?)

Username: [   ]

Password: [   ]   Login

Some courses may allow guest access:

Login as a guest

Forgotten your username or password?

Send my details via email

Hi! For full access to courses you'll need to take a minute to create a new account for yourself on this web site. Each of the individual courses may also have a one-time "enrolment key", which you won't need until later. Here are the steps:

1. Fill out the New Account form with your details.
2. An email will be immediately sent to your email address.
3. Read your email, and click on the web link it contains.
4. Your account will be confirmed and you will be logged in.
5. Now, select the course you want to participate in.
6. If you are prompted for a "enrolment key" - use the one that your teacher has given you. This will "enrol" you in the course.
7. You can now access the full course. From now on you will only need to enter your personal username and password (in the form on this page) to log in and access any course you have enrolled in.

Start now by creating a new account!

Figure 2-3. Login screen

You now have a verified account. Your account isn't automatically associated with the courses you're teaching. You'll need to find out from your system administrator how to enroll your account as an instructor in a course. By default, the system administrator will have to enroll you as an instructor in a course.

Editing Your User Profile

Once you have successfully confirmed your account and logged in, you will find yourself back at the main page. As Figure 2-5 shows, your username will now be displayed at the top of the screen.

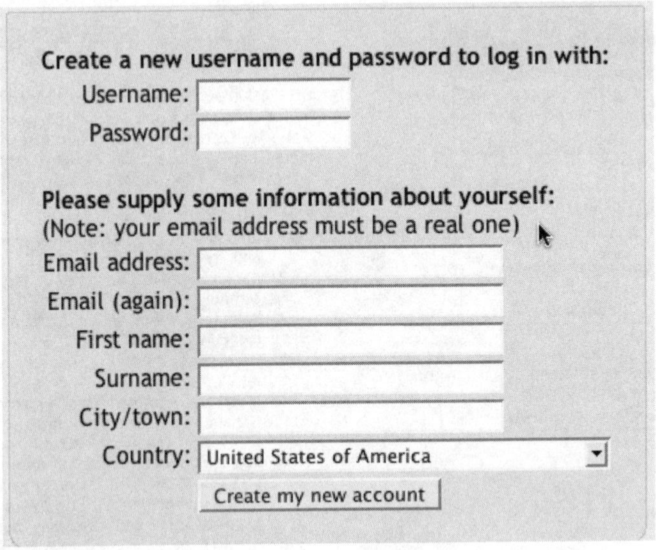

Create a new username and password to log in with:
Username: [   ]
Password: [   ]

Please supply some information about yourself:
(Note: your email address must be a real one)
Email address: [   ]
Email (again): [   ]
First name: [   ]
Surname: [   ]
City/town: [   ]
Country: [United States of America   ▼]
[Create my new account]

Figure 2-4. New account screen

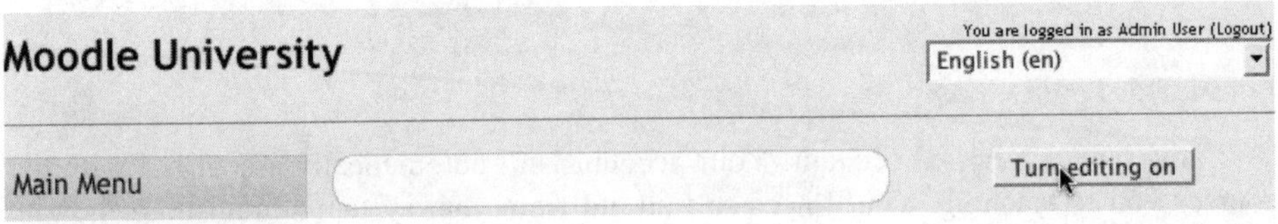

Moodle University

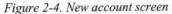

You are logged in as Admin User (Logout)
[English (en)   ▼]

Main Menu   [   ]   [Turn editing on]

Figure 2-5. Main screen after login

If you look at the upper-right corner, you'll see that the "Login" link has changed. It now reads "You are logged in as" and whatever your username is, highlighted as a clickable word. Click on your username.

Moodle will then present you with your user profile summary, like the one shown in Figure 2-6. You'll see your profile summary, and the last time you logged in. From this screen you can also edit your profile or change your password. Let's take a moment and edit your profile to customize the site and help other people get to know you.

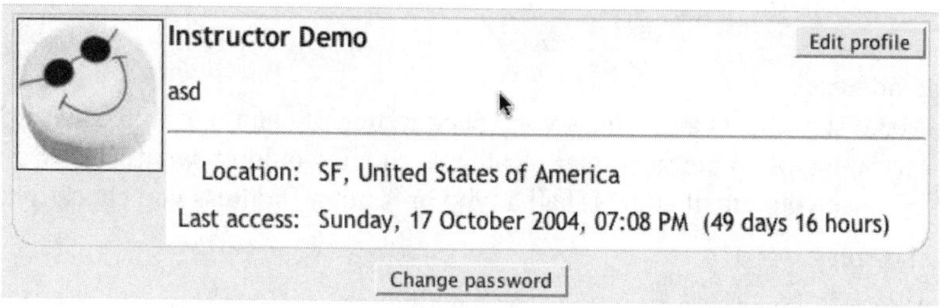

Figure 2-6. User profile page

To edit your user profile:

1. Start by click the Edit Profile button on the upper right hand side of the screen. Your user profile will look like Figure 2-7.

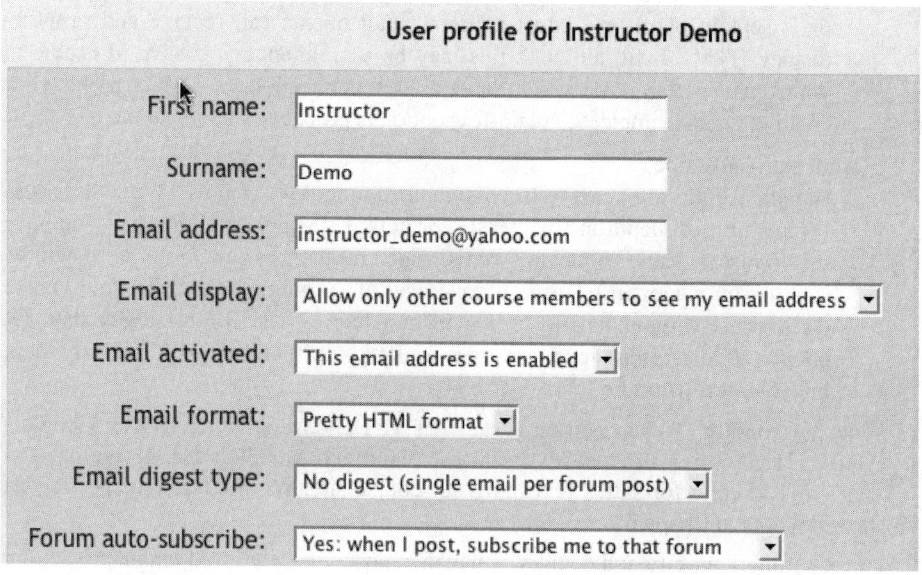

Figure 2-7. Editing your user profile

2. You'll see your username and a blank for your password. If you want to change either, do it here

3. You can then change the real name the system has stored for you.

4. The next four lines dictate how Moodle and other users can communicate with you through emails:

Email address

> Make sure this is an address you check frequently and that it is correct. Moodle has a lot of important email features, and I wouldn't want you to miss out because your email address had a typo or is not an address you check frequently.

Email display

> You can choose who can see your email address. Your choices are to hide your email from everyone, allow only the people in your classes to see it, or display it for everyone who logs in to the site. If you choose to hide your email from other people, they will not be able to send you email directly from Moodle.

Email format

> Here you can select whether mail sent from Moodle is formatted using HTML or is sent in plain text. Most modern email clients can receive and properly display HTML mail, although this may be a preference you have to enable in your email preferences. If you have a slow connection, or simply prefer your email plain and simple, the plain-text option is probably a good choice

Forum auto-subscribe

> Moodle forums are a powerful communication tool for classes. (We will discuss forums in great depth in Chapter 4. For now, I'll simply mention that you have the option of "subscribing" to forums, which means that new forum posts will be sent to you via email.) This is a great way of keeping current with your course discussions without having to log in and look at the forums every day. Of course, if your discussions really get cooking you'll end up with a lot of email, but at least it won't be spam.

5. The next option, "When editing text:," lets you choose whether to use Moodle's native HTML editor to enter text or to use plain text. Moodle's HTML editor is an easy way to enter formatted text into your course site. We'll cover the specifics of how it works in Chapter 3.

6. After setting your city and country, you can choose your preferred language. Setting your language here makes it your default language for all pages.

7. The timezone setting can be very important, especially if you're working with an international audience or will be traveling and accessing the system. Be sure to set the time zone to your local time, not the server's local time. I almost missed a meeting because I didn't set my time zone. The Moodle server we were using was in another country and I had left my profile setting on the default server's local time. The meeting was set for 11 p.m., which seemed odd to me. Then I realized I had the wrong time zone. When I changed the setting, I realized the meeting was scheduled for 8 a.m. my time!

8. The description box gives you a place to tell your Moodle community a little about yourself. If you don't feel comfortable writing a description, just put a couple of characters in here and the system won't complain.

9. The remaining optional fields allow you to include personal details about yourself, including your photo or a representative image, and contact information. Your picture will appear by your postings in the forums, in your profile, and in the course roster.

10. To upload a new picture, follow these steps:

    a) Prepare the picture you want to use by converting it to a gif or jpeg if you haven't already. It should be smaller than the maximum upload size (see Chapter 3 for more details).

    b) Click the Browse button and locate your prepared picture. Then click Choose in the dialogue box.

    c) Then click Update Profile at the bottom of the screen. Moodle will crop your picture into a square and shrink it to 100-by-100 pixels.

Moodle provides you with a number of ways to personalize your experience and share information about yourself with other people.

A First Look at a Course

On the left side of the main screen, you'll see a block that includes a list of all the courses you are teaching or taking as a student. You can access your courses by clicking on the course name in the block, as shown in Figure 2-8.

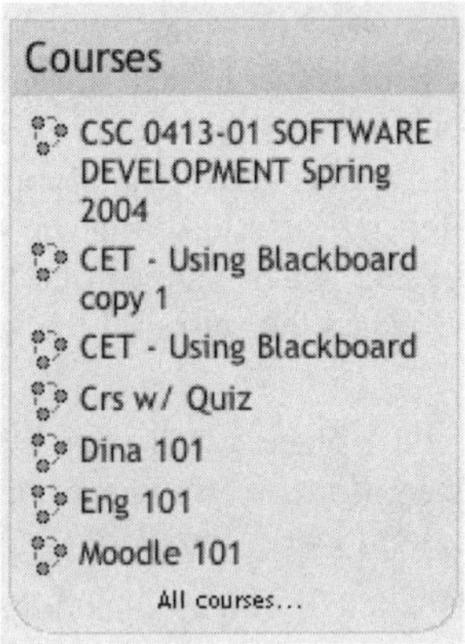

Courses

- CSC 0413-01 SOFTWARE DEVELOPMENT Spring 2004
- CET - Using Blackboard copy 1
- CET - Using Blackboard
- Crs w/ Quiz
- Dina 101
- Eng 101
- Moodle 101

All courses...

Figure 2-8. Main screen course list

Let's start with the upper lefthand corner of the course screen, as shown in Figure 2-9. There you'll see the name of your course as entered when the course was created. Either your system administrator entered your course name by hand or she got it from your institution's course database. (Read the "Course settings" section below if you need to change the name.)

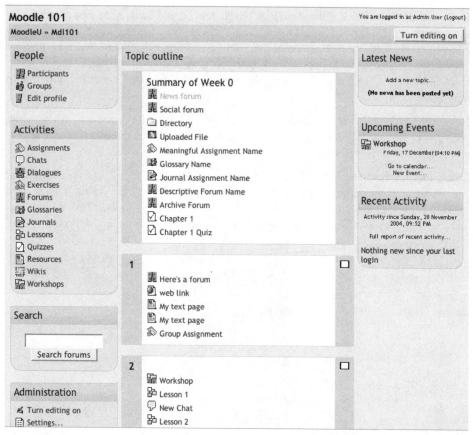

Figure 2-9. Course layout

Below the course name is a bar that fills with the hyperlinked names of pages as you navigate from one page to another. Also known as "breadcrumbs," these links track where you are in the course and allow you to easily to find your way back to where you started or to return to a page. Frequently, the best way to return to the course main page is to click on the course ID in the breadcrumb trail. For example, in Figure 2-9, you would click on Mdl101 to go back to the course main page from another page in the course.

Below the navigation bar are three columns, which are also shown in Figure 2-9. The far-left and far-right columns contain tool blocks, while the center block contains your course content and activities. The topmost tool block on the left is the People block. From here, you and your students can view the individual profiles of other participants in the course and check who is a member of student workgroups.

Beneath the People block is the Activities block. As you add forums, quizzes, workshops, assignments, and other activities to your course, the activity types will be listed here. By clicking on the activity type, students can view all of the activities of that type that are currently available to them. For example, if you gave a quiz every week, each content block would list a quiz, and all of the quizzes would also be listed under the quiz link in the Activities block.

Next in the column is the Search block. The single text-entry field currently allows only you or your students to search the forums. As I write this, a more general course search is currently under development.

Below the Search block is the Administration block (see Figure 2-10), from which you can set your course options, manage your roster, perform backups of the course, and manage student grades. In this chapter, we'll cover the first two tools, "Turn editing on" and "Settings," and we'll cover the rest in detail as they arise throughout the book.

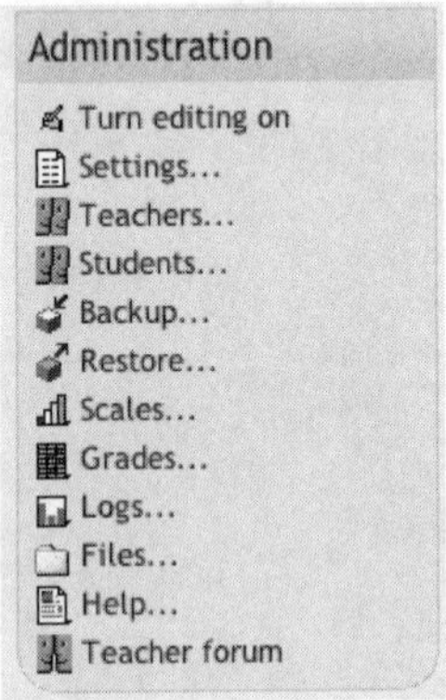

Figure 2-10. Administration block

The far-right column contains three blocks that report on activity in the course. The Latest News block lists the latest items added to the News forum, such as important news stories that pertain to the subject you're teaching. The Upcoming Events block lists events you've created in the calendar, such as exams and holidays. At the bottom of the block are links to view the calendar and add new events. Finally, there's the Recent Activity block, which lists the recent forum postings and uploads by you and your students.

The middle column is where the action is. This is where you add all of your content and activities, such as forums, quizzes, and lessons for students to access. Before we get to that, however, you need to make a choice about the format in which your course will be presented.

Course Formats

Unlike some CMSs that force you into one format, Moodle provides you with a number of options for the general format of your course. You can choose to order your course chronologically by week, conceptually by topic, or socially with a big forum as the central organizing principle.

Weekly format

> With this format, you specify a course start date and the number of weeks the course is to run. Moodle will create a section for each week of your course, as shown in Figure 2-11. You can add content, forums, quizzes, etc. in the section for each week. If you want all your students to work on the same materials at the same time, this would be a good format to choose.

Forums	Archive Forum	Recent Activity
Glossaries	Chapter 1	
Journals	Chapter 1 Quiz	Activity since Saturday, 4 December 2004, 10:45 AM
Lessons		
Quizzes	**1** 15 June - 21 June	Full report of recent activity...
Resources		Nothing new since your last login
Wikis	Here's a forum	
Workshops	web link	
	My text page	
Search	My text page	
	Group Assignment	
[Search forums]		
	2 22 June - 28 June	
Administration		
Turn editing on	Workshop	
Settings...	Lesson 1	
Teachers...	New Chat	
Students...	Lesson 2	
Backup...		
Restore...	**3** 29 June - 5 July	
Scales...		
Grades...		
Logs...		
Files...	OS in Higher Ed	
Help...	CNN	
Teacher forum	Wiki for essay 1	

Figure 2-11. A course in weekly format

Topics format

When you create a course using the topics format, you start by choosing the number of topics you will cover in your course. Moodle then creates a section for each topic, as shown in Figure 2-12. You can then add content, forums, quizzes, and other activities to each topic. If your course design is concept-oriented, and students will be working through a range of concepts but not necessarily according to a fixed schedule, this is a good choice.

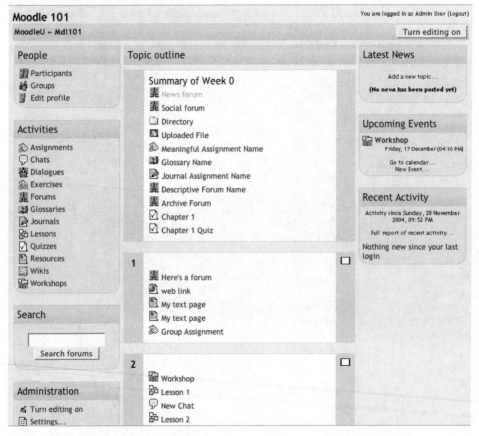

Figure 2-12. A course in topics format

Social format

The social format is based on a single forum for the whole course as shown in Figure 2-13. It's useful for less formal courses, or non-course uses, such as departmental sites.

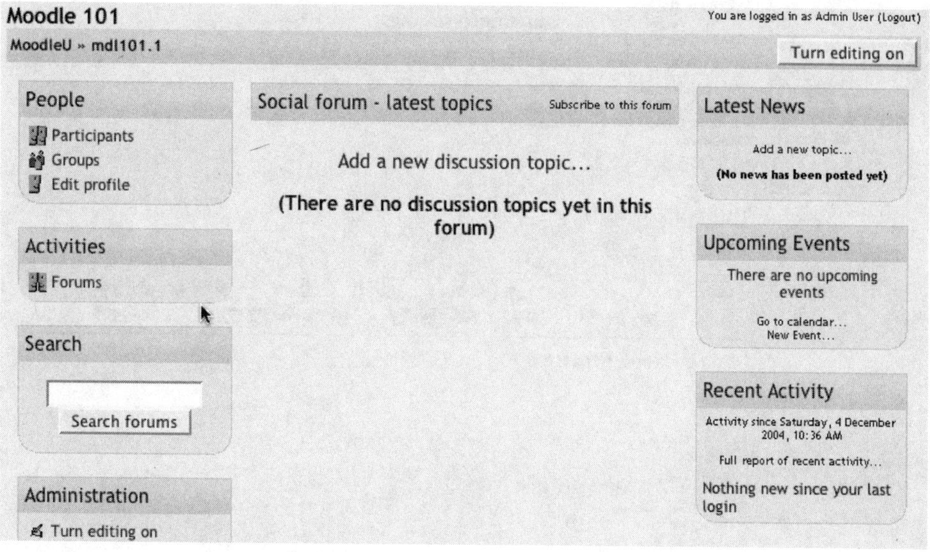

Figure 2-13. A course in social format

To set the course format:

1. Click Settings in the Administration block.

2. Select the course format from the dropdown list just below the course summary block (see Figure 2-14).

3. Enter the parameters for your course:

    a) For the weekly format, set the start date and the number of weeks.

    b) For the topic format, set the number of topics.

    c) For the social format, set the course start date. You don't need to worry about the number of weeks or topics.

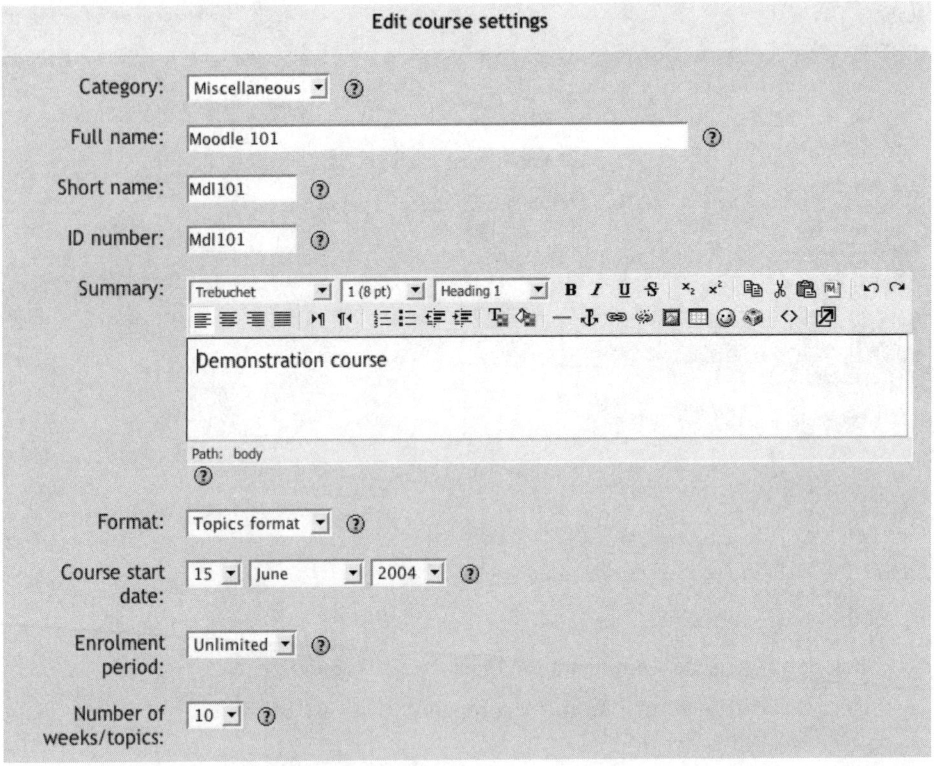

Figure 2-14. Course settings screen

Moodle allows you to switch between formats if you find that a given format isn't working for you. Simply follow the instructions above and select a different format. You can also add or remove topics or weeks at any time. So you don't have to worry too much about locking yourself into a format before you really understand the system.

Course settings

The settings area where you set the course format (see Figure 2-14) also gives you access to a number of important course options. You'll find it is important to take a moment to review the settings for your course to ensure that it behaves the way you want.

To change your course settings:

1. Click Settings in the Administration block.

2. Review each of the settings options to ensure they are correct for your course:

Category

Your system administrator may have created course categories, such as department or college labels, to help students and teachers find their courses. Depending on how your system is set up, you may be able to categorize your course by department, subject, or other organizational principle.

Full Name

This is the name that is displayed on the top header of every screen in your course. The name should be descriptive enough so students can easily identify the course in which they are working, but it shouldn't be too long. For example, use "English 400 – Beowulf" and not "ENG400 – Beowulf and the heroic poems of the ancient world."

Short Name

Enter the institutional shorthand for your course. Many students recognize Eng101, but not Introduction to Composition. The short name also appears in the breadcrumbs bar at the top of the screen.

Summary

The summary will appear in the course listings page when other users scan the course catalogs. A good one-paragraph summary will help communicate the essence of your course to your students.

Course Start Date

The start date is the day the course is first active.

Enrollment Period

The enrollment period is the number of days after the start of the course during which students *are* enrolled. After the enrollment period, all of your students will be unenrolled from the course.

Warning: Be very careful when using the enrollment period setting. When we first started using Moodle, we thought the enrollment period was how long a student had to enroll in a course, not how long she would stay enrolled. After 14 days, hundreds of students were suddenly unenrolled from their courses, causing headaches for weeks.

Group Mode

Moodle can create student workgroups. We will cover workgroups extensively in Chapter 13. For now, you need to decide if you want your groups to work independently or to be able to view each other's work. You can also set the group mode separately for many activities or force the group mode to be set at the course level. If everything in the course is done as part of a group, or you are running cohorts of students through a course at different times, you'll probably want to use the group mode to make management easier.

Availability

Use this setting to control student access to your course. You can make a course available or unavailable to students without affecting your own access. This is a good way to hide courses that aren't ready for public consumption or hide them at the end of the semester while you calculate your final grades.

Enrollment Key

A course enrollment key is a code each student enters when they attempt to enroll in a course. The key makes it more difficult for students who aren't officially in the class to gain access to your Moodle site. Create the key here and give it to your students when you want them to enroll in your Moodle course. They will need to use the key only once when they enroll.

Guest Access

You can choose to allow guests to access your course, either with an enrollment key or without it. Guests can only view your course and course materials; they can't post to the forums, take quizzes, or submit any materials.

Hidden Sections

When you hide an upcoming topic block to prevent your students from jumping ahead, you can choose to display the title as a collapsed section or simply hide the topic altogether. Displaying the collapsed sections will give your students a roadmap of the upcoming topics or weeks, so it's probably a good idea to leave this on the default setting.

News Items to Show

Use this setting to determine the number of course news items displayed on the default page.

Show Grades

This setting allows you to choose whether grades are displayed to students. If you are using the Moodle gradebook, I would recommend allowing students to view their grades. Checking grades has become one of the most popular features of CMS systems.

Show Activity Reports

This setting allows students to view their activity history in your course. This is useful if you want students to reflect on their level of participation, or if they are graded on participation.

Maximum Upload Size

This setting is used to limit the size of any documents you or your students upload to the class. The maximum size is set by your system administrator, but you can choose to limit students to files that are smaller than the system maximum. You can limit the amount of storage space each assignment can take or limit the size of picture or video files your students upload.

Your Word for Teacher/Teachers

> The next two settings allow you to enter the word you want Moodle to use for the singular and plural versions of the word that designates the teacher's role. You can call teachers instructors, facilitators, professors, etc.. Whatever you want to use, enter it here.

Your Word for Student/Students

> Again, you can choose the word you want Moodle to use for people in the student role, such as "participants" or "learners."

3. Once you've made all your selections, click Save Changes.

Editing Mode

Now that you've decided on a format and settings for your course, we'll look at how to add content to your course. To start the process, you'll first need to turn on *Editing Mode* (see Figure 2-15), which will allow you to add resources and activities to your course. On the left side of the screen of any course you are teaching, you'll see a link labeled, surprisingly enough, "Turn Editing Mode On." Clicking on this link will present you with a new array of options.

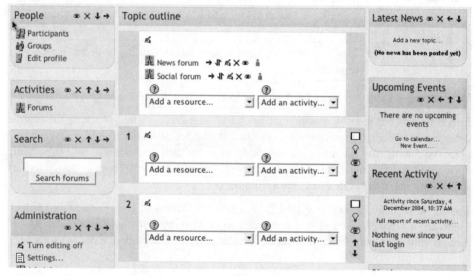

Figure 2-15. Editing mode

Starting at the top of the screen, let's look at what Editing Mode enables you to do. At the top of each block, you'll see an icon of a hand holding a pencil. When you click it, you are presented with a Summary text area. You can use this to label and summarize each topic or schedule blocks in your course. You should keep the summary to a sentence or two for each block to avoid making the main page too long. Click Submit when you've added your summary. You can go back and change it later by clicking the hand-and-pencil icon again.

On the lefthand side, next to the label for the People block, you'll see the icons described in Table 2-1.

Table 2-1: Block icons

Icon	Function
✖ ✖	Show or hide item. If you want to keep an item in your course, but don't want your students to see it, you can use this to hide it from them.
✗	Delete item. Removes the item or block from your course. Items will be permanently removed; blocks can be added again using the Blocks menu.
⇵	Move item. Clicking this will allow you to move an item to another topic or schedule block.
→ ←	Move right or left. You can move blocks to the left- or righthand columns. You can also use this to indent items in your content blocks
↑ ↓	Move up or down. Moves items and blocks up or down in their respective areas.

You will use these icons throughout Moodle to customize the interface for your needs.

In addition to the icons for manipulating the blocks, each content block in the middle column has two dropdown menus. On the left, the menu labeled "Add a resource..." gives you tools for adding static content, such as web pages and word-processing documents. On the right, the "Add an activity" menu gives you tools to add activities such as forums, quizzes, lessons, and assignments.

The resource menu, shown in Figure 2-16, gives you access to tools for adding content. There are a number of ways you can create content directly within Moodle, or link to content you've uploaded. We'll cover each of these tools in depth in the next chapter.

Compose a text page
> From here, you can create a simple page of text. It doesn't have many formatting options, but it is the simplest tool.

Compose a web page
> If you want more formatting options, you can compose a web page. If you selected to use the HTML editor in your personal profile, you can simply create a page as you

would using a word processor. Otherwise, you'll need to know some HTML for most formatting.

Link to a file or web site

If you want to upload your course documents in another format, you can save them on Moodle and provide easy access for your students. You can also easily create links to other web sites outside your Moodle course.

Display a directory

If you upload a lot of content, you may want to organize it in directories. Then you can display the contents of the entire folder instead of creating individual links to each item.

Insert a label

You can use labels to organize the links in your course's main page. The only thing they do is provide a label within the content block.

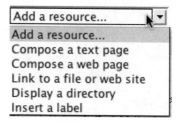

Figure 2-16. Resource menu

The Add Activity Menu, shown in Figure 2-17, allows you to add interactive tools to your course. The bulk of this book is dedicated to describing how each of these tools works and how to apply them in your course.

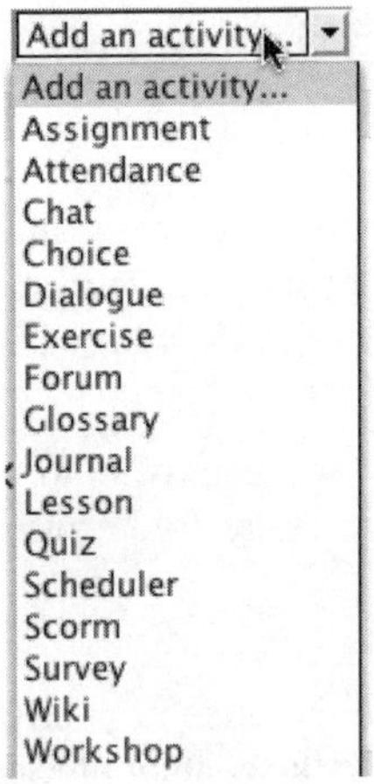

Figure 2-17. Add Activity menu

Table 2-2 explains each tool very briefly. We'll learn more about these tools as they arise later in the book.

Table 2-2: Activity types

Tool type	Description
Assignment	A basic task with which you can describe what you want the students to do or record a grade. You can also have the students upload a response and score it later.
Attendance	Used to manually or automatically track student participation in the class.
Chat	A group chat room where people can meet at the same time and send text messages.
Choice	A simple poll displayed within a content block.
Dialogue	Like a chat, but allows for one-to-one communication between students and teachers.
Exercise	A variant of the assignment tool with which you give students an exercise and they upload their work and then assess themselves. You can grade their work and their self-assessments.
Forum	Treaded discussion boards. They are a powerful communication tool.

Glossary	Dictionaries of terms that you can create for each week, topic, or course. You can have your students participate in building them.
Journal	Self-reflection is an important idea in social constructivism. Journals are free-response opportunities for students to reflect on the course materials.
Label	A way to insert text or other HTML elements into the content area.
Lesson	A set of ordered materials that use questions to determine what content the student sees next.
Quiz	A good, old-fashioned web quiz with a lot of flexibility.
Resource	A file, web page, link, or other content for students to view or download.
SCORM	SCORM is an acronym for Sharable Content Object Reference Model. It's a packaging standard for educational content. Moodle now has tools to allow you to upload content packaged as SCORM.
Survey	Gathers feedback from students using pre-packaged questionnaires.
Workshop	A very nice tool for student peer assessment. Students upload their work and score their peers' work using a scoring guide you create.

Adding Content to a Course

By now, you're probably wondering, "When the heck do I get to add stuff to my course?" I've provided a lot of background here so you'll understand some of the options you have. But now's the time to start building your course.

Let's start with a News item to announce to the world that your online materials are coming soon. The News forum is a special type of forum (for a full description of forums, see Chapter 4). The News forum is automatically created when the course is first generated. Everyone in the course can read the postings, and the news is automatically emailed to them. It's a good tool for making general announcements and sending reminders to students about upcoming assignments.

To add a news item:

1. Click News forum.

2. Click "Add a NewTopic." You'll see the screen to add a new topic such as the one shown in Figure 2-18.

3. Type your new message to your class.

4. Click Save Changes. You will now be back at the main News Page.

5. Click on your course name in the navigation bar at the top.

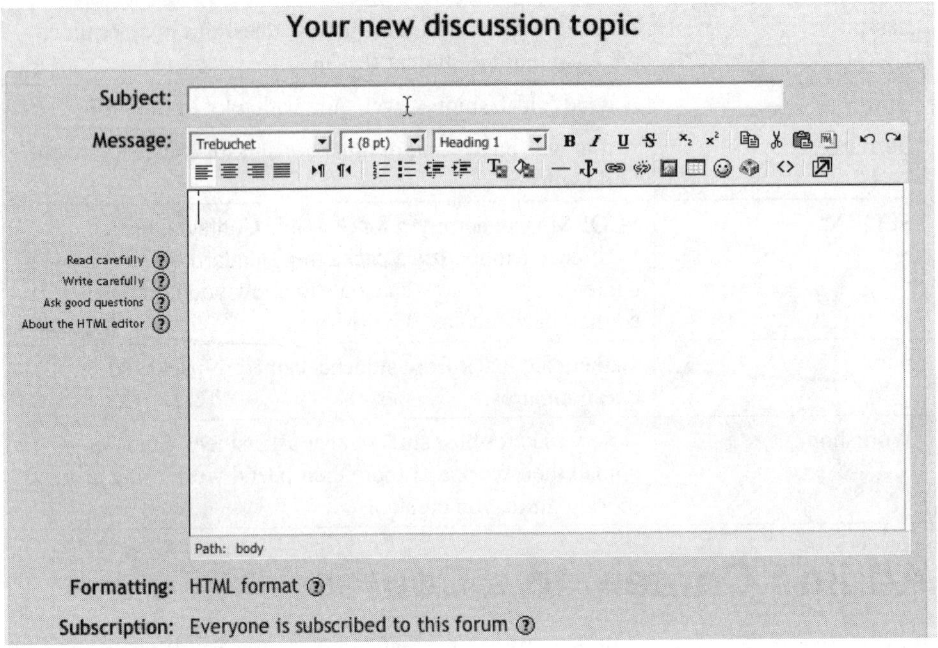

Figure 2-18. The News forum posting screen

Summary

In this chapter, we've looked at how to create your account and personalize your profile. We've become acquainted with Moodle's user interface and tools, and we got the format of your course set up the way you want it. In the next chapter, we'll start adding different types of content to your new Moodle course.

3

Creating and Managing Content

Adding Content to Moodle

The first thing most people want to do when they create a course in Moodle is add some content, such as syllabus or a course outline. As I explained in Chapter 2, you can add content to your course using the "Add a resource" menu in the content blocks of your course (see Figure 2-16). In this chapter, we'll use all of the tools in the resource menu. Chapters 4–12 will cover the tools in the "Add an activity" menu.

> *Tip: Remember that you need to turn Editing Mode on to see the "Add a resource" and "Add an activity" menus.*

The first two tools, "Compose a text page" and "Compose a web page," can be used to develop content directly in Moodle. The second two, "Link to a file or web site" and "Display a directory," are used to manage content developed in other programs, such as Word or PowerPoint. You can also add content from other web sites and take advantage of the rich library of information available on the Web.

Let's begin by creating a simple text page for your course.

Compose a Text Page

A text page is a simple plain-text page with little formatting, such as the example in Figure 3-1. You can add paragraphs and whitespace, but that's about it.

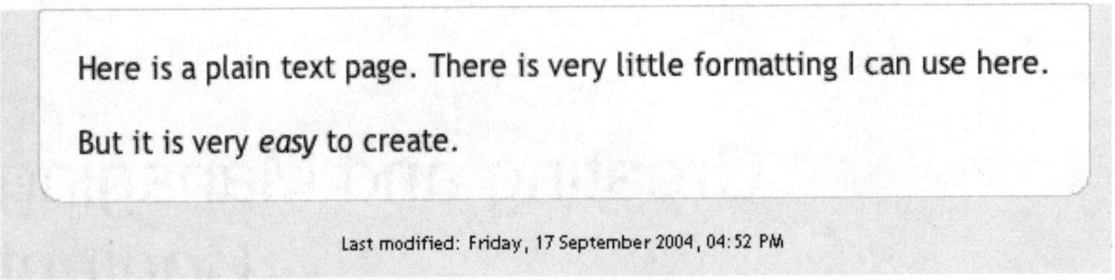

Here is a plain text page. There is very little formatting I can use here.

But it is very *easy* to create.

Last modified: Friday, 17 September 2004, 04:52 PM

Figure 3-1. A text page in Moodle

Text pages are very easy to create, however. To create one:

1. Turn Editing Mode on.
2. From the "Add a Resource" menu, select "Compose a text page." Moodle will then display the page to compose a text page like the one in Figure 3-2.

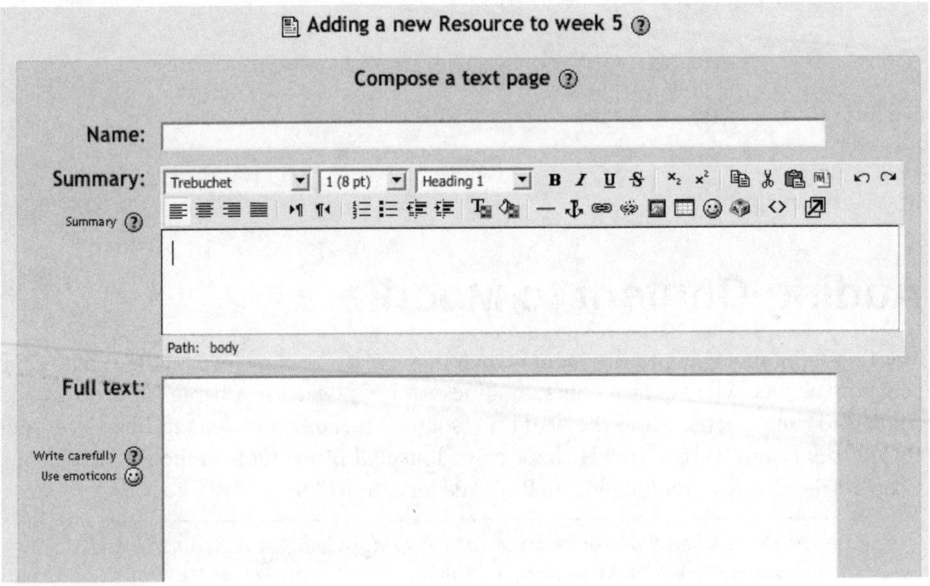

📄 **Adding a new Resource to week 5** ⑦

Compose a text page ⑦

Name:

Summary:
Summary ⑦

`Path:  body`

Full text:

Write carefully ⑦
Use emoticons ☺

Figure 3-2. Compose a text page

3. Enter a name for the text page.

> *Tip: The name you give the page will be displayed in the content block on the main page. Students will access your page by clicking on the name. Be sure to give the page a descriptive name so students will know what they are accessing.*

4. Write a summary of the page in the Summary field.

5. Add your text in the Full Text field. If you know some basic HTML tags, you could do some basic formatting in HTML.

6. Scroll down to the bottom of the page and click Save Changes

That's all there is to it.

Adding a Web Page

Adding a plain-text page to Moodle isn't the only way to add content. With Moodle, you can easily use an editor to create sophisticated documents which can be displayed in any web browser. The editor works like a word-processing application right in your browser, as you can see in Figure 3-3. Simply type your document directly into the text area and use the formatting tools to customize it.

Figure 3-3. HTML editor

Using the in-line HTML editor

> *Warning: The Moodle HTML editor doesn't work in all browsers. Currently, it works in Netscape 7, Internet Explorer 5.5 or later, Mozilla 1.7, and Firefox. It doesn't work in Safari, Camino, or Opera.*

To add content to a web page:

1. Click Turn Editing Mode On.

2. Select "Add Link to File or Web Page" from the "Add a resource" menu in the area where you would like to add the page.

3. Give the file a name and a summary. There's a good help file associated with the summary.

4. Create your document using the HTML editor.

5. Click Submit. Note on the next screen, you'll see a text area with the HTML editor (see Figure 3-3).

6. Type your document, format it, and click Submit.

The HTML editor provides the tools displayed in Table 3-1. Your students will be able to access your new content by clicking on the title in the Topic area where you created the document.

Table 3-1. HTML editor icons

Trebuchet ▼	Font
1 (8 pt) ▼	Font size
Heading 1 ▼	Style
B *I* <u>U</u> S̶	Bold, italic, underline, strikethrough
x₂ x²	Superscript or subscript
≡ ≡ ≡ ≡	Left, center, right, or full justify
≣ ≣ ⋹ ⋹	Number or bullet lists
T◨ ◈	Change text of background color
— ⬍ ∞ ⬩		Horizontal rules and anchors
▣	Images
▦	Tables
☺	Emoticons

Window Options

Any text pages or web pages you create, or web sites you link to, can be displayed in a new window. You can choose to open a new window to display any resource you created.

To display a resource in a new window:

1. Click Show Settings next to the Window label.

2. Select the New Window radio button.

3. Select the options for the window:

    Allow the window to be resized
        Checking this will allow the user to change the size of the window after it has opened. Unless you have a specific reason for not allowing the user to resize, you should leave this checked.

Allow the window to be scrolled
> You can prevent the user from scrolling the new window. Again, unless you have a specific reason to prevent the user from scrolling, leave this checked.

Show the directory links
> This will display the user's bookmark or favorites bar in her browser.

Show the location bar
> You can hide the address bar, and thus the site's URL, in the pop-up by unchecking this box.

Show the menu bar
> The menu bar is the browser menu that allows the user to set bookmarks, print, view the page source, and perform other browser functions.

Show the toolbar
> The browser toolbar has the back and forward buttons, as well as the reload and stop buttons.

Show the status bar
> The status bar is the lower area of the browser that shows how much of the page has loaded and the target of a link.

Default window width and height
> You can set the size of the new window to match the size of the linked page.

Create Link to File or Web Site

You don't have to create all of your content in Moodle. You can also upload and store any digital content that you have created in other applications. Documents you create in a word processor or presentation package can be shared with students in your course. You can also easily add links to other web sites to give your students access to important web resources.

Uploading Other Documents

Although it's easy to generate content directly in Moodle, you can also upload any type of electronic file you like. All you need to do is make sure your students can access it with the appropriate software on their computers.

Once you've added a file to your files area, you can easily add it as a resource for your students. There are two resource types you can use to add files. The first method is to add an "Uploaded File" resources (see Figure 3-4):

1. In Editing Mode, select "Add Link to File or Web Site" from the Resource menu from the content block where you want to add the link to the file.

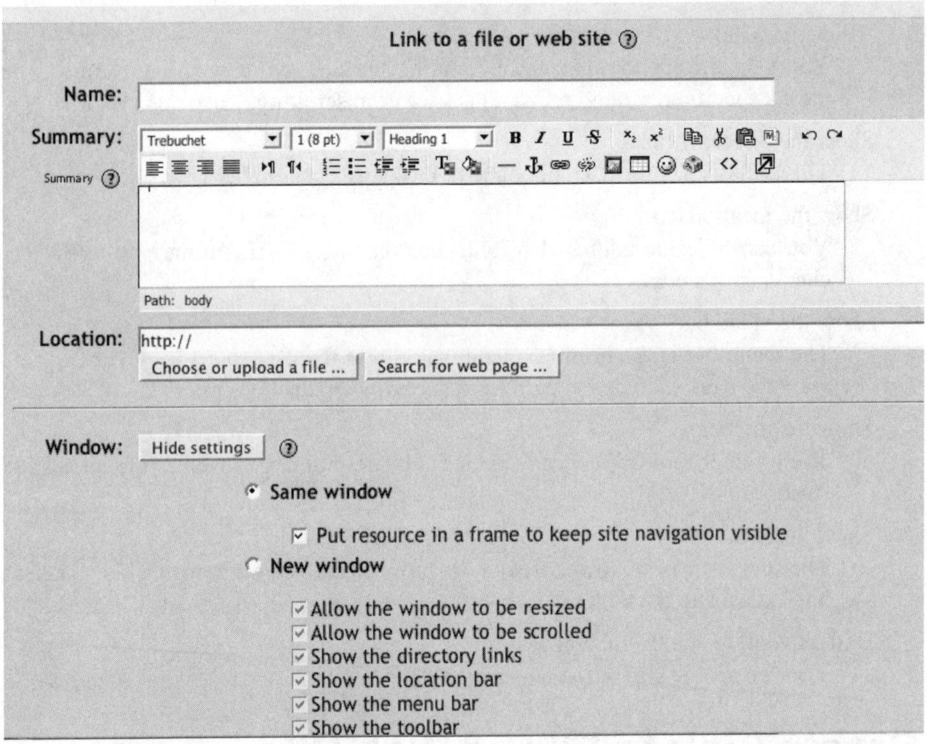

Link to a file or web site ⑦

Name: [   ]

Summary: [Trebuchet ▼] [1 (8 pt) ▼] [Heading 1 ▼] **B** *I* <u>U</u> S̶ x₂ x² ...

Summary ⑦   ≡ ≡ ≡ ≡ ¶ı ı¶ ⦂ ⦂ ⊒ ⊒ ... — ⚓ ∞ ⚓ ▣ ▢ ☺ ⬡ <> ▨

Path: body

Location: [http://   ]

[Choose or upload a file ...] [Search for web page ...]

Window: [Hide settings] ⑦

    ⦿ **Same window**

        ☑ Put resource in a frame to keep site navigation visible

    ◯ **New window**

        ☑ Allow the window to be resized
        ☑ Allow the window to be scrolled
        ☑ Show the directory links
        ☑ Show the location bar
        ☑ Show the menu bar
        ☑ Show the toolbar

Figure3-4. Adding a new resource

4. On the Edit page, click the "Choose or upload a file" button. A new window will pop up with the files area directory structure.

5. Find the file you want to add in the files area. You can also upload a new file here if you'd like .

6. On the right side of the files list, you will see a "Choose" link in bold (see Figure 3-5). Click that link. The Files window will close, and the path to the file will be entered into the filename.

7. You can choose to display the file in a new pop-up window. Most of the time, you won't need to worry about this with uploaded content.

8. The name of the resource will now be an active link in the content block.

Mdl101 -> Files			
Name	**Size**	**Modified**	**Action**
☐ 🗀 Folder	-	19 Sep 2004, 02:52 PM	Rename
☐ 🗀 backupdata	-	17 Oct 2004, 09:51 PM	Rename
☐ 🗀 glossary	-	21 Oct 2004, 12:07 PM	Rename
☐ 🗀 moddata	-	27 Oct 2004, 04:09 PM	Rename
☐ 🗀 presentation	-	6 Dec 2004, 10:07 AM	Rename
☐ 🗀 quizes	-	27 Oct 2004, 04:09 PM	Rename
☐ 🖼 DCP_1632.JPG	378.6Kb	28 Sep 2004, 11:45 AM	Choose Rename
☐ 🖼 Sample.jpg	9.7Kb	27 Oct 2004, 04:09 PM	**Choose** Rename
☐ 📦 backup-dina_101-20041027-0207.zip	2Mb	27 Oct 2004, 04:07 PM	**Choose** Unzip List Rename
☐ 📄 left_index.html	2.5Kb	6 Dec 2004, 10:26 AM	**Choose** Edit Rename
☐ 📄 main_pres.html	31Kb	6 Dec 2004, 10:26 AM	**Choose** Edit Rename
☐ 📦 new.zip	2.4Kb	8 Jul 2004, 08:12 PM	**Choose** Unzip List Rename
☐ 📄 presentation.html	183 bytes	6 Dec 2004, 10:26 AM	**Choose** Edit Rename
With chosen files... ▾		Make a folder	Upload a file

Figure 3-5. Choose file link

Adding a Directory

The other option for displaying files is to create a link to the entire files area or to a subset of the directory structure. To add a file directory:

1. In Editing Mode, select "Display a Directory" in the Resource menu from the content block where you want to add the link to the file.

2. On the Edit page (see Figure 3-6), select the folder you want the students to be able to browse. If you leave the default Main files directory selected, students will be able to browse the entire course files area.

3. When a student clicks on the resulting link, he will see a list of all the files in that folder, as shown in Figure 3-7. He will be able to browse any folders underneath it.

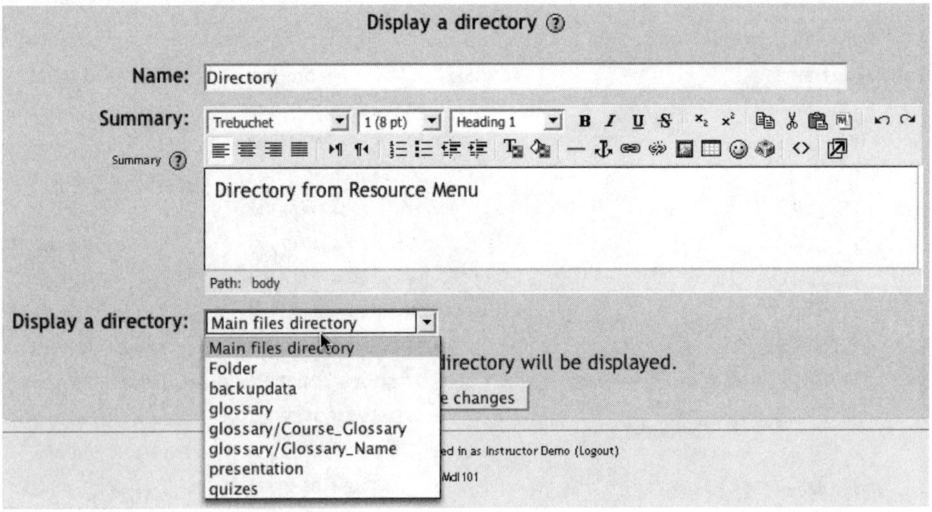

Figure 3-6. Display a directory

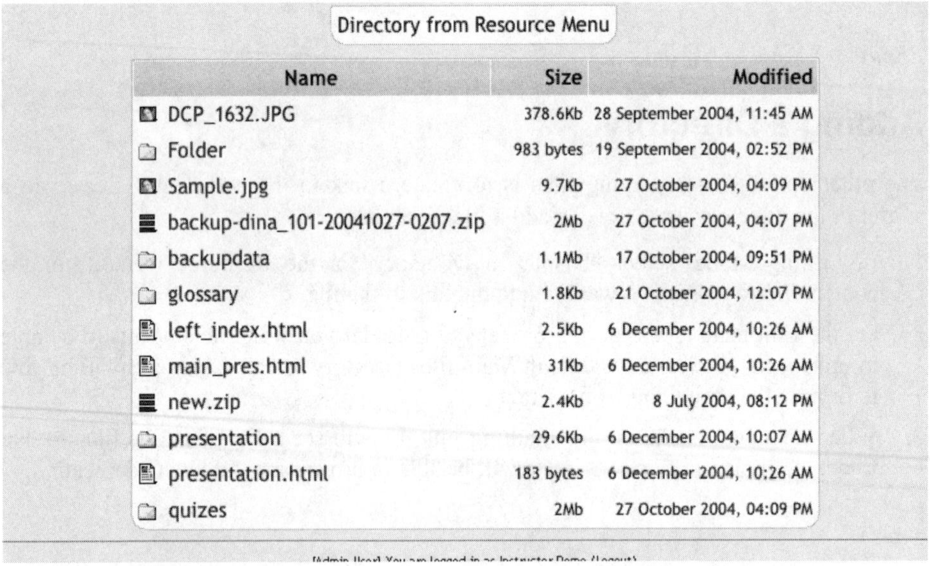

Figure 3-7. Viewing a directory

Creating Links to Other Web Sites

Creating links to other web sites is very similar to adding your own HTML. If the address of the page you want to link to isn't simple, such as *http://www.moodle.org/*, it's probably best to cut and paste it from the address bar of your web browser. That way, you're not typing a weird, long URL into the link text box.

To add a link to another web site:

1. Click Turn Editing Mode On.

2. Select "Link to a file or web site" from the Resource menu in a Topic or Schedule block.

3. Give the new link a name and Summary in the fields at the top of the screen, as shown in Figure 3-8.

4. In the location field, enter the address of the page you want to link to. If you want to look for the address, click the Search button, and Moodle will open a new window and take you to Google.

5. After you have selected the options you want, click Save Changes.

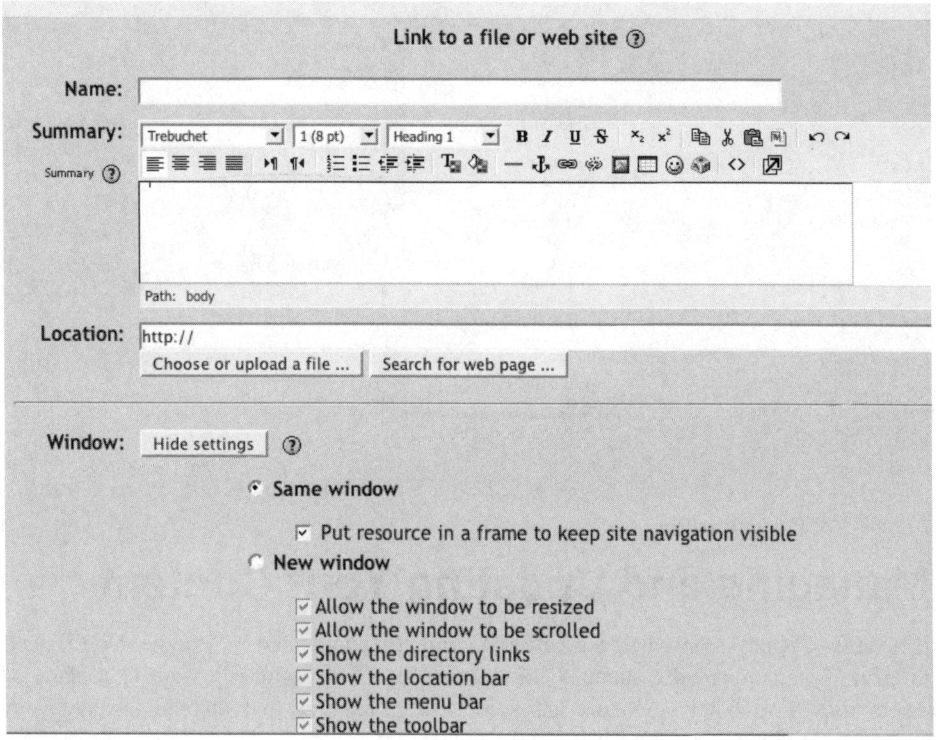

Figure 3-8. Adding a new web link

After you enter the link, you'll see the name of the resource listed in the content block. It is now an active link. If you've selected the window pop-up option, a new window will pop up when the user clicks the link.

Parameters

When you create a link to another web site, you can also easily send data about the student and the course to the receiving site. For example, if you want to create a link to another site in your university that use the same username as your Moodle site, you can send the student and the student's username to the other server. This makes it easier to utilize other dynamic web sites that share data with your Moodle site.

To send data to another server using parameters:

1. At the bottom of the link page, click the "Show settings" button next to the parameters.

2. Select the data you want to send from the list shown in Figure 3-9.

3. The variable name is the name of the variable that the receiving server is expecting. For example, if you're sending the student's username and the server wants a variable called userID, select username in the parameter list and put userID in the Variable name field.

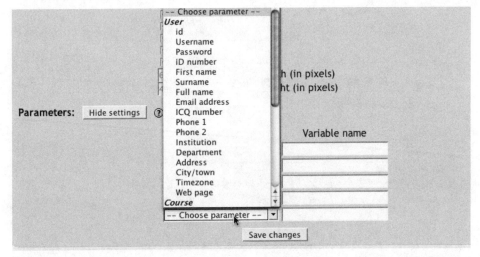

Figure 3-9. Parameter list

Managing and Updating Your Content

Uploading content is only half the battle of content management in Moodle. You'll need to ensure your uploaded content is current, and you'll occasionally want to replace or delete files. Fortunately, Moodle has some useful features to help you manage your content once it's on the server.

File Area Tools

Once you've uploaded your files, they are stored in the Files area. When you create a link to a file, you store the file in the Files area and create a link for your students to access it.

To access the Files area, click the Files link in the Administration block, as shown in Figure 3-10.

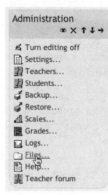

Figure 3-10. Files link in the Administration area

Each uploaded file and file folder has a checkbox beside it. You can select one or more files and then move or archive them using the tools in the dropdown menu on the lower-left side of the file list. By default, it reads "With chosen files...." If you click on the menu, you'll see three things you can do with your chosen files:

Move to another folder

To move uploaded content to another folder in the Files area:

1. Select the file(s) you want to move.

2. Select "Move to another folder."

3. Navigate to the folder where you want to move the selected files.

4. You'll see a new button at the bottom of the screen that says "Move Files here." Click the button, and the files will move to the new location.

Delete completely

This will remove all trace of the file from your Moodle site.

Create zip archive

A zip archive is a compressed file that holds the files you've selected. It's an easy way to create an archive of older files or create an easy-to-download collection of documents, such as all of the images for a lecture. Once the archive has been created and moved to the target computer, you'll need to unzip it to access the content inside. If you want students to download the archive, they will need an unzipping utility such as WinZip, MacZip, or Stuffit Expander to unpack the archive. Modern versions of Windows and Macintosh have built-in zip utilities. Moodle has a built-in zip utility as well that will allow you to unzip the archive directly into your files area. As Figure 3-11 shows,there are a few new options that come with a zip archive. The options include:

Unzip
>   This will unpack your archive into your files area.

List
>   Clicking this will display a list of files stored in the archive. You cannot access files through this list.

Restore
>   If you've backed up your Moodle class and uploaded the zip archive of the backup, you can restore your content using this command. We'll cover this in more detail in Chapter 13.

☐ left_index.html	2.5Kb	6 Dec 2004, 10:26 AM	Edit Rename
☐ main_pres.html	31Kb	6 Dec 2004, 10:26 AM	Edit Rename
☐ new.zip	2.4Kb	8 Jul 2004, 08:12 PM	Unzip List Restore Rename
☐ presentation.html	183 bytes	6 Dec 2004, 10:26 AM	Edit Rename

Figure 3-11. Zip file options

Tracking Versions

One of the biggest challenges you will face in keeping your content organized is dealing with versioning. As the semester progresses, you may have multiple versions of your syllabus which reflect changes to the calendar. Or you may have multiple versions of a presentation that has evolved over the years. There are a couple of strategies you can use to track versions and ensure that your students are accessing the correct version.

The easiest way is to develop a naming scheme for your files. While many people will attach a version number, I recommend using a date stamp. A date stamp lets people know just how recent the version is, and you don't have to track the current version number. To add a date stamp, simply add the date you saved the version to the end of the filename name. For example, the first version of a syllabus for your fall course may be called Syllabus_8_30.rtf. Later in the semester, you may post a revised version named Syllabus_9_21.rtf. Date versioning helps you keep track of the version on the server and the latest version on your computer.

There are also a number of tools in Moodle to help you deal with versioning. I recommend creating a folder in your course to archive older versions of documents. To create an archive folder:

1. Click on the Files link.

2. Click the Make a Folder button.

3. Name the folder Course Archives and click Save Changes.

Later, you can use the File tools to move old versions of a file into the archives area, which will enable you to keep a record of older versions while keeping only the latest version in the active area.

Effective Content Practices

There are a few effective practices that can make life easier for you and your students. First, there are file format tricks to ensure your students can download and use your content. Second, make sure the bit size of your files is as small as it can be so your students won't grow old waiting to download tomorrow's lecture notes. Third, there are creative ways to use static content in your courses to help you and your students succeed.

File Formats

Every file you create and save on your computer has a specific file format. For example, Word files are saved in Word format, and can be opened only in a compatible version of Word. However, this can cause problems if your students don't have the same version of Word you do. A solution is to continue to create your documents in Word but save them as Rich Text Format, or RTF, a format that can be opened by a wide variety of word processing programs. In most versions of Word, you can save a file as RTF by following these steps:

1. Select Save As… from the file menu.
2. Choose RTF from the file type dropdown.
3. Save the RTF copy of your document.

There are a number of file formats for displaying text and images that almost everyone can open, regardless of their computing platform, and you should strive to use these whenever possible. These formats include RTF, Hypertext Markup Language (HTML), Postscript Display Format (PDF), and picture formats, including pict, tiff, jpeg, gif, and png.

Table 3-2 describes some common file formats.

Table 3-2: File types

File type	Description	Software needed to use the file
RTF	A word-processor format that is readable by a wide range of applications. You can save Word and PowerPoint documents as RTF.	Most modern word processors will read RTF. In Windows, the free WordPad utility will open RTF. On Mac OS X, TextEdit will open these files.
HTML	The language of the Web. Every web page displayed in a browser is created in HTML. Moodle has a built-in HTML editor you can use to create documents directly in Moodle.	Any web browser. Some word processors will also read HTML documents.
PDF	Adobe has created a format that is very portable but can be difficult to create. If you have Acrobat (not the reader but the professional package) or are using Mac OS X, you can usually use the print function from within Word or other application to create a PDF	Acrobat Reader is a free download from Adobe.
PowerPoint (ppt)	As the most widely used presentation-creation software, PowerPoint files are natural candidates for upload. The presentations are easy to share, but be careful about file size and access.	PowerPoint or PowerPoint viewer. Some newer versions of PowerPoint allow you to generate a self-playing file (which tend to be big).
Pictures (pict, tiff, jpeg, gif, png)	There are a lot of graphic file formats. Generally, only gif, jpeg and png are viewable directly in a browser.	gif, jpeg, png require a browser. Other formats require appropriate external viewers.

Audio files (wav, mp3, ram, mov)	Audio files can be large, depending on your bit rate and compression format. Be sure the file size is smaller than the maximum file upload size for Moodle. Check with your system administrator.	Your students will need media player software. Many students will be able to play audio in mp3 format.
Video files (mov, wmv, rv)	Your Moodle server may not accept a large video file. Before you attempt to upload a large video file, ask your system administrator about file size limits. Your students will need to download the entire video, which may be a problem with a slow dial-up connection	To view a video, your students will need a media player that can play the appropriate format. Know whether your movies can play in Quicktime, Windows Media Player, or Real Player.

Reducing File Sizes

Equally important to creating files your students can open is getting them to a manageable size. Usually, graphics are the biggest offenders, and they crop up in some unlikely places. There are three strategies that will give you the best results for the effort.

Strategy 1: Save your PowerPoint presentations as RTF

In my experience, big PowerPoint files are the worst file size offenders. It's easy to add cool transitions, clip art, and images that will cause a simple hour-long presentation to balloon into a multi-megabyte behemoth that will take an hour to download. Not a good use of time for something that students will simply print out and bring to class.

I strongly recommend saving your slides as an RTF text outline. Students will get the benefits of the outline of the lecture and be able to use them to take notes, but the file will be quick and easy to download and viewable in a wide range of applications. Outline format is a text format. You'll lose all of your nifty transitions and the images in the presentation. But the advantages of a quick download and having an outline for note taking usually outweigh the lost information.

If you have important images or diagrams in the presentation, add them to your Moodle course separately. Students can then download them individually if they choose.

To save your PowerPoint as RTF:

1.   From the Files menu, select Save As.

2. In the Save As window, select Outline (Rich Text Format) from the Format menu.

3. Click Save to save your outline.

Strategy 2: Scan articles as text, not images

There are many good articles that just aren't available in electronic format. If you want to avoid printing an entire reader, scanning articles is an easy way to give your students access to important resources. Many libraries now have electronic reserve services that will scan them for you.

Scanning articles can result in very large files because most scanner software, by default, scans everything as a graphic. So when you scan a page, you're really creating a picture of the page that is much larger than a text version. The computer has to store information about every dot on the page, not just information about the characters and their placement on the page.

The solution is to use a software tool called Optical Character Recognition, or OCR. This great tool recognizes the shape of the letters and gives you a text version of the article. You can then manipulate the text version in the same way you'd edit any other text document. It has the added advantage of being accessible to screen readers for students with visual disabilities.

OCR software is probably available somewhere on your campus. OmniPage Pro is currently the most popular OCR package. It's come a long way in the last few years and is now very powerful. If you have a relatively clean photocopy of the articles you want to share, scanning them will be a very fast process.

Strategy 3: Reduce your image size and use compression

Finally, if you have digital images, it's very important to optimize their size and resolution for sharing over the Web. Modern digital cameras and scanners can produce amazing, crystal-cear images, but at a price of very large file sizes. A full resolution photograph in a modern camera can be 4 megabytes, which will take more than 5 minutes to download on a 56k modem.

Most cameras and scanners come with free utilities that enable you to manipulate images. Other programs such as Photoshop are fully featured, professional packages with lots of tools. To reduce your file size, you only need some very simple tools that most image-manipulation software provides.

The key to getting manageable images is to first reduce the size of the image. If your image will be primarily viewed on the screen, you can make it 72 dpi and it will still be viewable. If you plan to have your students print the image, then it will need to be higher resolution. Experiment with some different sizes and resolutions to get a result you're happy with.

When your image is the right size, save it at the minimum quality as a web-compatible format such as jpeg or gif. These formats will make your file size even smaller by eliminating unnecessary and redundant data.

By reducing the size of your files, you'll make life easier for yourself and your students. But the smallest, most portable files in the world don't mean much if your students can't use them successfully in your class. Next, we'll discuss some interesting ways you can use content to make your Moodle class a valuable resource for your students.

Creative Content

Moodle allows you to upload just about any file that resides on your computer. However, the key to a successful content strategy is knowing what content helps your students be successful, and what content is unnecessary or confusing. Below are two best practices for adding content to your course. These practices work well in a range of course designs, but there are other practices that might work just as well for your particular course.

Uploading lecture notes

One of the easiest ways to use Moodle to increase student learning is to upload your lecture notes before the lecture. Providing access to your lecture outlines *before* a class meeting gives your students a tool to prepare for class and structure their class notes. If students know which topics you consider important enough to include in your lecture, they are more likely to pay attention to those areas in any assigned readings. During class, they can use the lecture notes as a base outline and concentrate on elaborating the main ideas with examples. Lecture notes are also a useful tool for students whose first language is different from that of the speaker. If they get lost during a lecture, they can refer to the notes to get back on track.

If you use PowerPoint in your lectures, a simple way to create and upload lecture notes is to save your slides as an RTF file. This will eliminate graphics and other extras and provide the students with a plain-text outline. It will be easy to download and print for class.

External web sites

Effectively using the Web means you don't have to create or photocopy everything you want to use in your class. There is a lot of quality content available on the Web, if you know where to look and how to evaluate it. A full discussion about vetting online resources is beyond the scope of this book, but your institution's librarian can recommend some sources to get your started.

Most newspapers and news magazines have online versions you can bring into your class for discussions of current events. Universities, schools, and non-profit organizations publish huge amounts of content available for you to use free of charge.

Here are a couple of good sites where you can begin your search for other sites:

http://www.merlot.org
  A community dedicated to sharing and evaluating educational resources, simulations, and other materials

http://www.wikipedia.org
> An online encyclopedia developed by thousands of volunteers

http://www.eoe.org
> An online repository of Java learning objects submitted by educators from around
> the world

This list is by no means exhaustive. Simply using Google as a tool in your class would vastly expand the amount and variety of content available to your students.

Summary

Ultimately, the content you develop and share in your Moodle course is up to you. Static Moodle content provides resources for students as they engage in the learning process. In this chapter, we've looked at how to upload and create content for your Moodle course. In the next chapter, we'll discuss some of the dynamic activities you can add to your class to make it truly compelling.

4

Using Forums, Chats, and Dialogues

Forums are a powerful communication tool within a Moodle course. Think of them as an online message board where you and your students can post messages to each other while easily keeping track of individual conversations. Forums are the primary tool for having a discussion online and are the central organizing feature in the Social course type. In fact, you've already posted your first message to a forum back in Chapter 2. When you posted your news item, you were posting to a special forum used in every course for announcements and news.

Forums allow you and your students to communicate with each other at any time, from anywhere with an Internet connection. Students don't have to be logged in at the same time you are to communicate with you or their classmates. Figure 4-1 demonstrates how conversations are tracked through time, and readers can review the history of the conversation by simply reading the page. Those of us in the computer biz call this type of communication "asynchronous," meaning "not happening at the same time." This can be compared to a synchronous forms of communication like a chat room, instant messaging, or a face-to-face conversation.

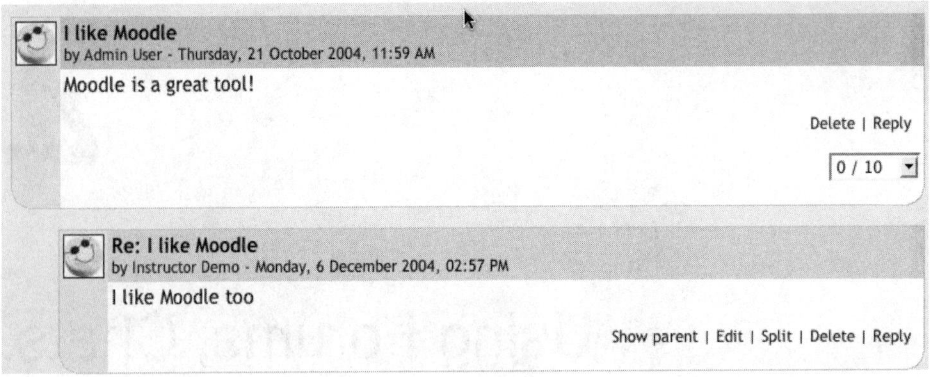

Figure 4-1. Forum posting

Because forums are asynchronous, students can take their time composing a reply. There is a lot of research indicating more students are willing to participate in an asynchronous forum than are willing to speak up in class. For learners for whom English is a second language, for people with communicative disabilities, and for the just plain shy, forums offer a chance to take as much time as they need to formulate a reasonable reply. Other students who might be afraid of embarrassing themselves by making a mistake when they speak up in class can double-check their responses before they send them in.

These features create many opportunities for you not only to replicate the conversations you have in class, but also to create entirely new activities that are difficult to do in a classroom setting.

Forums

Before we start creating a forum, it is important to make sure we're using the same vocabulary. It might be useful to think of the forums module in terms of a party. Each forum is a room at the party; there's a living room, a kitchen, and a dining room. In each room, there are groups of people having discussions. Each discussion has a thread to the conversation with everyone replying to each other about the topic. Without people having discussions, a forum is an empty, quiet space. Each forum can contain one or more discussions which are comprised of one or more posts and replies.

Moodle forums also allow subscriptions. When a user subscribes to a forum, all new posts are automatically sent to the email address stored in his user profile. This makes it easy to keep track of what's happening in the forums without constantly logging in.

Creating a forum is relatively easy. The key to success is choosing the right options for the type of forum you want to create. Moodle has three basic forum types:

A single, simple discussion
> You can create only one discussion in this forum.

Each person posts one discussion

Each person on the class can start only one discussion. This would be useful when each person needs to post an assignment or a question. Each discussion can then have multiple replies.

Standard forum for general use

There can be one or more discussions in this forum, and anyone with permission can post multiple discussions.

To add a forum to your class:

1. Click Turn Editing Mode On.

2. Select Forum from the activity menu in the Topic or Schedule section where you would like to add the forum.

3. On the resulting page, shown in Figure 4-2, give the forum a descriptive name.

4. Select the forum type you want to use.

5. Write a descriptive summary.

6. Choose the options you want to use for this forum.

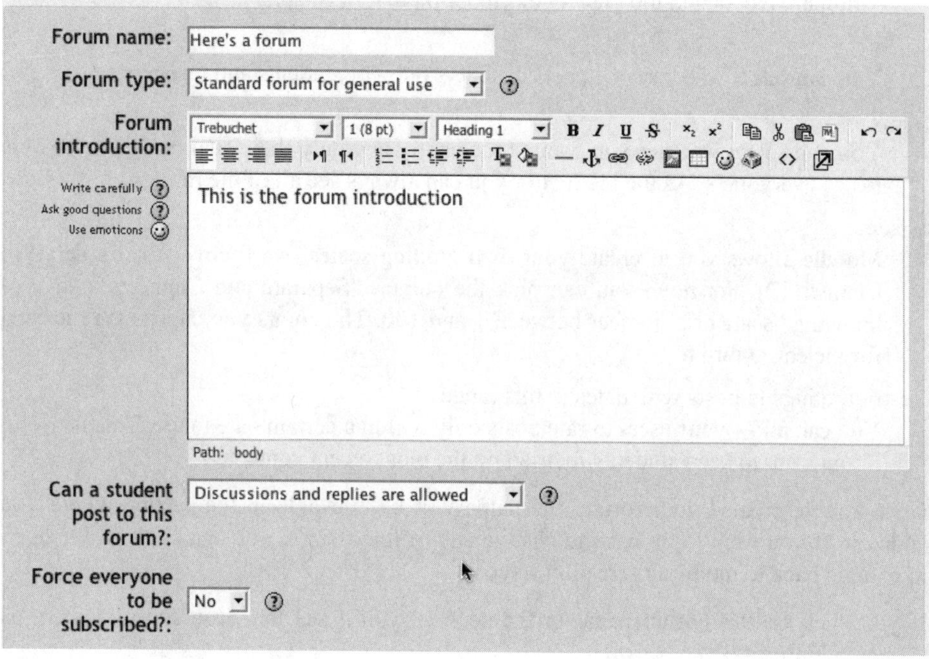

Figure 4-2. Adding a new forum

Forum Options

Can a student post to this forum?

There are three levels of permission you can give your students for a given forum:

- Discussions and replies are allowed. Students can post both discussions and replies.

- No discussions, but replies are allowed. Students can't start new discussions, but they can reply to discussions you start.

- No discussions, no replies. Students can read the forum but can't post anything. This is usually used for a teacher only forum.

Force everyone to be subscribed?

If you select Yes, everyone in your course will automatically receive emails of new posts. Otherwise, people have the choice to subscribe or not.

Maximum attachment size

When students attach files to their posts, you'll want to limit the maximum size of their posts so you don't eat all of your server space. This is especially important if you are paying a commercial hosting company for your Moodle site.

Allow posts to be rated

Moodle's forums allow users to rate each other's posts. This is a useful tool for the interview ratings or for giving students participation grades. Any ratings given in the forum are recoded in the gradebook (more on that in Chapter 12).

Users

You can select who can rate posts: teachers only, or students and teachers.

View

You can select whether you want students to view only their own ratings or be able to see everyone's. As the instructor, you can always see all of the ratings.

Grade

Moodle allows you to create your own grading scales (we'll cover this in detail in Chapter 12). For now, you can pick the default "Separate and Connected ways of knowing" scale or a number between 1 and 100. The points you choose are the total for the entire forum.

Restrict ratings to posts with dates in this range

You can allow your users to rate posts only within a certain date range. This is useful if you want to keep students focused on the most recent content.

Once you've created your forum, the name will be clickable in the section where you added it. If you want to go back to change any of the options, you can click on the hand icon to go back to the forum-creation screen.

If you click on the Forum name in the section, you'll see the main forum screen, as shown in Figure 4-3.

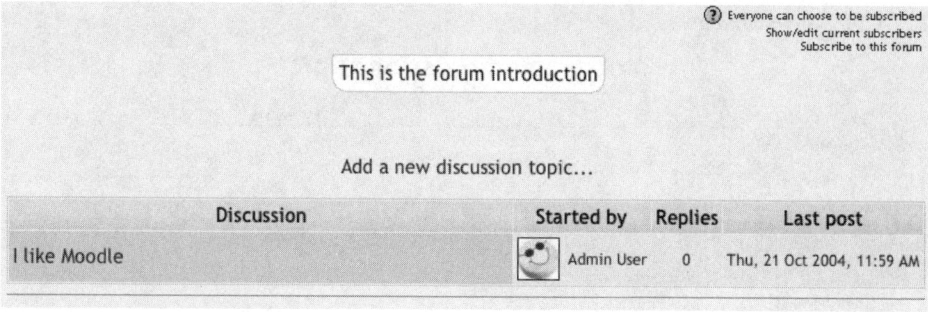

Figure 4-3. Forum main screen

There are some interesting features on this screen. Below the navigation bar at the top of the screen, you'll see a Help menu question mark button and three links. The first link with read "Everyone can choose to be subscribed" or "Everyone is subscribed to this forum," depending on whether you are forcing everyone to subscribe or not. If you click on the link, you can flip back and forth between forcing subscription or not. If you aren't forcing users to subscribe, the next link will read "Show/Edit current subscribers," which will give you an interface for seeing who's subscribed and changing who is and isn't receiving email. The last link will read "Subscribe to this forum," which will subscribe you when you click it.

Below the subscription links, you'll find the forum description you wrote when you created the forum. Below the description, you'll see a link labeled "Add a new discussion topic…." You can use this to create the first discussion in the forum. If you've prohibited students from creating discussions, you'll need to create one to allow anyone to use the forum.

To create a new post:

1. Click on the "Add a new discussion topic…" link.

2. On the new discussion topic page, shown in Figure 4-4, give your new discussion a subject.

3. Formatting: If you don't have the HTML editor enabled, you can choose the formatting type you used in your message. Most of the time, you'll want to leave it on Moodle Auto-Format, which will try to automatically recognize the format you used in the post.

4. Subscription: You can choose to subscribe to the forum if subscriptions were enabled when the forum was created.

5. Attachment: If you want to attach a file, such as an RTF document or a picture, click the Browse button, find your document on your computer, and click Open. Be sure your document is smaller than the maximum attachment size for the forum.

6.   Click Save Changes.

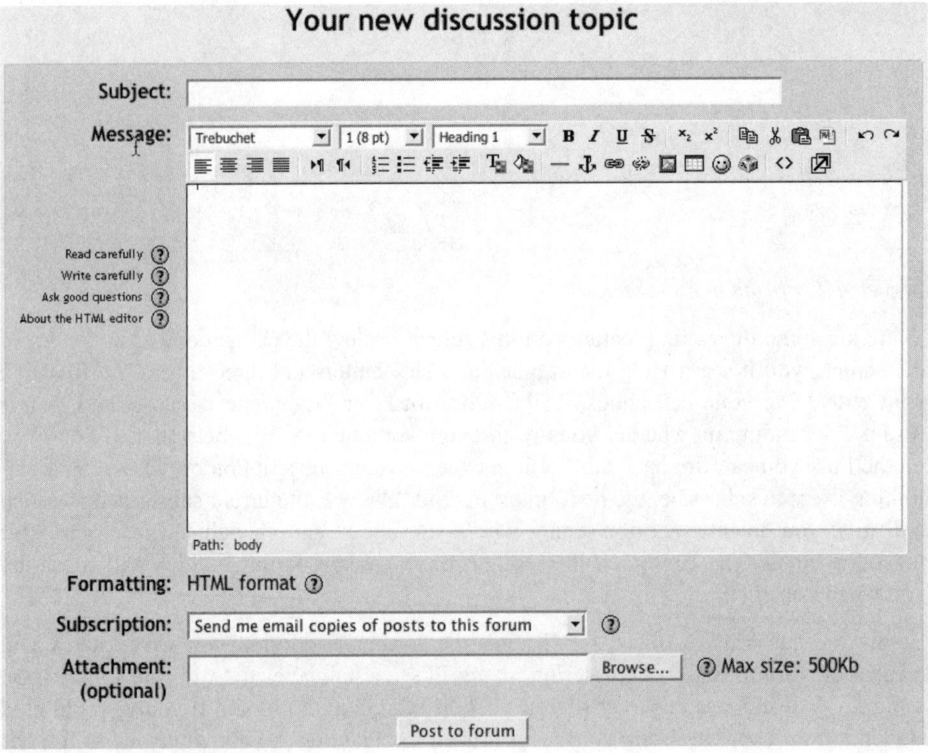

Your new discussion topic

Subject:

Message: [Trebuchet ▼] [1 (8 pt) ▼] [Heading 1 ▼]   **B** *I* <u>U</u> S̶   x₂ x²   [icons]   ↶ ↷

≡ ≡ ≡ ≡   ▶¶ ¶◀   ☰ ☰ ☰ ☰   Tₐ ◿   — ⚓ ∞ ✷ ▣ ▭ ☺ ⊕ <> ◪

Read carefully ⑦
Write carefully ⑦
Ask good questions ⑦
About the HTML editor ⑦

Path: body

Formatting: HTML format ⑦

Subscription: [Send me email copies of posts to this forum ▼] ⑦

Attachment: [_____] [Browse...] ⑦ Max size: 500Kb
(optional)

[Post to forum]

Figure 4-4. New forum post

Once you submit your discussion topic, you'll see a screen telling you the post was successfully saved and how long you have to make changes to your post. The time you have to make changes is set by your system administrator for the whole Moodle site. The default is 30 minutes, so most of the time you'll have a half hour to go back and edit your post before it's mailed to the subscribers. After it's been sent, you can't edit.

> *Warning: Your post won't be mailed to subscribers until the editing time has passed. Unless your system administrator has changed the default, your forum posts won't be sent out for at least 30 minutes.*

The success screen should automatically send you back to the main screen for your forum. You'll see the discussion you just created. If you click on the discussion name, you'll see the message you wrote with any attachments in the upper righthand corner of the message body (see Figure 4-5).

If you can still edit the post, you'll see three links at the bottom of the message body. You can choose to edit or delete the post, or post a reply.

After the editing time has passed, your message will be emailed to all subscribers. If a student or instructor has opted to receive HTML-formatted email, they will receive an email that looks just like the posting in the browser. Otherwise, they will receive the plaintext version. As Figure 4-6 illustrates, the email will have a link labeled "Reply to forum," which will bring them right to the message in the forum so they can post a reply.

I like Moodle
by Admin User - Thursday, 21 October 2004, 11:59 AM
Moodle is a great tool!
Delete | Reply
0 / 10
Re: I like Moodle
by Instructor Demo - Monday, 6 December 2004, 02:57 PM
I like Moodle too
Show parent | Edit | Split | Delete | Reply

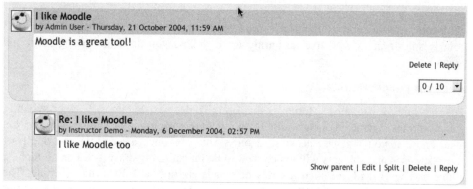

Figure 4-5. Discussion post

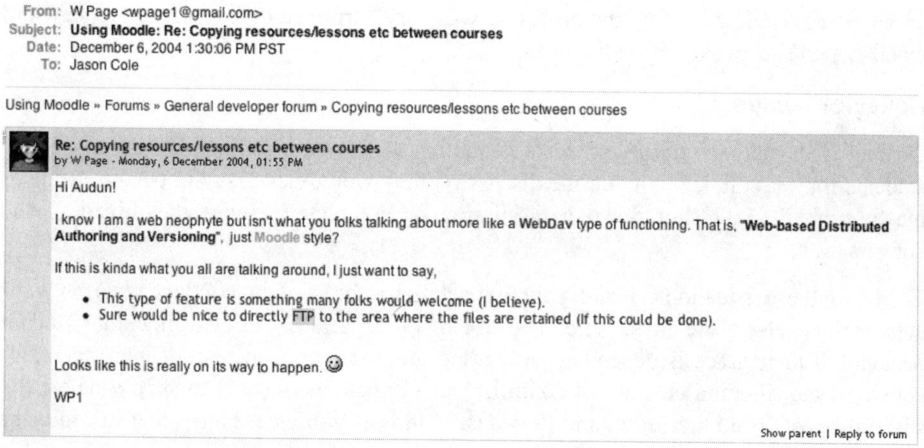

From: W Page <wpage1@gmail.com>
Subject: Using Moodle: Re: Copying resources/lessons etc between courses
Date: December 6, 2004 1:30:06 PM PST
To: Jason Cole
Using Moodle » Forums » General developer forum » Copying resources/lessons etc between courses
Re: Copying resources/lessons etc between courses
by W Page - Monday, 6 December 2004, 01:55 PM
Hi Audun!
I know I am a web neophyte but isn't what you folks talking about more like a WebDav type of functioning. That is, "Web-based Distributed Authoring and Versioning", just Moodle style?
If this is kinda what you all are talking around, I just want to say,
This type of feature is something many folks would welcome (I believe).
Sure would be nice to directly FTP to the area where the files are retained (If this could be done).
Looks like this is really on its way to happen.
WP1
Show parent | Reply to forum

Figure 4-6. Emailed discussion posting

If you've enabled ratings, you'll also see a drop-down menu at the lower righthand side of the message body with the scale you've chosen. At the bottom of the screen, below all the posts in the discussion, you'll see a button labeled "Send in my latest ratings." If you select a rating for the post and click the button, you'll submit your scores for the posts. The scores are the stored in the grade book (more on that in Chapter 12).

Once you've submitted a rating, it will appear next to the rating menu. If you click on the rating, you'll see everyone's ratings for that post.

Managing Forums

Once you've created forums for your students, you will need to manage them during your course. As I discussed earlier, forums are great tools for getting people to participate who don't usually talk in class. If you make your discussions an important part of your class, you can really get people talking.

Of course, a lot of people talking in a forum means there's more to manage. Forums can quickly sprout and spread like an unruly weed, unless you do some management and pruning.

Managing expectations

The first key to managing a forum is managing student expectations. In your syllabus, you should let students know how often you intend to respond to questions and posts. Let them know if you will be checking in once a day or once a week. If you don't set expectations, some students will expect you to be on call 24 hours a day. For example, a professor I work with received a series of emails starting at 1:30 in the morning. The student wrote a question at 1:30, asked again at 2 a.m., and sent an annoyed message at 2:30. Finally, at 3 a.m., the student sent an email saying he was going to bed and was very upset the instructor had not answered hid question in time for him to complete the assignment. Needless to say, the professor was very surprised to find the entire series of emails when she awoke the next morning.

Behavior issues

Dealing with rude and unruly students is another challenge of online discussions. Some students may say things in an online discussion they would never say in person. Rude or hurtful remarks can shut down a discussion or completely divert the thread of the conversation.

To avoid these situations, make your expectations for student conduct clear in your syllabus and elsewhere in the site. The use of rating scales can also moderate student behavior if their grade is dependent on getting good ratings from you or their peers. Of course, if the situation gets out of control, your ultimate recourse is to simply delete the students' posts from the forum and then deal with it as you would any other disciplinary issue.

Archiving forums

Once forums get too long, you may want to archive them and start up the conversation again with a good summary. While there is no built-in tool for creating archives, with a little ingenuity, you can easily create a repository for old conversations.

To archive a discussion:

1. Create a forum named Archive Forum somewhere in your class (the first or last content block is a good idea), as shown in Figure 4-7. You'll probably want to prohibit students from posting new discussions or replies.

Figure 4-7. Archive link

2. Go to the forum with the discussion you want to archive.

3. Enter the discussion by clicking on the discussion name. At the top-right corner of the screen, you'll see a menu labeled "Move this discussion to…" (see Figure 4-8).

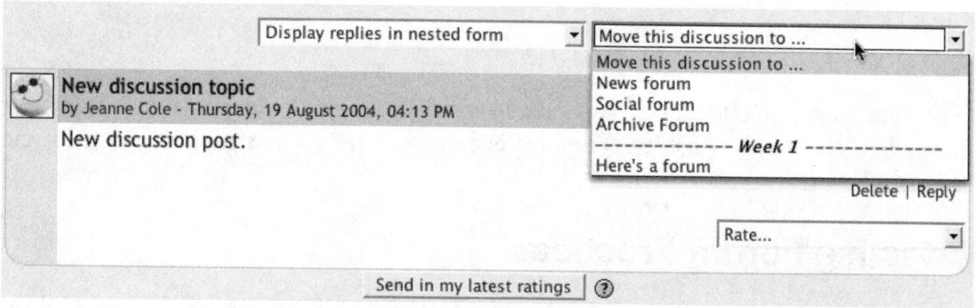

Figure 4-8. Discussion move menu

4. Select "Discussion Archives" forum from the list, as shown in Figure 4-9.

5. You'll now see the discussion in the Archive forum. Click the Forums link in the navigation bar and select the original forum from the list.

6. Post a summary of the archived discussion in the original forum to restart the discussion.

Using an archival forum allows you to keep the discussions manageable, while retaining all of the detail of the original. It's also an easy way to move good discussions from class to class or semester to semester.

Managing discussions is also easier with some help. A number of studies have reported the benefits of assigning groups of students to moderate duties for discussions around given topics. If a group of students knows they are responsible for being able to discuss an issue intelligently with their classmates, they are much more likely to be sure they've done the reading and really understand the topic. They can be responsible for moving the conversation along, answering basic questions, and archiving and summarizing a discussion.

General forums			
Forum	**Description**	**Discussions**	**Subscribed**
Archive Forum		0	No
Descriptive Forum Name	Descriptive forum summary.	1	No
News forum	General news and announcements	0	Yes
Social forum	An open forum for chatting about anything you want to	2	No
Teacher forum	A forum for teacher-only notes and discussion	0	No

Learning forums			
Forum	**Description**	**Discussions**	**Subscribed**
1 Here's a forum	This is the forum introduction	1	No

Figure 4-9. Forum list

To create student moderator groups, assign a small team of students to each forum or discussion. Be sure to enable ratings by everyone, to allow the student group to rate ratings.

Effective Forum Practices

Forums are an important tool in your Moodle toolbox. They are the primary method for students to communicate with you and each other. Social constructivism is all about discussion and negotiated meaning. I would argue that good moderation and intelligent deployment of discussion opportunities are more important to the success of a course than the static content.

> *Tip: MIT has said the same thing. It is posting many of its course syllabi, problem sets, and lecture notes through its OpenCourseware initiative (*http://ocw.mit.edu*). Anyone can download course materials from over 700 courses for free. MIT does this because the value of an MIT education is not in the content, but in the interaction between students and the instructor. Moodle's forums are the key tool for you to add the same value to your course.*

Getting students to participate in online forums can be a big challenge. If you simply create a forum and expect students to communicate online, you will be sadly disappointed. Many times instructors create a forum, give some vague instructions, and then complain that the students aren't spontaneously communicating with each other.

Encouraging participation

The key to student participation in online forums is tight integration with your course goals. The forums should be a practice activity and a resource for students. Of course, it is important to distinguish between which forums are for practice and which are resources to engage in effective practice.

Let's take an example to help make this clearer. Suppose you have a weekly reading you want students to discuss online before meeting face to face. There are two possibilities for this forum. As a practice exercise, you'll want the forum to be a place where students can practice applying the new ideas they encountered in the reading. So you may want to make each week a discussion of a case study. If you want the forum to be a resource, you may want each student to post a question about the reading. You can then use the questions as a basis for discussion in class.

Of course, being clear about the goal of the forum is only one step. As we've discussed earlier, your goals for the class may be very different from your students' goals. To help encourage alignment between your goals and your students' goals, you will need to have a grading strategy for student participation. Moodle has some great tools to help you create and manage graded forums. To be successful, you will need grading criteria for each forum type. Are you just going to grade practice forums? Give extra credit for good resource postings? How much of the grade will be based on forum participation? How will you and any student raters distinguish between good posts and poor ones?

The final strategy for encouraging participation is to engage with the forums yourself. If your class meets face-to-face, bring up important postings and discussions in class. By merging the online environment with the face-to-face environment, you show your students their participation is valued. One of the best examples of merging online discussions with a course happened in a management course of 400+ students. The instructor assigned groups of students to small discussion groups. She and her teaching assistants randomly read a subset of the discussions each week for assessment. The instructor would also bring the best questions and discussions into her lecture, frequently devoting half of her lecture to talking about what was happening online.

Creative Forum Uses

There are many creative uses of forums, so I can only present a few of the most common here. Moodle forums are so flexible, there's really no limit to the types of activities you can develop to take advantage of the technology.

Interviews

Bringing outside experts into your class can be difficult. You have to coordinate schedules, tear them away from their busy lives, and then hope your students are prepared enough to ask interesting questions. You can eliminate many of these problems by using the forums for communication between the students and experts. The easiest strategy is simply to invite the expert into your forums as a regular participant. Simply give her an account and enroll her in your class. She can then participate in the forum and elsewhere in the course.

However, some people will be reluctant to agree to such an open-ended discussion. As an alternative strategy, create a forum in which students can submit questions for an interview with an expert. They can then vote on the best questions. You select the top 10 questions and send them via email to the interviewee. Your expert can then respond when it is convenient for her and email back her responses. If you post her responses to a new forum, your students can respond to her answers and even prepare a second round of questions, if your expert is up for it.

Debates

While many instructors frequently hope some level of debate will spontaneously break out between students around controversial issues or new concepts, it's sometimes difficult to get the ball rolling. Try assigning your students to groups on different sides of an issue. Each post must be a reasoned argument for their side of the issue, supported by evidence. They can be graded on how well they reason and support their argument.

Frequently asked questions

How many times do you answer the same question from three different students? Frequently, many students have the same questions about assignments, difficult concepts, or grades. If everyone is meeting face to face, you can answer the question out loud, but other students may not be listening to the answer. A fully online environment is harder to manage when the questions from students arrive via email. Many teachers of fully online courses complain about the constant barrage of repetitious questions. I strongly recommend you create a forum in which students can ask questions about the administration of the course, and separate forums for questions about the subject matter. Have them consult the forums and the responses before sending you yet another email about the date of the final exam.

Reading study groups

A strategy to encourage students to do the reading they have been assigned is to create reading study group forums. This strategy works well with groups of three to five students who are collectively responsible for discussing a reading before class. Each student asks one question about the reading, and the group must answer all the questions before the start of the class session. This encourages students not only to read the assignment, but to think more deeply about it through the question-and-answer process.

Tip: This strategy of having groups of students asking each other questions about course material supposedly originated with a group of engineers who were taking a class together. They were all transferred as a group midway through the semester but didn't want to drop the class. The instructor agreed to videotape the lectures and mail them to the students. Very quickly, the instructor noticed the engineers' performance in the class was getting worse, so he insisted they watch the videotape together. He told them they had to stop the tape every 15 minutes, and each person was to ask a question about what they had just seen. They couldn't continue until every question was answered. By the end of the class, the remote group of engineers performed a third of a letter grade higher than the rest of the class.

Social forum

Although the majority of your forums will focus on the course material, it's important for your students to have an informal way to get to know each other, especially if the course is completely online. A social forum gives people a place to talk without worrying about being graded, or having to appear really smart. It's a good idea to start your social forum with some fun questions. Ask everyone to post an introduction telling the class where they are from, what they hope to get out of the class, and their favorite food, movie, or something interesting. The more interesting the introductory post, the more likely people will respond to it and get a real discussion going.

Chats

The Moodle chat tool is a simple synchronous communication tool allowing you and your students to communicate in real time. If you've every used an instant messaging system like AOL, MSN or iChat, you've used a system similar to the Moodle chat. In the forums, you and your students don't have to be logged in at the same time. In a chat, everyone needs to be logged in at the same time in order to communicate.

Creating Chats

To use the chat tool, you will need to create a chat room for you and your students and set a time when everyone will log in and meet in the chat room. You can create one session for the entire course or set up repeating sessions for multiple meetings.

To create a chat session:

1.   Click Turn Editing Mode On.

2.   Select Chat from the "Add an activity…" menu.

3.   In the create chat page, shown in Figure 4-10, give the chat room a name and provide directions on how to use the room in the Introduction text.

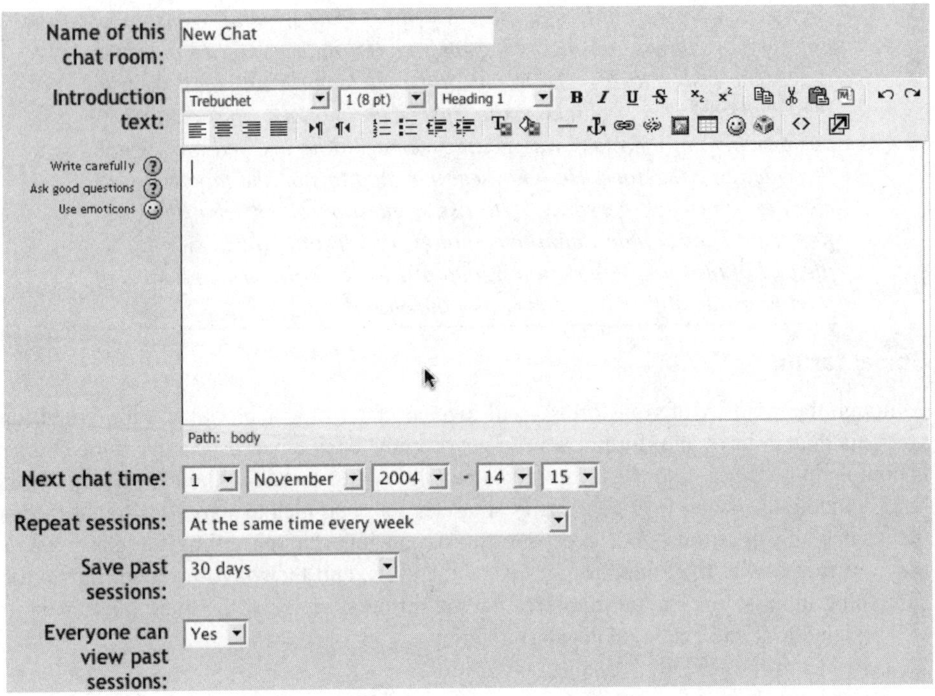

Figure 4-10. Create chat

4.   Set the time for the first chat session in the Next chat time.

5.   Set the options for the chat room:

Repeat sessions
    There are four options here:

Don't publish any chat times
    Creates a chat room that is always open and has no specified meeting times

No repeats
    Creates a one-time chat room that will meet only during the time specified in step 4

At the same time every day
> Creates an entry in the course calendar for a daily chat at the time specified in step 4

At the same time every week
> Creates a weekly entry in the course calendar

Save Past Sessions
> When a chat is complete, the transcript will be available for the amount of time specified here.

Everyone can view past sessions
> Determines whether transcripts are available to students or just the instructor.

6. Click "Save Changes".

The chat you created is now available.

Using Chats

Even if you've set chat times, the chat is always open to students. Moodle does not restrict access to the chat based on the times you set when you create the chat. Instead, it creates entries in the course calendar that remind people to log in for the chat at certain times. If a student wants to wander into the chat at another time, he could talk to himself or anyone else who wanders by.

During the chat, shown in Figure 4-11, there are two things you can do. You can type messages in the text field at the bottom of the screen or beep other users. I don't know why the developers thought it was important to include the beep function, but it's there and it can be annoying. You may want to remind students to keep the beeping to a minimum.

Figure 4-11. An ongoing chat

Once you type a message in the text area, hit Enter and your message will be broadcast to everyone logged in to the chat. The Moodle chat works by refreshing the screen every five seconds, so you may not see your message right away.

On the right side of the screen, Moodle lists the chat participants and how long they have been idle in the chat room.

The chat room is very basic. As of this writing, the community is looking at improving the chat functionality to bring it up to par with some of the better synchronous communication tools on the market.

Effective Chat Practices

While the chat room may not be very feature-rich at this point, it can still be an effective learning tool. I know of one professor who couldn't speak for a semester due to throat surgery. He posted his lecture notes to his course web site, and held class meetings in the chat room instead of on campus. The students were expected to come to the chat meeting having already read the materials. The chat was set up as a question-and-answer session in which students typed their questions and the professor typed his responses. The entire process was recorded in the archives. I was able to review the archives and I was amazed at the quality of the interaction. The chat room was an ideal tool for this type of interaction.

The key to a successful chat is good moderation. The nature of the chat room makes it difficult to track different conversations. If everyone in the class is talking at the same time, the conversation will go by too quickly. It's important to set some ground rules to make the chat useful for everyone. Try to keep everyone on the same track of the conversation. If the conversation starts to get out of control, gently try to bring people back to the main flow.

Creative Chat Practices

Online office hours

Many students may not be able to come to your office hours. For working students, it may be difficult to make it to office hours because they have arranged their schedules to make it to class. The chat room is an easy way to allow your students to contact you during a scheduled time to ask a quick question about an assignment or a lecture.

Group chats

If you've set up student groups, each group could have its own chat. Set up a chat room and set the group mode to separate or visible groups. Each group can then use its chat room for communication between group members.

Dialogues

The dialogue tool is a private communication channel between two people in your class. You can set up dialogues to allow student-to-teacher communication or student-to-student communication. Each dialogue you create can host a number of different conversations. You may only need to create one dialogue for the entire class, depending on how you want to use them.

Creating Dialogues

To create a dialogue:

1.   Click Turn Editing Mode On.

2.   Select Dialogue from the Activity menu.

3.   The Introduction text entered in the dialogue-creation screen shown in Figure 4-12 will be displayed when anyone enters the dialogue.

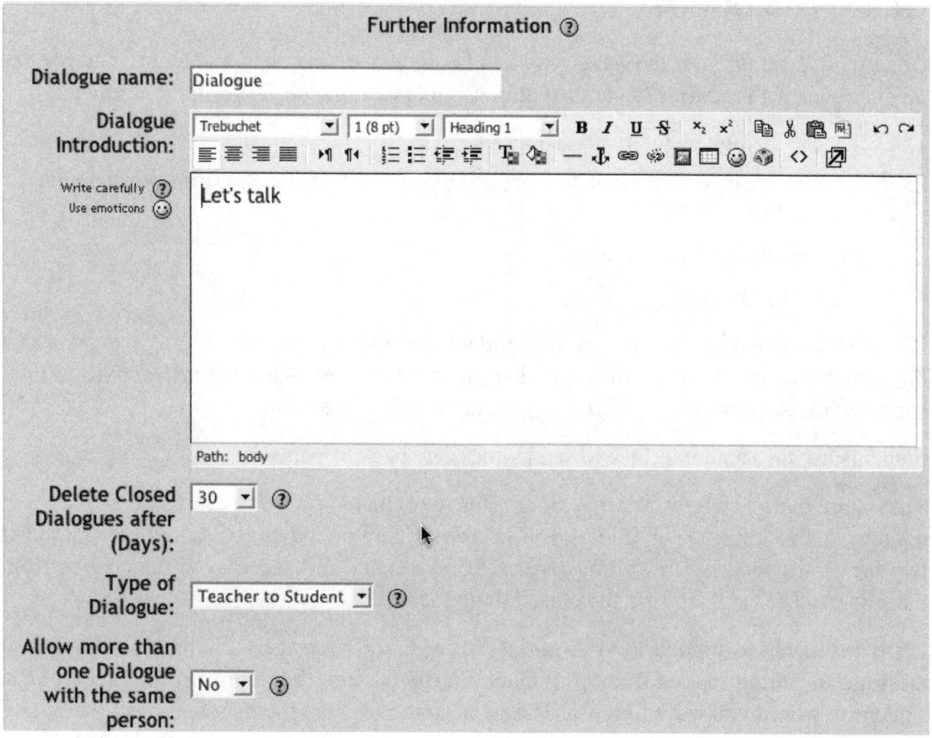

Figure 4-12. Dialogue creation screen

4.   Set the dialogue options:

Delete Closed Dialogues after (Days)
>   You can close dialogues after they are finished. After they've been closed, the participants can see the transcripts until they are deleted.

Type of Dialogue
>   This setting selects whether the dialogues should be teacher-to-student or student-to-student.

Allow more than on Dialogue with the same person
>   This setting determines whether you can have more than once conversation with a given person within a dialogue tool.

Mail Default
>   This setting selects whether mail notifications of dialogue postings should be
>   mailed to the participants.

5. Click Save Changes.

Once you've set up the dialogue, you and your students can begin communicating using
the dialogue.

Using Dialogues

Once you've set up your dialogue, you can begin conversing with a student. You can set
up dialogues with multiple students within a single dialogue tool. To start a dialogue:

1. Click the dialogue you created above.

2. Select the student you want to start a dialogue with from the drop-down menu, as
    shown in Figure 4-13.

3. Type your subject and message.

4. Click Open Dialogue.

If you've set email default to Yes, the student will receive an email telling her she has a
dialogue message. Moodle won't send her the text of the message but instead will tell her
she has a message waiting for her and give her a link to the dialogue tool.

Students use the same interface to send a message back to you.

The main dialogue interface has four tabs that help you keep track of the current
dialogues. The leftmost tab allows you to open a new dialogue with a student. The next
two tabs track messages awaiting replies from you and messages awaiting replies from
the student. The final tab lists the closed dialogues.

Once a student has replied to your initial message, the message will appear in the list of
messages awaiting replies from you. Click on the tab and then click on the name of the
student to whom you want to reply. The next screen will list the messages sent so far and
give you a text area to type your reply. In the upper left of the screen is a link to close the
dialogue.

Once a dialogue has been closed, it cannot be reopened. Both you and the student can see
the transcript of the dialogue until it is deleted at the end of the time frame you set in the
dialogue options.

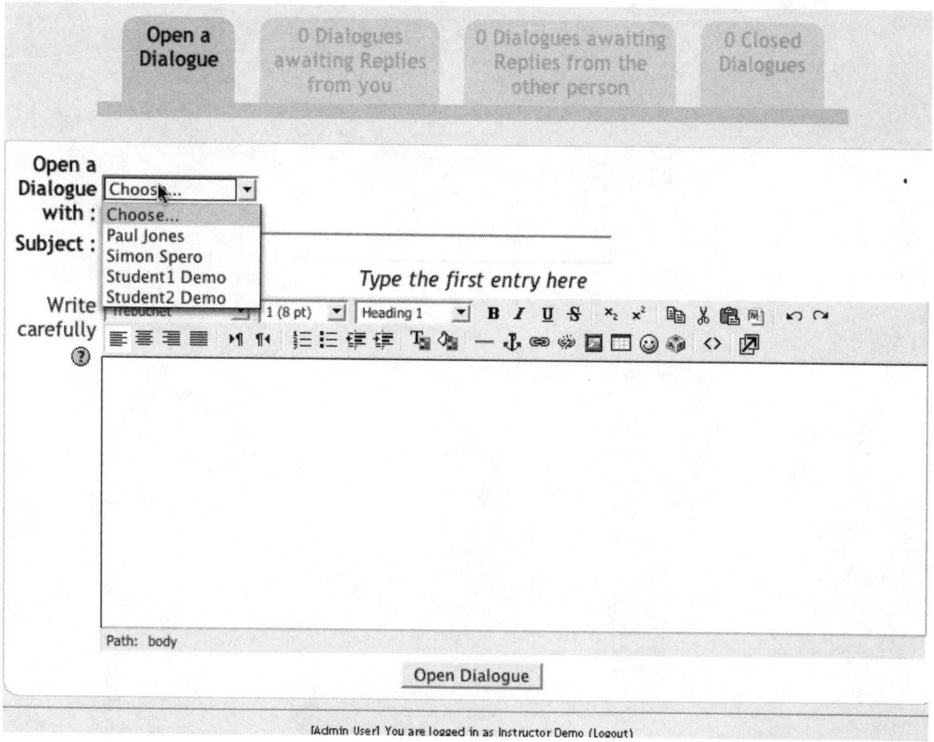

Open a Dialogue	0 Dialogues awaiting Replies from you	0 Dialogues awaiting Replies from the other person	0 Closed Dialogues

Open a
Dialogue
with :
Subject :

Write
carefully

Choose...
Choose...
Paul Jones
Simon Spero
Student1 Demo
Student2 Demo

Type the first entry here

1 (8 pt)   Heading 1   **B** *I* U S x₂ x²

Path: body

Open Dialogue

Figure 4-13. Main dialogue screen

Effective Dialogue Practices

The dialogue tool is designed to aid in communicating privately with your students. If you need such a communication channel, dialogues are a useful alternative to email because you can track all of your correspondence in once place without clogging your inbox.

Summary

Moodle provides three channels of communication for you and your students. Forums provide an asynchronous, public method for sharing ideas. The chats are a great way to have simultaneous conversations online with a group of people. Dialogues provide a private channel for you to communicate directly with your students. Communication is a key to success for any class, and it's even more important in an online environment.

5

Quizzes

Feedback on performance is a critical part of a learning environment, and assessment is one of the most important activities in education. As educators, we can't tell what's going on inside the heads of students, so we need a way for them to demonstrate what they understand and what they don't. A well-designed test, even a multiple-choice test, can give you critical information about student performance. If the feedback is rapid enough, it can also be a critical tool for students to gauge their own performance and help them become more successful.

Moodle's quiz module is one of the most complex pieces of the system. The community has added a large number of options and tools to the quiz engine, making it extremely flexible. You can create quizzes with different question types, randomly generate quizzes from pools of questions, allow students to retake quizzes multiple times, and have the computer score it all.

These features open up a number of strategies that usually aren't practical with paper-based testing. It's hard enough to score one batch of quizzes, and nearly impossible to score it 10 times for each student. When the computer does the work for you, it's easy to give students a chance to practice taking a test or give frequent small quizzes. We'll explore how to apply these advantages later in the chapter. For now, let's get started building your first Moodle quiz.

How to Create a Quiz

Moodle quizzes have two major components: the quiz body and the question pools. Think of the quiz bodies as a container for various types of questions pulled from the question pools. The body is what students see when they take the assessment. It also defines how the students interact with the quiz. The questions in a quiz body can be of any type, chosen manually or at random, and displayed in a set order or a random order. The question pools can contain questions arranged in a manner that makes sense to you. You can create pools based on chapters, weeks in the semester, important concepts, or any other organizational scheme. Pools can be reused in multiple quizzes, shared between classes, and moved between systems.

To start, we need to create a body for our first quiz.

Creating the Quiz Body

When you create the quiz body, you are creating a container for the questions and setting the rules for interacting with the quiz.

To create a quiz body:

1. Click Turn Editing Mode On.

2. Select Quiz from the add menu in the content section where you want to place the link to a quiz.

3. In the Quiz editing page, shown in Figure 5-1, give the quiz a descriptive name. We'll call this first quiz "Chapter 1."

4. Write an introduction for the quiz. Be sure to include any special instructions for taking the quiz, such as the number of attempts allowed or scoring rules.

5. Choose opening and closing dates for the quiz.

> *Warning: The default opening and closing dates are the same, and are set to the time you create the quiz. Be sure to change at least the closing date to some point in the future, or your students won't be able to take the quiz at all.*

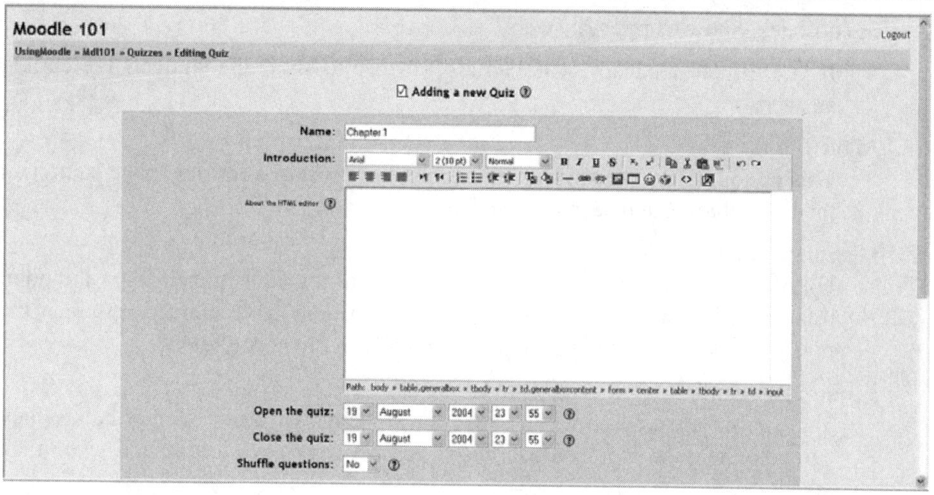

Figure 5-1. Quiz editing

6.   Choose the options you want to use for your quiz:

Time Limit
> Determines how long students have to complete the quiz. At the end of the allotted time, the quiz is automatically submitted with the current answers.

Shuffle Questions
> Set this to Yes to randomly order the quiz questions when they are displayed to the students.

Shuffle Answers
> This will shuffle the answer prompts within the question.

Attempts Allowed
> Use this option to set the number of times a student can take a quiz. You can set it to unlimited times or a number from 1 to 6.

Each Attempt Builds in the Last
> If you allow multiple attempts, you can choose to let students build their answers over time. If you set this to Yes, the student's responses from the last attempt will be visible the next time they try to take the quiz.

Grading Method
> If you allow multiple attempts, you can choose which score is recorded. Your choices are highest grade, average grade, first attempt, and last attempt.

After Answering, Show Feedback?
> Displaying feedback will show students which answers are right and which are wrong once they submit their quiz for grading.

In Feedback, Show Correct Answers?

If you display feedback, you can also choose to show the students the correct answers.

Allow Review

This option will allow students to review past quizzes after they have submitted them for grading and seen the feedback.

Maximum Grade

Use this menu to set the highest possible score for your quiz. This is the point total recorded in the grade book. If your questions have more points than the maximum, they will contribute proportionally to the max grade.

Require Password

You can set a password for the quiz that students will need to enter before they can take the quiz. You can use this to restrict who takes a quiz and when they take it.

Require Network Address

This option restricts access to the test to certain IP address ranges. If you want to require students to take a test from a certain lab on campus, set the network address range to cover the networks in the lab. For example, if you want to require access from computers with an IP range of 10.10.10.0 to 10.10.10.50, you would enter 10.10.10.0/50. To allow access from all computers in a subnet (say, on the campus), enter the partial address you want to use.

7.   Click the Continue button.

Once you click the Continue button, you'll see the second editing screen where you will write and select questions to include in the quiz body.

Creating Questions for a Quiz

You can create your quiz questions in the question-editing section. Here, you'll create and categorize your quiz questions and add them to the quiz body you just created.

On the left side of the screen, as shown in Figure 5-2, you'll see a block where the questions you've added to the current quiz are displayed. Since this is a new quiz, there are no questions there, and Moodle tells us this.

On the right side of the screen, you'll see a category selection menu labeled "Category" and a button labeled "Edit categories." Categories are used to organize your quiz questions for your course, and they can be a container for sharing questions between courses. By default, there is one category, called Default. If you click on the category menu, you'll see it as an option.

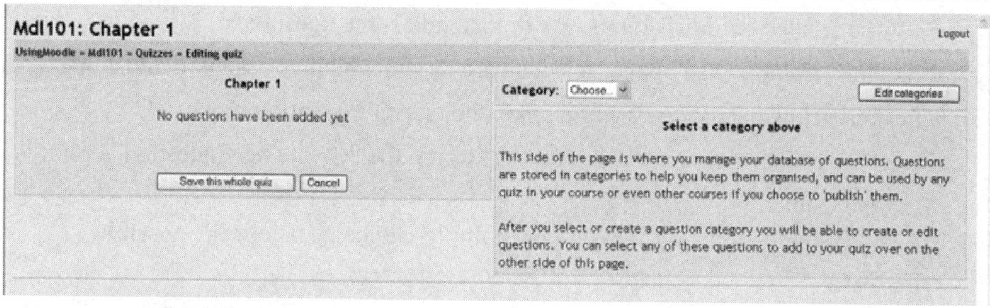

Figure 5-2. Add questions

> *Tip: It's good practice to create categories to organize your questions. The level of detail in the categories is up to you, but I tend to lean toward more detailed categories I can combine into larger groups later if I want to. For example, I'll break down questions related to a reading into a couple of concepts. It's easier to clump questions together later than it is to pull them apart.*

Let's start out by making a category to hold our questions for our Chapter 1 quiz:

1. From the Editingquiz page, click "Edit categories."

2. At the bottom of the list of current categories, as shown in Figure 5-3, you will see a blank line.

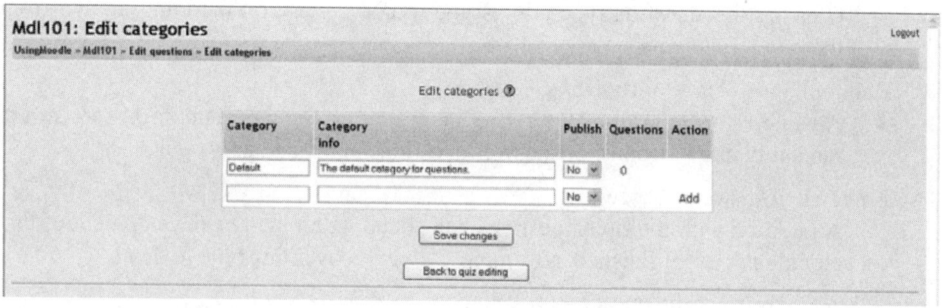

Figure 5-3. Edit categories

1. Type the name of your new question category in the first text box on the left.

2. Add a description for your class in the category info area.

3. If you'd like to share your question with the other classes on the server, select Yes in the Publish column.

4. Click the Save Changes button at the bottom,

5. If you want to add another category, a new blank line will appear at the bottom of the list.

6. When you are done adding categories, click the "Back to quiz editing" button. This will take you back to the "Editing quiz" page.

Once you've created your categories, it's time to add some questions:

1. From the "Editing Quiz" page, select a category to which you want to add a question.

2. The area below the category will display the question-creation block.

3. Select the question type you want to create from the "Create new question" option:

    Multiple Choice
    > Both single- and multiple-answer multiple-choice questions are possible.

    True/False
    > A simple multiple-choice question with only two possible answers.

    Short Answer
    > Students answer this question by typing a word or phrase. You need to provide a list of acceptable answers.

    Numerical
    > A short-answer question that accepts a numerical value instead of a word.

    Matching
    > A standard two-column matching question.

    Description
    > This embeds some text into the quiz. It's not a question but it's useful for giving mid-quiz instructions.

    Random Question
    > Creating this question type allows you to add a question randomly drawn from the category to your quiz.

    Random Short-Answer Matching
    > An interesting question type. The subquestions for the matching exercise are randomly drawn from short-answer questions in the category.

    Embedded Answers (Cloze)
    > A question with multiple questions embedded within it. The development of this module is not yet finished, so I'm not going to cover this type in depth.

4. Fill in the form for the question type you are creating.

5. Click Save Changes at the bottom of the form.

Each question type has its own form and options. We'll spend the next few pages detailing the options for each question type.

Multiple-choice questions

Moodle provides you with a lot of flexibility when creating this common question type. Figure 5-4 shows an example question. You can create single- and multiple-answer questions, display pictures in the question, and give relative grading weights to individual answers.

To create multiple-choice questions:

1. Figure 5-5 shows the multiple-choice question-editing page. Start by giving the question a descriptive name. You'll use the name to track your questions later, so "Question 1" isn't a good idea.

2. Create the question text. If you're using the HTML editor, you can format the question just like a word-processing document.

3. If you want to add an image to the question, you have two options:

   • If you've already uploaded an image to your Files area (see Chapter 4 for details), it will be available to add to the question stem in a dropdown menu under the Question text area.

   • If you're using the HTML editor, you can click the image icon. This will pop-up the Insert Image window. You can choose to upload an image into your Files area from this window or add the URL of an image on the Web. If you add a file to your Files area, click the name of the file after you upload it to insert the link into the URL text entry at the top of the screen. Then click OK.

4. Choose whether students can select only one answer or multiple answers.

5. Write your first response in the Choice 1 text field.

6. Select a grade percentage for the answer. This is the percentage of the total points possible for the question selecting a given answer is worth. You can select negative percentages as well as positive percentages. So if a question is worth 10 points, selecting one correct response out of two in a multiple-choice question may give you 50% of the possible points (i.e., 5 points). Selecting a wrong answer may take away 10% (i.e., 2.5 points).

7. If you wish, you can add feedback for each response.

   > *Tip: It may be a bit more work, but it's good practice to tell the students why each answer is right or wrong using the feedback area. If students know why an answer is right or wrong, they can analyze their own thinking and begin to understand why an answer is correct. Your feedback will be displayed only if you select Show Feedback in the quiz body option.*

8. Fill in the response choices in the rest of the form. Any unused areas will be ignored.

9. Select the Save Changes button at the bottom of the screen.

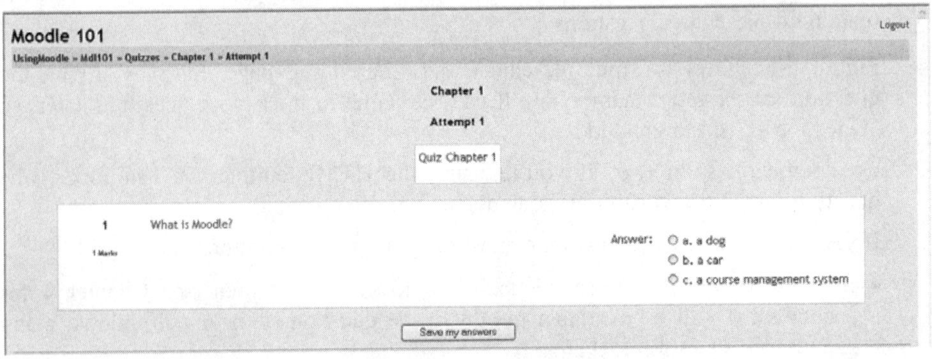

Figure 5-4. A multiple-choice question

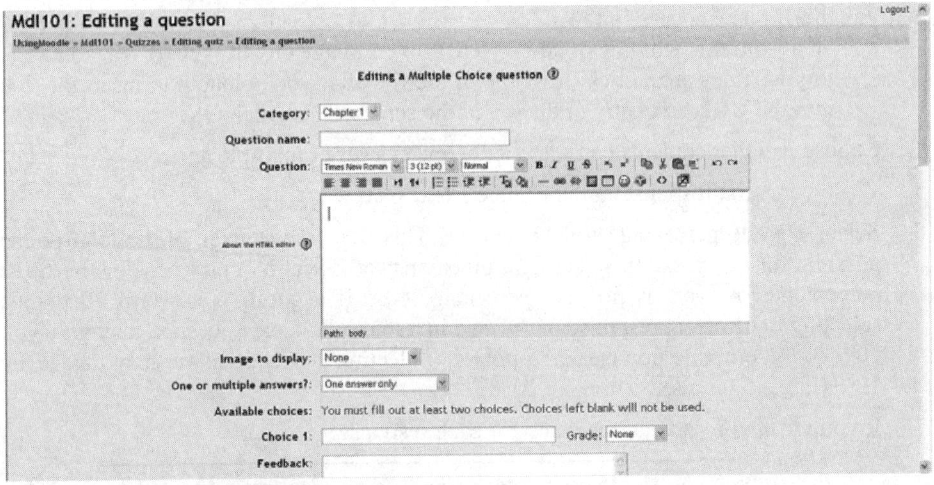

Figure 5-5. Editing a multiple-choice question

You have now added a multiple-choice question to the question category.

Short-answer questions

Short-answer questions require the student to type an answer to a question, as shown in Figure 5-6. The answer could be a word or a phrase, but it must match one of your acceptable answers exactly. It's a good idea to keep the required answer as short as possible to avoid missing a correct answer that's phrased differently.

> *Tip: I like to prototype my short-answer questions to catch common acceptable answers I hadn't thought of. To do this, start by creating a few acceptable answers and include the question in a quiz for no points. Be sure to tell students you are testing a new question. Once the quiz is over, review students' answers and add their acceptable answers to the list.*

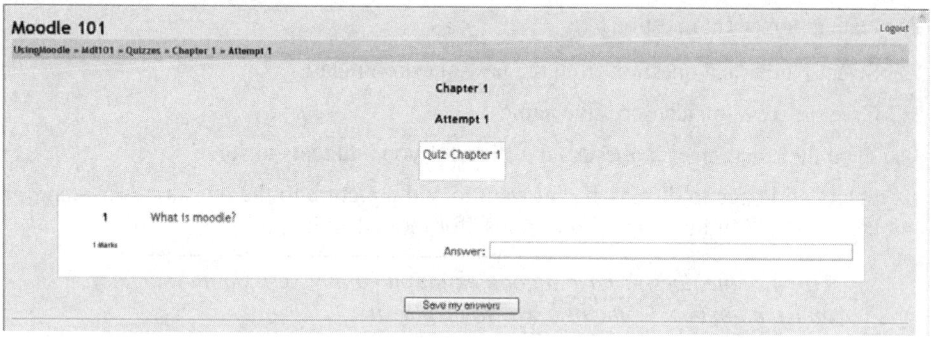

Figure 5-6. A short-answer question

To create a short-answer question:

1. Give your question a descriptive name.

2. Create the question stem. If you want students to fill in a blank, use the underscore to indicate where the blank is.

3. Select an image to display if you want to add a picture to the question (see step 3 in the previous section for more details).

4. Choose whether capitalization is important. Case-sensitivity can be tricky. Will you accept "george Washington" as well as "George Washington" as an answer?

5. Fill in the answers you will accept. Give each answer a percentage of the grade if required. You could give common misspellings partial credit with this option.

6. Create feedback for each acceptable answer.

7. Click Save Changes to add the question to the category.

Numerical questions

Numerical questions are a lot like short-answer questions for equations such as the one shown in Figure 5-7. You can create a question with an equation, and your students type in a numeric answer. Students will get credit for answers within the range of answers you specify.

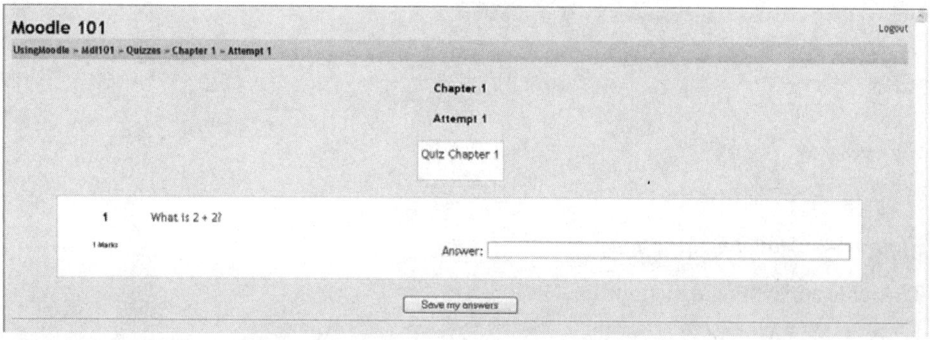

Figure 5-7. Numerical question

To create a numerical question:

1.   Select Numerical question from the new question menu.

2.   Give the question a descriptive name.

3.   Type the equation or numerical question for your students to solve.

4.   Select an image to display if you want to add a picture to the question (see step 3 in
     the section "Multiple-choice questions" for more details).

> *Tip: Moodle doesn't have a good equation editor (yet). So an image of
> an equation may be the best way to display it.*

5.   Enter the correct answer (you can add only one correct answer).

6.   Enter the accepted error, i.e., the range above or below the correct answer. For
     example, if the correct answer is 5, but you will accept 4 or 6 as answers, your
     accepted error is 1.

7.   Enter feedback for the question.

8.   If you want to accept answers in multiple units (e.g., metric or English units), specify
     the unit multiplier and the unit label in the areas.

9.   Click Save Changes to add the question to the category.

Matching questions

Matching questions ask students to match multiple question stems to multiple possible
answers (see Figure 5-8). They are useful for testing students' understanding of
vocabulary and their ability to match examples to concepts. Setting up a matching
question in Moodle is a bit different from setting up other types of questions.

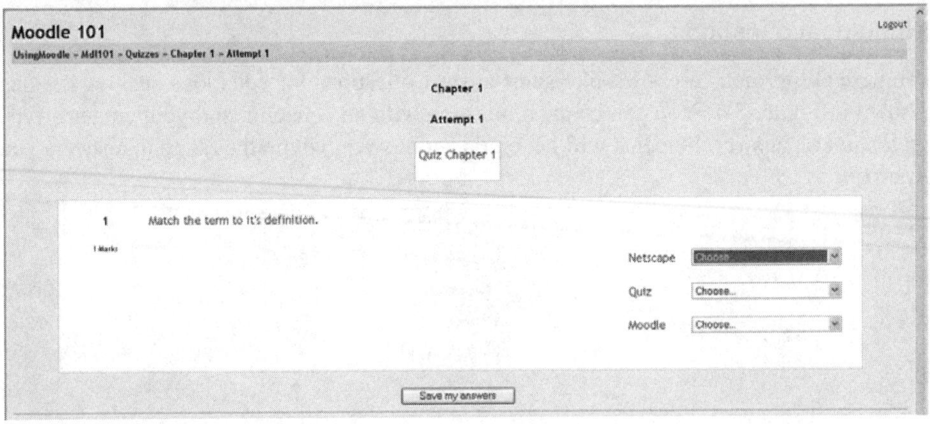

Figure 5-8. Matching question

To create a matching question:

1.   Select Matching question from the new question menu.

2.   Give the question a descriptive name.

3. Enter the question stem to tell the students what they are matching.

4. Select an image to display if you want to add a picture to the question (see step 3 in the section "Multiple-choice questions" for more details).

5. For the first matching item, enter the question and a matching answer.

6. Fill in at least three questions and answers. You can enter as many as 10 items.

7. Click Save Changes to add the question to the category.

Moodle will display the question in two columns. The first will contain the questions. The second will display a dropdown menu for each question with all possible matching answers as options.

Random questions

A random question is a placeholder for a randomly selected question. One of the advantages of a computer-generated quiz is the ability to generate a quiz from questions randomly selected from a category. Each random question will pull a question randomly from the question category and insert it into the quiz whenever a student takes the quiz.

Each random question can be inserted into a quiz only once, so you'll need to create a random question for each question you want randomly inserted into the quiz. Fortunately, it's easy to create a random question or even a bunch of them at once.

To create a random question:

1. Select "Random question" from the new question menu.

2. Give the question a descriptive name.

3. Click Save Changes to add the question to the category.

To create multiple random questions:

1. Click the Create multiple questions button below the new question menu.

2. Select the number of questions you want to create on the screen shown in Figure 5-9.

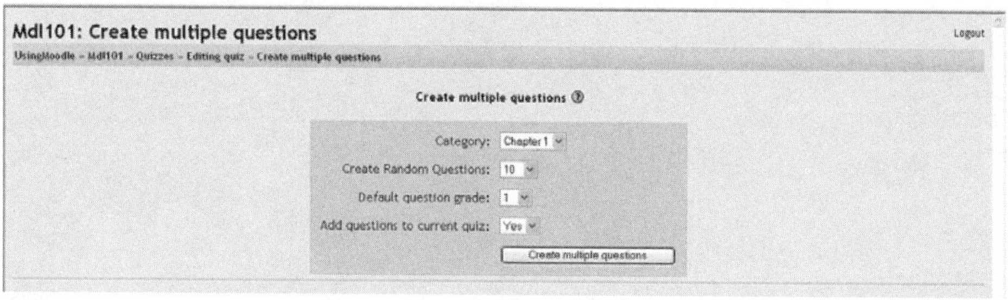

Figure 5-9. Create multiple questions

3. Enter a default point value for each created question.

4. Choose to add questions directly to the current quiz or leave them in the category for inclusion later.

Random short-answer matching questions

This is an interesting question type. You take random multiple short-answer questions and their correct answers and create a matching question out of them. It's an interesting way to reuse your short-answer questions in a new format.

To create a random short-answer matching question:

1. Select Random Short-Answer Matching from the new question menu.

2. Give the question a name.

3. Select the number of questions you want to add to the matching question.

4. Click Save Changes.

Calculated questions

Calculated questions are the newest addition to the Moodle quiz. A calculated question is a mathematical equation with placeholders for values that will be pulled randomly from a dataset when a student takes the quiz. For example, if I want to create a large number of multiplication problems to drill my students, I would create a question with two placeholders and a multiplication sign such as {a} * {b}. When a student takes the test, Moodle will randomly select values for a and b. The test will very rarely appear the same way twice.

To create a calculated question:

1. Select Calculated question from the new question menu.

2. Give the question a name on the editing screen shown in Figure 5-10.

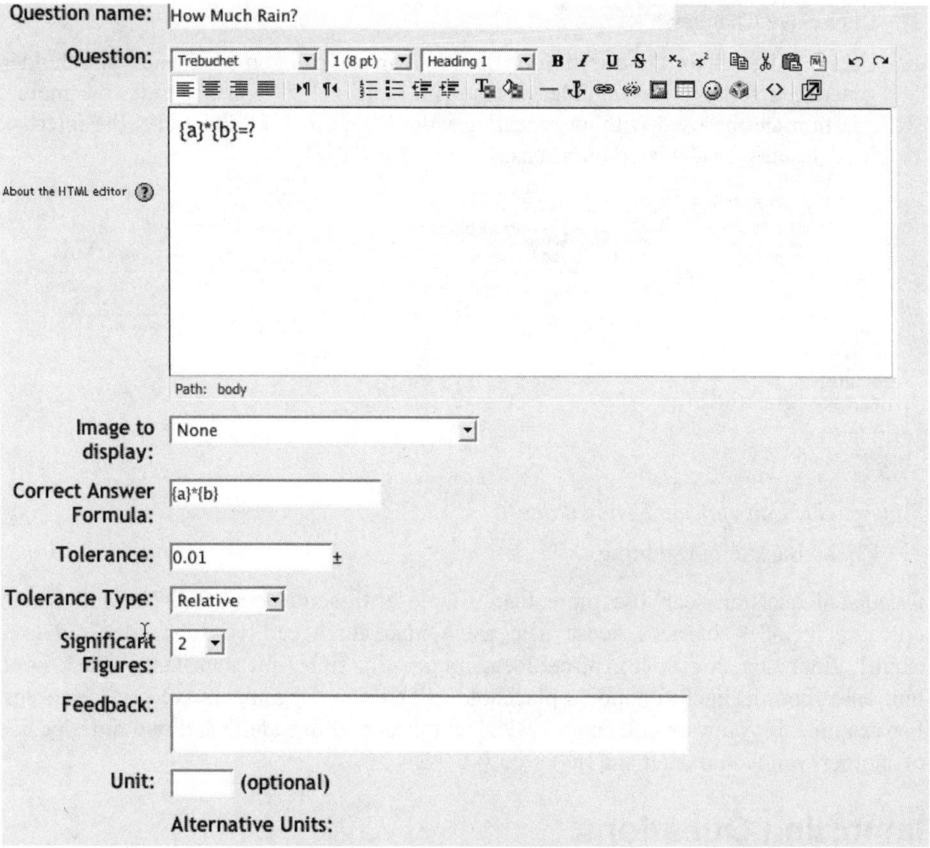

Question name: How Much Rain?

Question:

{a}*{b}=?

About the HTML editor ②

Path: body

Image to display: None

Correct Answer Formula: {a}*{b}

Tolerance: 0.01 ±

Tolerance Type: Relative

Significant Figures: 2

Feedback:

Unit: (optional)

Alternative Units:

Figure 5-10. Creating a calculated question

3. Enter your question into the question field. All variables you want Moodle to replace with generated values must be placed in curly braces.

4. Enter the formula for the answer. Be sure to use the same placeholders so Moodle can substitute the same values.

5. Determine the tolerance for error that you will accept in the answer. The tolerance and tolerance type combine to give a range of acceptable scores.

6. Select the number of significant figures you want in the correct answer.

7. If you want, type some feedback for the student.

8. Enter the units for the answer (e.g., meters, kg., ft., etc.). Moodle will look for the correct units. If you want to enter other acceptable units, such as metric versus English distances, enter them along with a conversion factor.

9. Click Save Changes.

10. On the next screen, choose whether to create substitution values for each placeholder only for this question, or for other questions in the same category.

11. Click Save Changes.

12. Create a dataset for the question or questions in the category. For each placeholder, generate a series of acceptable values. The more values you generate, the more a question can be used without repeating values. Figure 5-11 illustrates the interface for datasets for calculated questions.

Action	Number	a	b
		Generate a new value between	Generate a new value between
		1.0 & 10.0 with 1 ▾	1.0 & 10.0 with 1 ▾
		decimals, from a uniform distribution ▾	decimals, from a uniform distribution ▾
Add ⊙ reuse previously removed ○ force regeneration	1	7.7	9.1

Figure 5-11. Calculated question dataset

13. Click "Back to quiz editing."

Calculated questions can use more than simple arithmetic operators. The full list of operators includes abs, acos, acosh, asin, asinh, atan, atanh, ceil, cos, cosh, deg2rad, exp, expm1, floor, log, log10, log1p, rad2deg, round, sin, sinh, sprt, tan, tanh, atan2, pow, min, max, and pi. Each function's placeholders and other arguments are in parentheses. For example, if you want students to calculate the sine of one angle and two times cosine of another, you would enter sin({a}) + cos({b}*2).

Importing Questions

If you have questions from a textbook question bank, or if you don't want to use the web interface to create your questions, you can import them from a text file. Moodle supports eight native formats and provides an easy way to create new importers if you know a little PHP.

Once you get to know a format, it may be easier simply to type the questions into a text file than to use the web interface. You can just keep typing instead of waiting for new web pages to load for each question.

The default formats include:

GIFT
> With GIFT format, you can write multiple-choice, true/false, short-answer, matching, and numerical questions.

Aiken
> Aiken format provides an easy way of writing multiple-choice questions for import. It's a very easy, readable format.

Missing-word

> If you're going to write a lot of missing-word multiple-choice questions, the missing-word format is an easy way to create them.

AON

> This is the same as the missing-word format, except it creates matching questions from the multiple choice questions.

Blackboard

> If you're converting from Blackboard to Moodle, you can export your course and import the question pools into Moodle using the Blackboard format.

WebCT

> Currently, the WebCT format supports only the importing of multiple-choice and short-answer questions.

Course Test Manager

> This format enables you to import questions from the Course Test Manager from Course Technology.

Embedded answers (Cloze)

> The Cloze format is a multiple-answer question with embedded answers. These questions can be a bit tricky to develop, but they are a unique way of asking questions.

Click the help button next to the Import File button for more details about each format.

Adding Questions to a Quiz

Once you've created your questions, you'll need to add them to the quiz.

The buttons at the bottom of the question are used to add questions to the quiz. You can select individual questions using the checkboxes on the left of the question list. Select the individual questions and click the "Add selected to quiz" button at the bottom of the list, as shown in Figure 5-12.

If you want to add all of the questions you created to the quiz, click the "Select all" button and then click the "Add selected to quiz" button.

Once you've added a question to the quiz, it appears on the left side of the screen in the quiz question list. The question is still selectable on the right, but you can add it to the quiz only once. If you select the question in the category list again and add it to the quiz, nothing will happen.

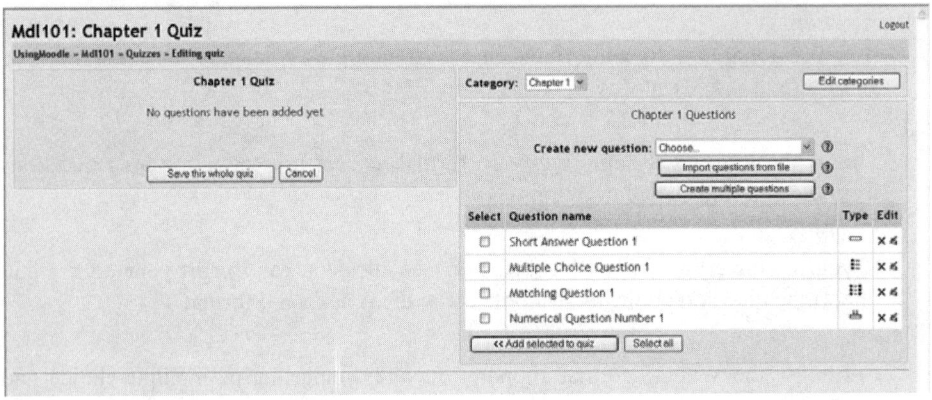

Figure 5-12. Quiz editing screen

Once you've added the questions to the quiz, you can change the order of the questions by clicking the arrow buttons on the left side of the list of quiz questions (see Figure 5-13).

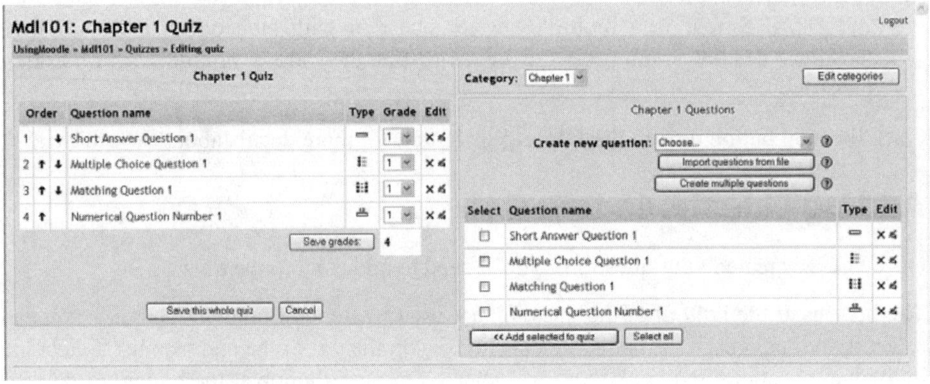

Figure 5-13. Editing quiz with questions

You will also need to set the grade for each question. You can set the number of points for each question in the dropdown menu in the Grade column. You may want to make certain questions or question types worth more than others. Remember, the questions will be weighted to match the total points possible for the quiz you set in the quiz body.

When you're done, click "Save this whole quiz."

You'll then be taken back to your course's main page. If you click on the quiz link from the content block, you'll see the quiz intro page. You can preview the quiz by clicking on the "Attempt quiz now" button. Figures 5-14 and 5-15 show the quiz as your students will see it

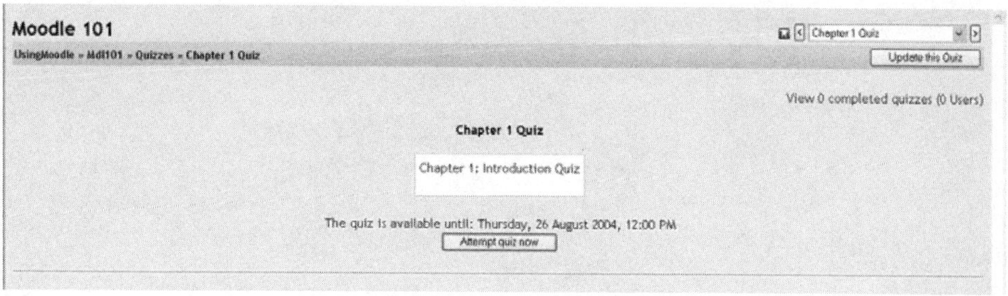

Figure 5-14. Quiz introduction

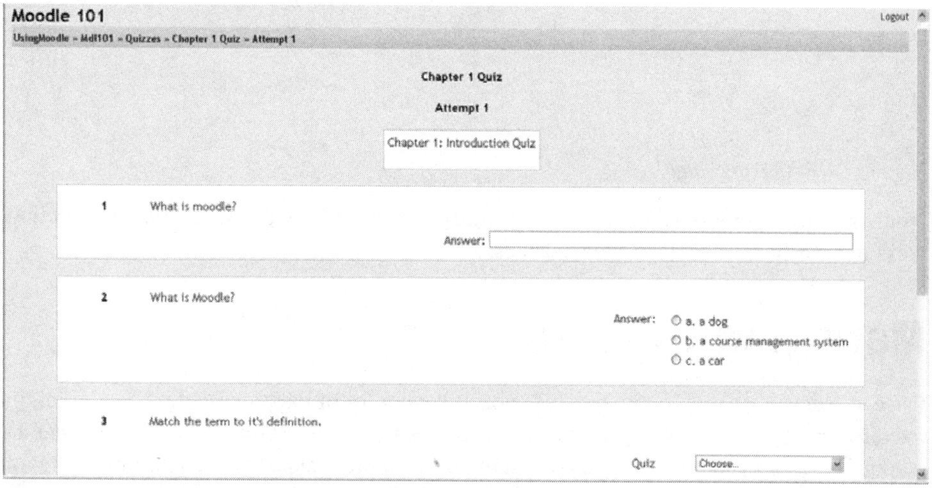

Figure 5-15. Quiz attempt

If you answer the questions, you can submit the quiz and see the feedback and responses your students will see. Your students will see two scores at the top of the page. The first is the raw score representing the total points they scored out of the maximum possible points from each question. The second score is the weighted score representing the number of points out of the maximum possible points for the quiz.

If you've enabled feedback after answering, each question will be displayed below the scores with the answers marked correct or incorrect, as shown in Figure 5-16. If you've enabled the display of correct answers, they will appear highlighted in green.

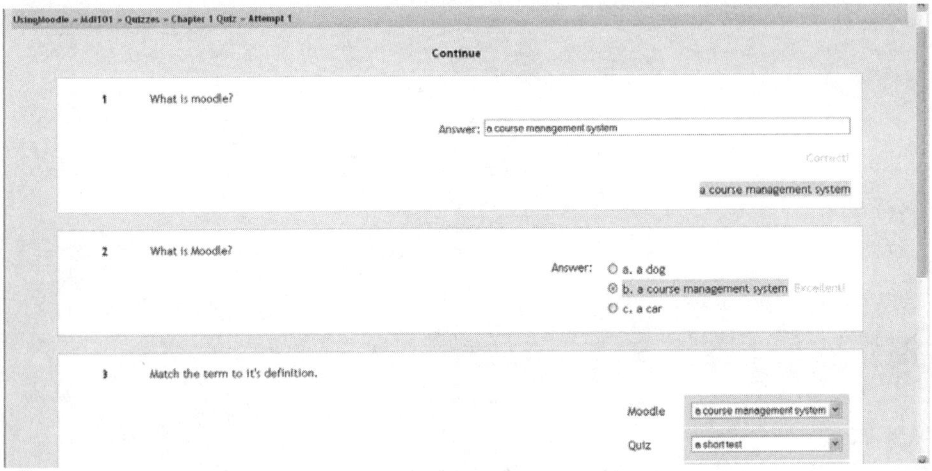

Figure 5-16. Quiz results

Your preview scores will be recorded with the students' attempts. In the next section, we'll discuss how to manage your quizzes.

Managing Quizzes

Once students start to take the quizzes, you'll have a lot of data available. If you click on the quiz link in the content block of your course's main page, you'll immediately see the number of quizzes that have been completed by your students. If you click on the attempt summary, you'll see the quiz report screen as shown in Figure 5-17. From here, you can see every quiz attempt and drill down into the individual responses. Clicking on the date and time of the attempt provides each question and answer.

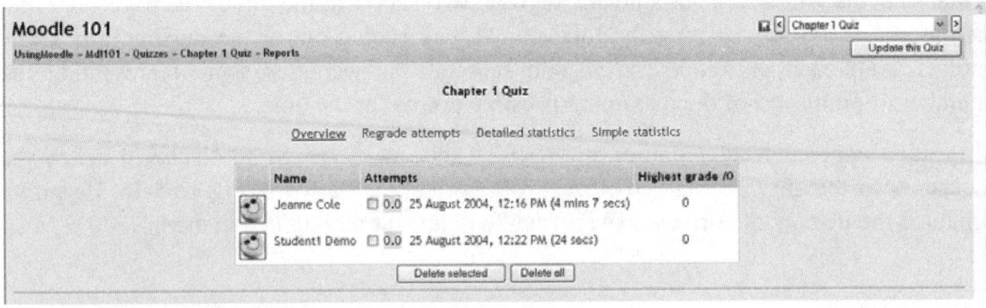

Figure 5-17. Quiz reports

If you want to delete an attempt by a student, click on the checkbox between the student's name and the grade and then click the "Delete selected" button below the attempts list. This is a good way to get rid of your own preview attempts so you have clean data in your reports.

Above the attempts list, there are four links to aggregate reports. These reports are a great way to monitor your students' performance. The first link, Overview, links to the list of completed attempts you saw when you first clicked on the completed quiz link.

The next link, "Regrade attempts," will recalculate the quiz grades if you have changed the possible number of points for the quiz or a question.

The next two reports give you detailed statistics about the quiz results. The first table displays the responses to each question individually. You will only see the results of the non-randomly selected questions. The random questions will appear as blanks in the table. The report also displays incorrect or partially correct responses. Correct responses are displayed as a double dash, except for numerical and short-answer questions. The reports for these two question types always display the student's answer. This report gives you an easy way to tell at a glance where students are having problems.

The next table is the item response analysis as shown in Figure 5-18. This is a great tool for evaluating the reliability of your questions. You can see the three most common answers to each question, the percentage of students who got each question correct, and the discrimination index. The discrimination index correlates students' overall performance on the quiz to their performance on each item; stronger students should have a better chance of getting each individual question correct, and weaker students should be have a lower chance of getting each item correct. If the distribution of correct and incorrect responses is flat (everyone has an equal chance of being correct), then everyone is guessing. If everyone is getting it right (or wrong), then the question is too easy (or too hard). The higher the discrimination index, the better the question is at providing useful data about student performance.

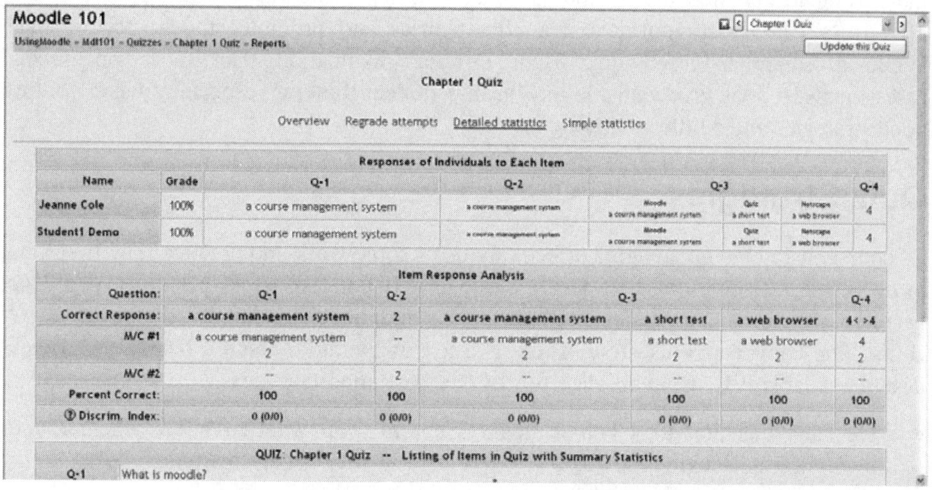

Figure 5-18. Detailed statistics report

The final table displays the questions used in the report. Multiple-choice questions also display the responses and the number of people who selected each wrong answer.

The simple statistics report shown in Figure 5-19 simply lists the number of points each student received from each question. This tells you at a glance which items students got right and wrong. Use this data to make informed decisions about your students' performance on quiz items. Bring the data back into the class and reinforce confusing concepts, and spend less time on concepts your students already understand.

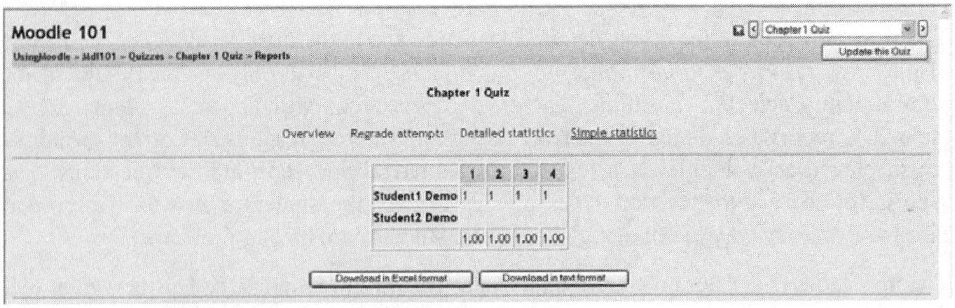

Figure 5-19. Simple quiz stats

Each statistical report can be downloaded into Excel or a text file for use in other programs. You can download the simple statistics report and generate your own statistics in Excel or another statistical package.

Effective Quiz Practices

As we've seen, the Moodle quiz engine is a powerful, flexible tool for monitoring and diagnosing a student's understanding of certain types of knowledge. Using this tool effectively can boost your course's effectiveness and promote student performance. While a computer-scored quiz is a different evaluation than more open-ended assessments, it does give valuable insight into student thinking, especially when you use good strategies and a little creativity.

Quiz Strategies

Of course, using the quiz engine effectively takes some work and practice. The first thing to do is use effective question-design strategies. If you ask good questions, you'll get useful data about your students' performance and understanding of the material. Of course, the converse is also true. There is a ton of literature about effective assessment design available. I'll just highlight a few of the most important ideas:

- Tie each question to a course goal. After all, you want to know whether your students are achieving the goals of the course, so why not ask them directly?

- Try to ask multiple questions about each important idea in the class. This gives you more data points about a student's understanding.

- When writing a multiple-choice question, be sure each wrong answer represents a common misconception. This will help you diagnose student thinking and eliminate easy guessing.

- Write questions requiring your students to think at different levels. Include recall questions, comprehension questions, and application and analysis questions. You can determine where students are having problems in their thinking. Can they recall the material but not apply it?

- Test your questions. After you've established an initial question bank, use the system reports to determine which questions are useful and which aren't. As you write new questions, give them a lower point value and throw in a few to establish their reliability.

Once you have a few well-written test banks, be sure to use the quiz reports and statistics to monitor your classes' performance. The detailed reports and statistics are valuable tools for measuring your students' understanding of the material.

Creative Quiz Uses

With the Moodle quiz engine, it's easier to utilize educationally sound assessment strategies that would be too difficult to implement with paper and pencil. Most people think of tests as an infrequent, high-stakes activity, e.g., mid-terms and finals. Better strategies involve frequent, low-stakes assessments you and your students can use to guide their performance during the course of the semester.

Creating a series of mini-tests gives you a very flexible system for gauging performance and keeping students engaged in the class. Here are a few ideas for quick quizzes you can use as part of a larger assessment strategy.

Chapter checks

Getting students to complete reading assignments has to be one of the hardest motivational tasks in education. Reading is critical to understanding most material and fundamental to success in many classes. The problem for most students is there is no immediate punishment for procrastinating on a reading assignment. If you haven't done the reading for a class discussion, you can either keep quiet or, as I used to do occasionally, wing it by skimming in class. If you have a lecture course, there's almost no need to do the reading since the lecturer usually covers most of the material in class anyway.

Creating a mini-test for each reading assignment solves a number of problems. First, it encourages students to do the reading so they can do well on the quiz. Second, it gives the students feedback on how well they understood the reading assignment. Third, it gives you data about which aspects of the reading students found confusing, and which they have already mastered so you can refocus your class activities.

For a reading mini-test, I would recommend setting a limited time quiz students can take only once. Because it's a low-stakes activity, you want students to use for self-assessment, I would also display feedback and correct answers. If you're concerned about students sharing answers after they've taken the quiz, randomize the question and answer order. If you have a test bank, make some of the questions random as well. As an additional assignment, students should write down one question about a question they got wrong and bring it to class.

Test practice

They key to effective practice is to have a realistic practice environment. Many students worry about tests, especially high-stakes tests, because they have no idea what to expect. What question format will you use? How detailed will the questions be? What should they study?

You can help alleviate test anxiety by creating a practice test students can take to help answer these questions. These tests are usually based on old questions similar to the upcoming test questions. Using last years final as an example test will force you to write new questions every year. This is a good idea anyway, since you can be sure someone has a copy of last year's test and are sharing it with others.

To set up a practice test, I'd create a zero-point test with questions from the year before in random order with random answers. I would also allow students to take the test as many times as they'd like so they can test themselves as much as they need. Display feedback, but not correct answers so it presents more of a challenge.

Data gathering

As an expert, you know a lot about your field. Your challenge as a teacher is to translate your knowledge for a novice who doesn't share your conceptual understanding or experience. An example or lecture you think is brilliant may leave your students completely confused. It can be hard to tell what students really understand and what's leaving them baffled.

A data-gathering quiz is similar to a chapter check, but it takes place after a class meeting or lecture. Your goal is to quickly get some feedback on your students' understanding of a lecture. What did they really understand? What do you need to spend more time on? I've found many instructors have trouble gauging what students find difficult, and what the students find so easy they are bored by it.

Setting up a post-class, data-gathering quiz is similar to creating a chapter check. Set the quiz for a limited time, such as a day or two before the next meeting. Allow your students to take it once and display feedback and correct answers.

Quiz Security and Cheating

Of course, online testing also presents another chance for the cheaters in your classes to try to game the system. Most online quizzes are meant to be taken at home, or at least outside of class. Students can download the questions and print them out. They can take the tests with other students, or while reading their textbooks.

Fortunately, you can counter many of these strategies, making them more trouble than they are worth to students. Let's look at a few strategies for countering most cheating schemes:

Printing and sharing questions

> If you display feedback and correct answers, students can print the results page and share it with their friends. Or they can simply print the questions themselves directly from the quiz. The key to discouraging this behavior is to randomize the question order and answer order. It makes the printouts a lot less useful. Creating larger question banks and giving tests with random subsets is also an effective strategy. If students can print only a small number of questions at a time, they will need to view the test again and again, and then sort the questions to eliminate duplicates.

Using the textbook

> Students will frequently look up the answer to questions in the textbook or a reading. If you are giving a chapter-check quiz, then this is what you want them to do. Otherwise, you need to come up with creative ways to make the textbook less directly useful. Timed quizzes are the single most effective tool for eliminating this strategy. If you include enough questions and make the time to take the quiz short enough, students won't have time to look up all the answers. I usually allot about 30 seconds per multiple-choice question. If they answer them faster and have time to look up some answers afterward, I figure they knew enough to deserve the option of looking up an answer or two.

> *Warning: Assume there will be printed copies of your questions available to students who want them. Most instructors don't realize students frequently have copies of old paper-based tests, and delivering a test electronicly is another way for students to get copies of the questions. I know one professor who had over 1,100 questions in his online test bank. At the end of the semester, he confiscated a printout from a student. It had every question with the correct answer, neatly formatted and divided by textbook chapter. We decided if students wanted to memorize 1,100 questions to the level where they could answer a small number of them displayed at random, then they would have learned more than if they had just studied. Of course, we used timed quizzes and other strategies to minimize using the printout as a reference manual.*

Asking students to apply their knowledge to novel situations can also make a difference. Synthesis and application questions can't be looked up. Students have to understand the material and apply it creatively to answer the questions. So while they may take the time to review the text, they will still need to understand what they've read to successfully answer the question.

Working with friends

If your students are on the same campus, they may meet in a lab and try to take the quiz together. This strategy is easily thwarted with random question order, random answer order, and random questions pulled from a test bank. If my screen doesn't look like yours, then it's harder for us to quickly answer all of the questions. A timed quiz also makes it harder for the two of us to cheat if we have different questions and only a short amount of time to answer.

Have someone else take the test

The old adage goes, "On the Internet, no one knows you're a dog." And no one knows who is actually taking the test. Students will sometimes pay classmates, or others who have taken the course in the past, to take online quizzes for them. There are two ways to counter this strategy. One, have an occasional proctored exam where students need to show ID. If they haven't taken the quizzes or done the work until then, they will do poorly on the proctored exam. Second, to eliminate current classmates from taking each other's quizzes, make them available only for a short time. You could require everyone to take the test within a two- to four-hour block. If the test is properly randomized, it will be very difficult to take it more than once during the testing period. The test-taker will worry about his own grade first, then about his employer's grade.

Obviously, there are many strategies students can use to cheat. While it would be naïve to assume there isn't cheating, the vast majority of your students want to succeed on their own merits. The anonymity of the online environment may open up new avenues for the cheaters, but it's not really much different from your face-to-face classes. A few people will go to great lengths to cheat, but most will be honest as long as it's not too easy to get away with it. A few precautions will eliminate most of the cheaters, and the classic strategies will work for the others.

6

Workshops

The workshop activity is the most complex tool currently available in Moodle. Workshops are designed so a student's work can be submitted and offered for peer review within a structured framework. Workshops provide a process for both instructor and peer feedback on open-ended assignments, such as essays and research papers. There are easy-to-use interfaces for uploading assignments, performing self-assessments, and peer reviews of other students' papers.

The key to the workshop is the scoring guide, which is a set of specific criteria for making judgments about the quality of a given work. Open-ended assessments are difficult to score reliably, unless there are very specific performance dimensions the reviewers should follow, such as the presence of a thesis and strong evidence supporting each point. For example, if a grader receives 15 student essays, she may review each one in turn. She will probably spend more time on the first few papers, carefully marking the grammar and structure of the essay. As the grader becomes fatigued, she may move to a more holistic scoring heuristic, deciding if an essay is "good" or "bad." The level of feedback given to each student can vary depending on where they are in the pile.

Good scoring guides ask specific questions about the work being evaulated. Making a judgment about whether there is a clearly written thesis statement in an essay is a much easier task than deciding if an essay is "well written." As you develop your workshop, you will create a set of scoring criteria that you and your students can follow when evaluating submitted assignments.

Workshops also allow students to evaluate example assignments uploaded by an instructor. You can upload good and bad examples of an assignment so students can practice critiquing. This gives students a valuable opportunity to calibrate their judgments against your expert opinion. If they realize their evaluation of a work is significantly different from yours, they can work with you to figure out why.

Setting up and managing workshops is a complex process. It can take a while to figure out how the system works. Once you get it up and running, however, it is a powerful learning tool.

How to Create a Workshop

Preparing a workshop so students can begin submitting their assignments is a three-step process. First, you need to add the workshop to your course. Second, you need to create the scoring guide you and your students will use to evaluate submissions. Third, if you want students to critique your example assignments, you need to upload those as well.

Adding a Workshop

To create a workshop for peer review of materials

1. Click Turn Editing Mode On.
2. Select Workshop from the Add Activity menu in the section where you want to place the link.
3. On the Workshop page, shown in Figure 6-1, add a title and description.

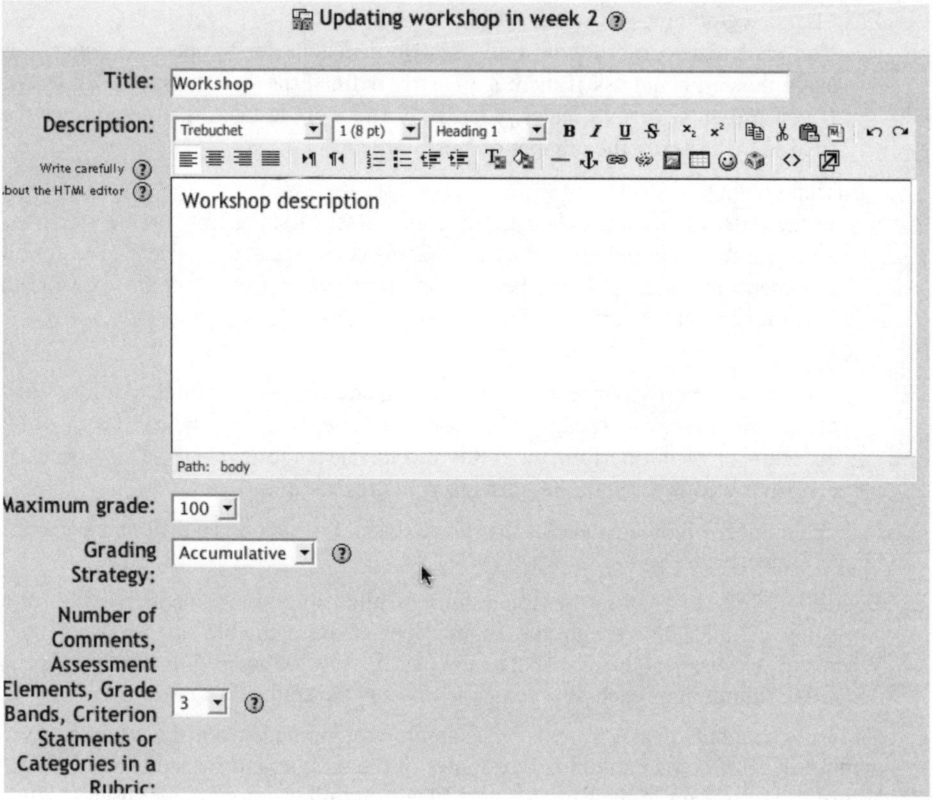

Figure 6-1. Add a workshop

4. Select the maximum grade for the workshop assignment.

5. Choose a grading strategy from these five options:

    No grading
        Students who review assignments don't give each other grades, just comments.
        You can then grade the comments, which will give the commenting student his
        final grade.

    Accumulative grading
        Later in the process, you can create a multidimensional scoring rubric for
        students to score each other's work. Accumulative grading calculates the
        submitting student's final grade based on the cumulative grades received from
        her peers within each of the dimensions. You assign a scale and weight to each
        dimension when you develop the scoring guide.

Error Banded grading

>   You can create a rubric with only Yes/No decisions for the peer reviewer. For example, you could ask if there's a clearly defined thesis statement in an essay. If you use only Yes/No scales, you can create a grade table that determines the final score based on the number of Yeses or Nos.

Criterion grading

>   In the criterion grading scheme, you create a set of statements used to rank the assessment. Each statement has an associated suggested grade. The criterion statements and grades should be in order so reviewers can select the appropriate grade for the statement.

Rubrics

>   Rubrics use performance examples that guide decisions about quality. Each element in a rubric is scored on a five-point scale, with each point illustrated by an example of the performance. Reviewers select the level of quality on each element by comparing the submission with the example.

6. Pick the number of dimensions for the rubric. Each dimension is a different aspect of the performance.

7. Decide if you will allow resubmissions. Unlike the assignment module, the workshop module allows multiple submissions to be available at the same time. When the submissions are distributed for peer review, Moodle will randomly pick one of the submissions each time someone reviews the student's work.

8. Choose a number of assessments of example assignments from the teacher. As I mentioned above, you can upload examples of the assignment for students to assess before they move on to their peers' work. These training scores can be used to fine-tune a student's critical eye.

9. Determine the number of peer reviews a student must perform.

10. Choose whether self-assessment is required. Self-assessment always adds one assessment to the number of reviews of exemplars and peer reviews a student must perform.

11. Select whether assessments must be agreed on by peers. This feature requires the reviewer and the reviewee to agree on the reviewer's assessment before it is calculated. The student who submitted the assignment may disagree with the reviewer and send it back for reevaluation. This can continue until the deadline. If there is no agreement before the deadline, the review isn't used. If you're using assessment agreement, you can hide the grades before agreement. Students will have to reach an agreement on the comments only. Once they've agreed the comments are fair, the grade is revealed to the submitting student.

12. Set a maximum upload size for an assessment. The upper limit for the system is set by the system administrator.

13. Set the deadline for submission and review of the assignment.

14. Click Save Changes and you will be taken back to the course's main page.

Obviously, there's a lot here to make sense of without having seen the rest of the process. Bear with me for a bit while we look at how to set up the rest of the workshop, and this will become more obvious.

Creating Scoring Guides

Creating the workshop shell is only the first step. Once you've created the shell, you'll need to set up your rubric, upload exemplars, and finish setting up the workshop for your students.

To create a scoring guide for an accumulative grading scheme:

1. Click on the workshop you created in your main course page. You will then be taken to the Editing Assessment Elements page.

2. For each rubric dimension you created when you set up the workshop, you will see a description, scale, and weight entry, as shown in Figure 6-2.

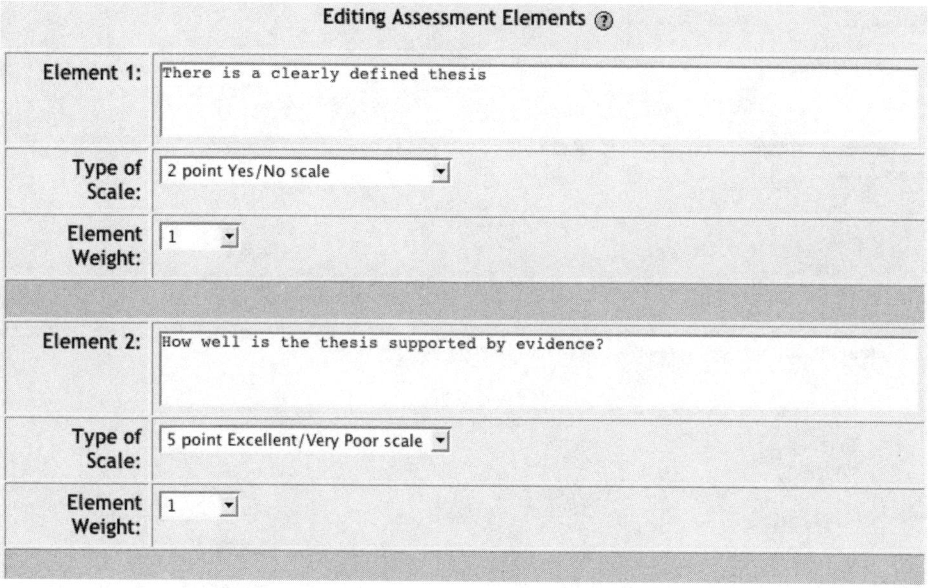

Editing Assessment Elements

Element 1:	There is a clearly defined thesis
Type of Scale:	2 point Yes/No scale
Element Weight:	1

Element 2:	How well is the thesis supported by evidence?
Type of Scale:	5 point Excellent/Very Poor scale
Element Weight:	1

Figure 6-2. Accumulative grading scale

3. Enter the first performance dimension you want students to assess when looking at their peers' work. Each dimension should evaluate a critical aspect of the performance.

4. Select a scale for the element. Remember, the scale itself doesn't affect the weight given to that element. A 2-point Yes/No scale can be worth as much or more than a 100-point scale.

5. Set the weight of the element. The weight scale can be between 1 and 4 (the default is 1).

6. Repeat the process for each element you selected for your rubric.

7. Click Save Changes.

To create a scoring guide for the error-banded scoring guide:

1. Click on the workshop you created in your main course page. You will then be taken to the Editing Assessment Elements page.

2. Enter a description of each element as shown in Figure 6-3. These are the elements reviewers will make yes/no decisions about.

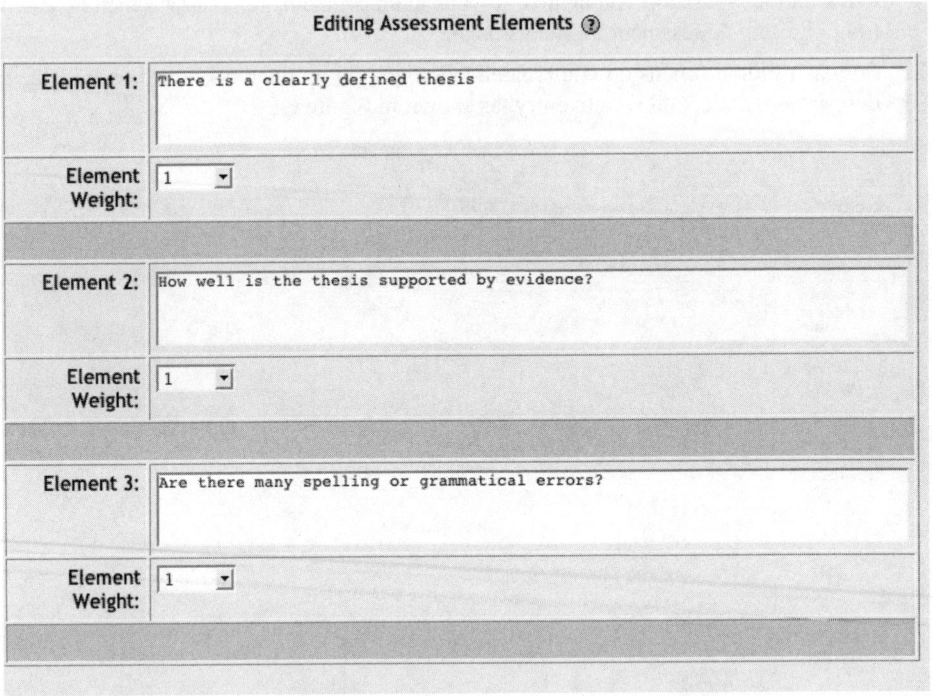

Editing Assessment Elements ⑦

Element 1:	There is a clearly defined thesis
Element Weight:	1 ▾
Element 2:	How well is the thesis supported by evidence?
Element Weight:	1 ▾
Element 3:	Are there many spelling or grammatical errors?
Element Weight:	1 ▾

Figure 6-3. Error banding grading scale

3. Click Save Changes.

To create a criterion scoring guide:

1. Click on the workshop you created in your main course page. You will then be taken to the Editing Assessment Elements page.

2. Enter a set of criteria for grading the submission (see Figure 6-4). Criteria can be cumulative or self-contained and should be in order of either increasing or decreasing quality.

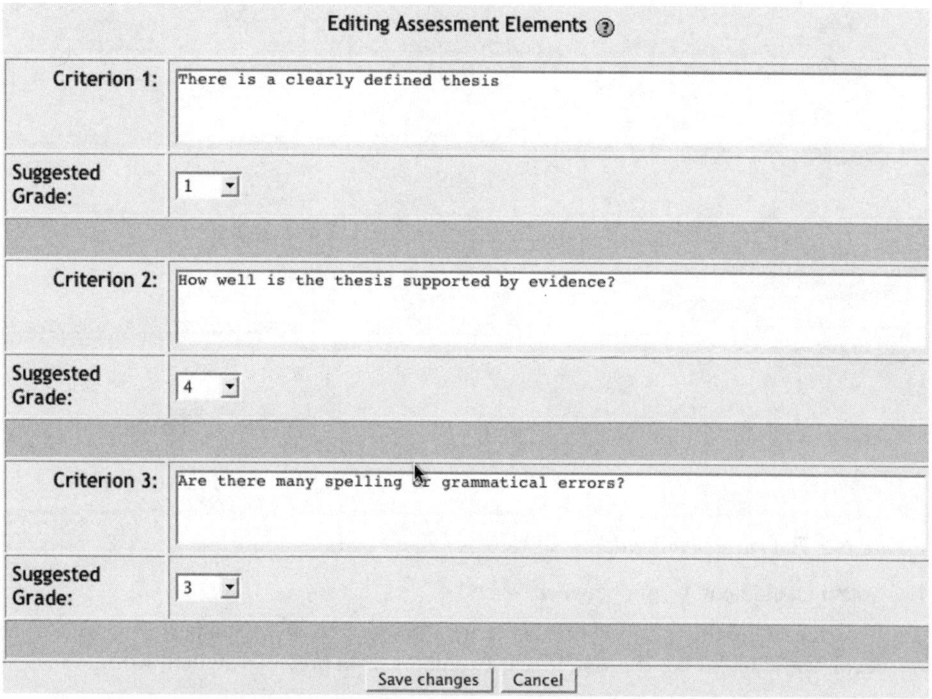

Editing Assessment Elements ⑦

Criterion 1:	There is a clearly defined thesis
Suggested Grade:	1 ▾
Criterion 2:	How well is the thesis supported by evidence?
Suggested Grade:	4 ▾
Criterion 3:	Are there many spelling or grammatical errors?
Suggested Grade:	3 ▾

Save changes   Cancel

Figure 6-4. Criterion scoring guide

1. Enter a suggested grade for each criterion. The grades should also be in order.

2. Click Save Changes.

To create a scoring guide for the rubric grading scheme:

1. Click on the workshop you created in your main course page. You will then be taken to the Editing Assessment Elements page.

2. Enter a description for the first element in the rubric form, as shown in Figure 6-5.

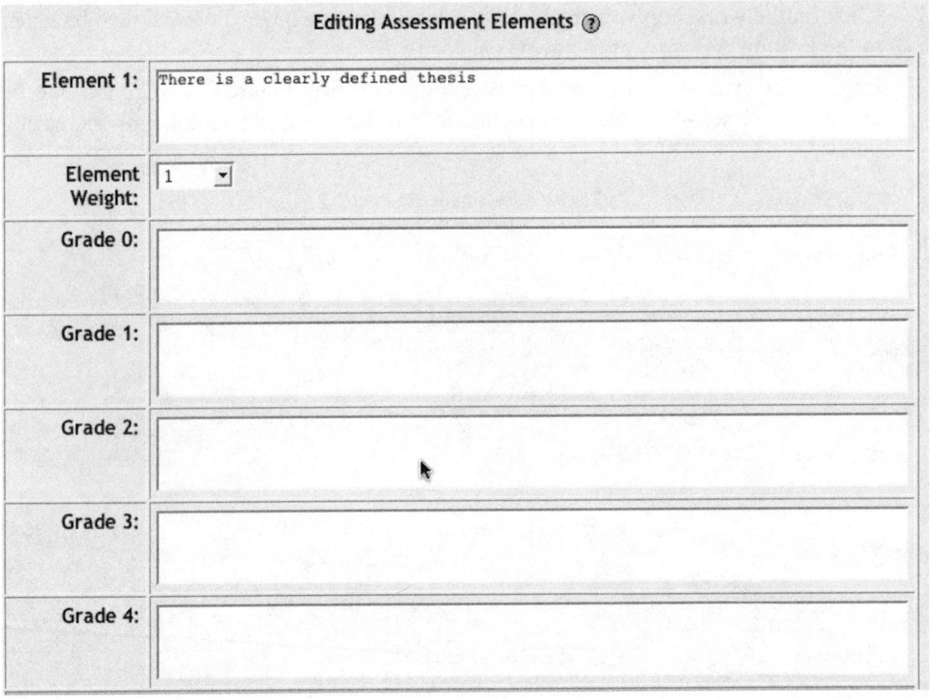

Editing Assessment Elements ⑦

Element 1:	There is a clearly defined thesis
Element Weight:	1 ▾
Grade 0:	
Grade 1:	
Grade 2:	
Grade 3:	
Grade 4:	

Figure 6-5. Rubric scoring guide

1. Select an element weight between –4 and 4.

2. For each of the four grade elements, write a description of what a performance at that level would look like. If possible, use examples from previous student work.

3. Click Save Changes.

Once you've clicked Save Changes, you'll be taken to the Managing the Assessment Page. Below the assignment-description block, you'll see six tabs displaying the steps of the workshop setup and delivery process, as shown in Figure 6-6. Each tab enables different capabilities for you and your students.

Set Up Assignment
    This tab gives you the links to upload your example work for students to review.

Allow Student Submissions
    When this tab is activated, students can score the instructor's examples, upload their own submissions, and complete self-assessments. They will not see other students' submissions for peer review, however.

Allow Student Submissions and Assessments
> During this phase, students can perform the actions listed above as well as score other students' work.

Allow Student Assessments
> Once this phase is activated, students can only score instructor examples and perform self-assessments and peer reviews.

Calculation of Final Grades
> Once all of the assessments are completed, you can set weights for each of the components.

Display Final Grades
> After you've set the weighting for the final grades, the last phase displays the results.

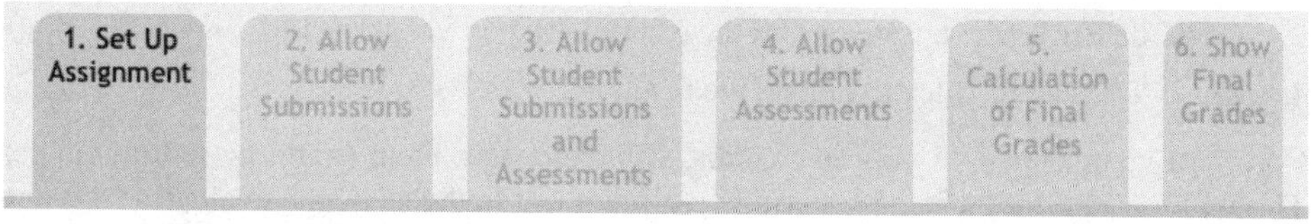

Figure 6-6. Workshop process tabs

After you've set up your scoring guide, you'll need to upload example assignments for students to review before they can review their peers' submissions.

Uploading Example Assignments

Below the six workshop process tabs, you'll see four links. The one we're interested in right now is the Submit Example Assignment link. Example assignments are graded by students before they move on to their peers' submissions. You may want to use examples from previous semesters, or you can create your own exemplars.

The idea behind using example assignments is to give students a chance to practice evaluating other assignments. Example assignments should contain both positive and negative examples of the scoring criteria so students can practice rating on both ends of the scale. For example, you may want to include one essay with a well-written thesis and a lot of good supporting material, but a number of spelling and grammatical errors as well. Alternatively, you can include an example with few errors and a good writing style, but a weak, poorly supported thesis.

To upload an example for assessment:

1.   Click Submit Example Assignment.

2.   Give your example a title. You *must* give your example a title or Moodle will reject it (see Figure 6-7).

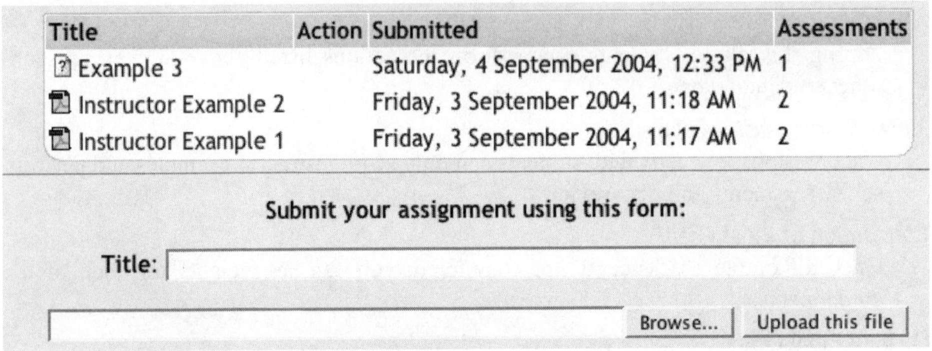

Title	Action	Submitted	Assessments
⬚ Example 3		Saturday, 4 September 2004, 12:33 PM	1
📄 Instructor Example 2		Friday, 3 September 2004, 11:18 AM	2
📄 Instructor Example 1		Friday, 3 September 2004, 11:17 AM	2

Submit your assignment using this form:

Title: [   ]

[   ] [Browse...] [Upload this file]

Figure 6-7. Upload example file

3. Click the Browse... button to find the example file on your desktop.

4. Click "Upload this file" to upload the example.

Once you've uploaded all your exemplars, you can assess them using the scoring guide. This will be important when comparing your judgment to the students' evaluation of your examples.

To score the example assignments:

1. Click the Teacher Submissions for Assessment link below the Submit Example Assignment link.

2. For each element in your scoring guide, rate your submitted example.

3. Give feedback for each rating.

4. Add general comments about the example.

5. Click Save my Assessment.

> *Tip: As you rate your example, give detailed feedback about why you are giving each rating. If students can see your reasoning, they will find it easier to apply the same reasoning to their own peer evaluations.*

Once you've uploaded and scored all your examples, you are ready to move the workshop to the next phase.

Managing Workshops

Once you've set up your workshop, you will need to manage student submissions and evaluation. Fortunately, the workshop makes it easy to track student activity as it happens. You can also choose how much feedback you give to students at any given time.

Workshop Phases

The six tabs on the workshop screen represent the six phases of a workshop. We've just completed phase 1. Phases 2 through 4 allow students to interact with the workshop. Phase 2 allows students to upload their submissions and perform instructor and self-assessments but does not distribute submissions for peer review. Phase 3 allows students to do everything in phase 2, but also distributes submissions for peer review. Phase 4 allows only self- and peer-assessments.

You may not want to use all three phases. There are two strategies for managing workshop phases. The easiest, but not necessarily the best, is to use only phase 3 after you've set up the workshop in phase 1. This gives students maximum flexibility. They can upload their assignments at any point before the due date. The problem occurs when students begin to peer-review each other's work. If students are permitted to peer-review before all of the submissions are in, the submissions won't be distributed randomly. The students who submit and review early will see only other early submissions. Late submitters will see only late submissions. Students who submit too close to the deadline may not give their peers enough time to review their work.

The alternative strategy uses only phases 2 and 4. You can set an interim deadline for student submissions and only accept student work before this due date. After the submission deadline, you'll set the workshop to phase 4 and students will only be allowed to perform peer reviews. This strategy will help ensure an even distribution of student work for evaluation and ensure that everyone has sufficient time for review.

Student submissions

Once you've activated the Allow Student Submission tab, students can begin to interact with the workshop. If you've required students to assess instructor examples, they will need to complete that assessment before they can upload their own work.

The student view of the workshop is very different from your own. Students see a gradual process in which they must first evaluate the instructor examples. Once they've completed these, they will then see the interface to upload their own assignments. Only after they've uploaded their assignments can they access the link to perform self-assessments (see Figure 6-8).

```
                        Workshop

    Due date: Friday, 17 December 2004, 04:10 PM (10 days 17 hours)
    Maximum grade: 100
    Details of Assessment: Specimen Assessment Form

  Workshop description
```

Your Assessments of Examples from the Teacher

Title	Action	Comment
📄 Instructor Example 1	View	Graded by Teacher

Assessments by Teachers

Title	Action	Comment
📄 Student Essay 1	View	Friday, 3 September 2004, 11:41 AM

No Submissions available for assessment

Your Assessments

Title	Action	Comment
📄 My Essay	View | Re-assess	Assessed on Saturday, 4 September 2004, 01:33 PM; Graded by Teacher; Assessment not yet agreed
📄 Student Essay 1	View | Re-assess	Assessed on Friday, 3 September 2004, 11:47 AM; Own Work; Graded by Teacher; Assessment not yet agreed

Figure 6-8. Student view of a workshop

> *Warning: Student submissions do not immediately appear in the instructor's workshop interface. The workshop module depends on a process on the server that runs on a regular basis (called a cron job) and won't update the interface until the cron job is complete. Your system administrator can tell you how often the process runs and how often you can expect the workshop to be updated.*

Student assessments

Your view of student activity takes place on the main workshop page. Below the six workshop process tabs, you'll see three links that will help you track the workshop shown in Figure 6-9:

Ungraded Assessments of Teacher Submissions
From here, can access student evaluations of your example submissions. You give each evaluation a grade and give the students feedback.

Ungraded Assessments of Student Submissions
Like the assessment of instructor examples, you can grade the students' peer-review evaluations.

Student Submissions for Assessment
Use this link to grade the students' submissions directly. Later, you can use your rating to influence the final grade for the workshop.

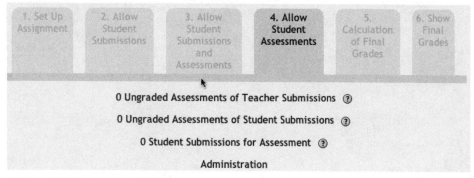

Figure 6-9. Student activity links

Each of these grading opportunities is optional. Which you choose depends on how you want to calculate the final grade for the workshop. Each of these grades can be used in calculating the final grade, which I'll discuss below.

When you assess a student assignment, you'll see the same scoring guide you set up in the beginning of the workshop (see Figure 6-10). You'll use it to give the student a score for his work. Later, you can choose to include your assessment directly as part of the final grade or include it with the other peer reviews.

Administration

The administration area serves two important functions. First, below the tools, there is a complete record of all student submissions and evaluations. The system first lists your submissions and their assessments. Below your submissions is each student's assessment. It's easy to see the ratings each student has completed and get a quick overview of their scores. Finally, you'll see a list of each student's submissions with corresponding assessments.

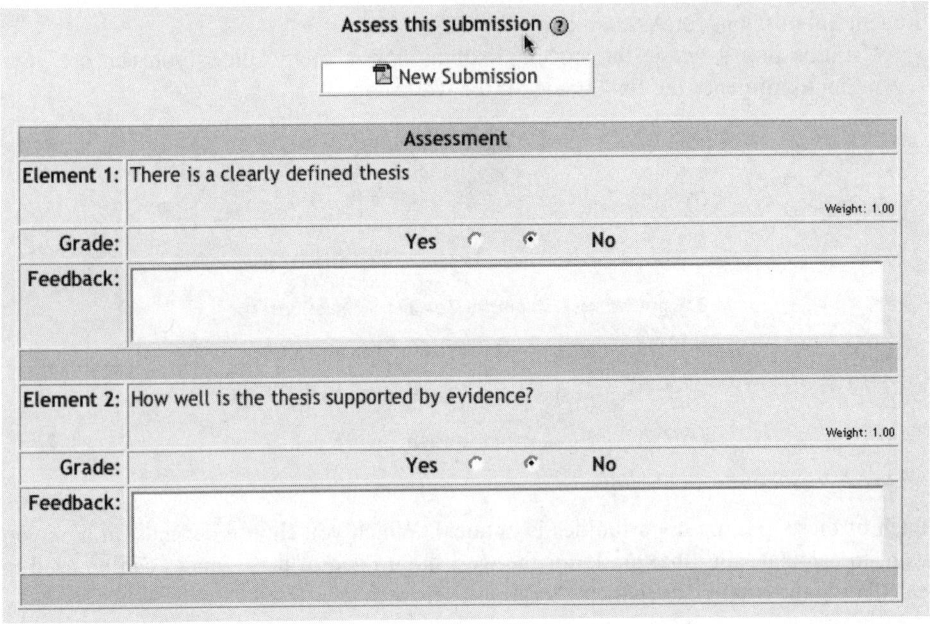

Figure 6-10. Assess student work

The administration area also holds two important tools shown in Figure 6-11. The first tool sets the over allocation level. Over-allocation is the amount any given student submission will be assigned for peer review over the level needed for an even distribution of assignments. If the over-allocation is set to 0, then each submission is assigned the same number of times. Over-allocation greater than 0 allows each assignment to be assigned one or two more times more than the even distribution level.

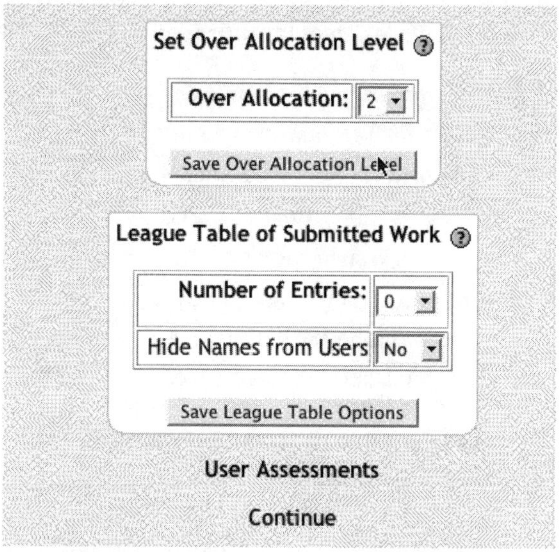

Figure 6-11. Workshop administration tools

If you allow submission and peer review at the same time, increasing the over-allocation level will increase the chances a student won't have to wait for all the submissions before she receives her full quota of peer-review submissions. The disadvantage is that some students will receive one more or one less review of their assignment than their peers.

The other tool in the administration area creates a league table of student submissions. Like the standings in a sports league, a league table lists the highest-scoring papers. You can set the number of submissions listed and whether the students can see the names of the submitters.

Calculation of final grades

Once the workshop is completed, you can configure the calculation of the final grades by moving to phase 5. There are a number of factors you can weigh when assigning the final grade for the workshop, as shown in Figure 6-12. Each item is assigned a relative weight on a scale from 0 to 50. If each of the items is assigned a weight of 1, they will all factor equally into the score. The same will hold true if all the items are set to the same nonzero number. An item set to a weight of 10 will have 10 times the impact on the student's final grade than an item with a weight of 1, but 1/5 the impact of an item with a weight of 50.

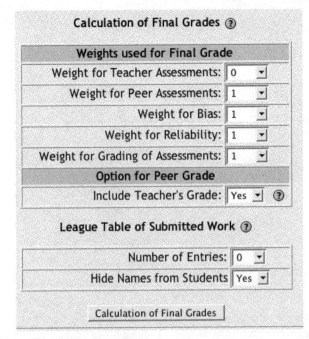

Figure 6-12. Calculation of final grades

Weight for Teacher Assessments
: Teacher assessments are your grades for the students' submissions. Set this weight to a nonzero number to include your score as a separate factor.

Weight for Peer Assessments
: Assign a weighting factor for the scores from the peer-review process.

Weight for Bias
: This factor measures the bias of the student receiving the grade. Bias is measured as the difference between the student's rating of peer submissions and the peer averages for those assignments. So if a student consistently rates their peers higher or lower than the average, they will receive a lower bias score. The workshop developer recommends *not* giving the bias factor a high weight.

Weight for Reliability
: Reliability is another measure of how well the student's peer reviews compare to the average reviews. The reliability measure averages the difference between the student's grade and her peers' average grades after discounting for bias. So if a student closely follows the average score for all the assignments she assessed, she will get a good reliability rating.

Weight for Grading of Assessments
> This factor calculates how much weight your grades for student assessments will carry in the final calculation.

Option for Peer Grade: Include Teacher's Grade
> You can choose to roll your own grade of the student's submission into the peer assessments. If you feel the averages for peer assessments are too high or too low, you can add your own score for a student's submission into the average.

Once you save your final weights, you'll see a grade sheet listing each student in the class, the scores of each factor, and a final grade. If you're not happy with the grade calculation, you can go back and change the weighting before you determine the final grades.

Under the grade-weighting table, you'll also have the opportunity to create a new league table that will be visible when you publish the final grades.

After you've completed the grade weighting, you can display the final grades to the students by moving to the sixth and final phase, Display of Final Grades.

After the final grades are displayed, students can view their grades and the detailed score for each factor by clicking on the workshop link again.

Effective Workshop Practices

The workshop is the most complex tool we've looked at so far. The extensive setup and management process can be daunting, which is why it is especially important to have a plan for how you will use the workshop before you start working. If you know in advance how you want the workshop to function, the important evaluation criteria, and how the students will interact with the submissions and with each other, you'll save yourself a lot of potential confusion later.

There are a few important decisions to make before you get started:

*   How many instructor examples do you want students to practice on?

*   How many peer reviews can you reasonably expect them to perform?

*   How long will you give students to submit? How long to perform assessments?

*   How will you control the quality of the student assessments, i.e., how will you prevent students from just giving each other A's?

*   Do you want the workshop to focus on peer assessment or instructor assessment?

Once you've made these decisions, you have the beginning of a plan for your workshop. The last decision is critical in determining the shape of your workshop. I've been in classes where peer review was required but didn't influence the grade. I've also been in classes where peer assessment counted for half of the grade I received on a paper. It's important to decide this ahead of time so students know how much their peer ratings will influence the final grades.

If peer review is very important to the assignment, be sure to put measures in place to moderate student assessments. Plan on adding your assessment of a student's submission to the peer-review pool. This will help pull the average toward a score you think is reasonable without completely overriding the consensus view.

Creative Workshop Practices

Once you've mastered the basics of creating and managing a workshop, you can begin to use them in creative ways. I've detailed a few ideas below.

Intermediate steps

Writing, and many other creative processes, is an iterative endeavor. It takes multiple revisions of a work to make it the best it can be. Early in the process, it is useful to receive feedback from peers and experts about the structure and direction of the work.

To facilitate a continuous feedback process, consider setting up workshops for the intermediate steps in projects during the semester. For example, if students are writing an essay, you could set up a workshop for the topic proposal. Students could evaluate each other's proposals according to the dimensions you think are important. Later, they could submit outlines or early drafts for feedback as well.

For early work, you may want to make a student's grade more dependent on the feedback they give their peers than on the quality of the work itself. Later on, you could increase the value of the assessment of the work itself. Students won't have to submit perfect work right away, and the early grading and feedback on their assessments will help them calibrate their responses.

Presentations and performances

Most instructors use the workshop module to assess written work, but a workshop is not limited to just written assignments. Just like the assignment module, the workshop module can accept any electronic document smaller than the maximum upload limit. You could also submit links to media stored on other servers if a video or audio file is too large.

You can use the workshop module for peer feedback on presentations and performances. If students are required to give a presentation in class, you could set up a workshop for peer review and self-assessment. Students would submit their presentation slides or notes. The scoring guide could ask students to rate each other on both the live presentation and the submitted materials.

Randomly assigning assessments can be a useful motivational tool in this context. If students don't know in advance which presentations they will be required to assess, they are more likely to pay attention to all of the presentations and take good notes so they can articulate an informed judgment later.

7

Assignments
and Exercises

Assignments

After looking at the complex and powerful workshop and quiz modules, assignments will be a refreshingly simple method for collecting student work. Assignments are a simple and flexible catch-all for things you want to grade, but don't fall into any of the other tool types.

The assignment module gives you an easy way to allow students to upload any digital content for grading. You can ask them to submit essays, spreadsheets, presentations, photographs, or small audio or video clips. Anything they can store on their hard drives can be submitted in response to an assignment.

Assignments don't need to require uploads. You can create offline assignments to remind students of real-world assignments they need to complete. Currently, these "offline" assignments are used to record grades online for activities that don't have an online component.

Assignments are a simple, useful tool you can use in creative ways to collect more authentic responses from your students than is possible with the quiz engine.

How to Create an Assignment

Compared to some of the other tools we've looked at, assignments are easy to create. Basically, you create a description of the assignment and a place for students to upload their responses. There is no special processing or a lot of options.

To create an assignment:

1. Click Turn Editing Mode On.

2. Select Assignment from the Add menu.

3. On the Editing Assignment page, shown in Figure 7-1, give your assignment a meaningful name.

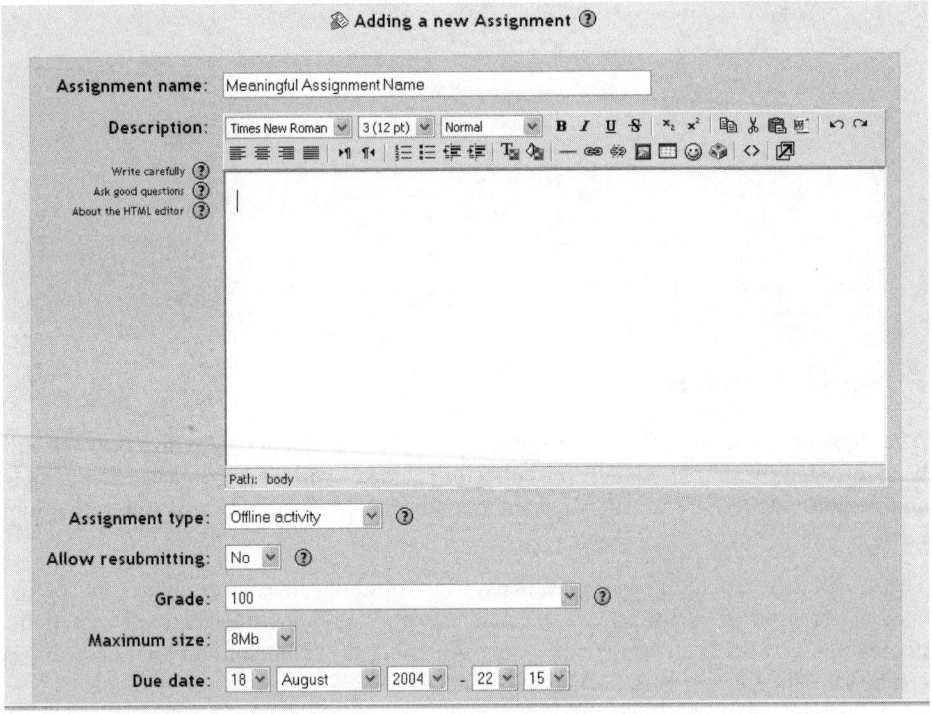

Figure 7-1. Add an assignment

4. In the Description area, carefully describe your assignment. It's a good idea to be very detailed here, even if you've already detailed the requirements in your syllabus. In fact, you might want to copy and paste from your syllabus to avoid confusion.

5.   Choose the assignment type: offline or an uploaded file. Offline assignments are descriptions and a column in the grades module. Uploaded assignments require students to submit an electronic file for grading.

6.   If you want students to be able to upload multiple revisions of an assignment, set Allow Resubmitting to Yes. Otherwise, leave it on No.

7.   Choose the grade scale you want to use for the assignment.

8.   Set the maximum size for a file upload. The top of the scale is set by your system administrator.

9.   Set the due date and time for your assignment.

10. Click Save Changes to make your assignment available.

Your assignment will appear in your course's main page. It will also be added to your course calendar and will appear in the Upcoming Events block to remind students when it's due.

Later, we'll take a look at how to combine these options in creative ways to help your students engage in some interesting tasks. But for now, let's look at how to manage the responses to the assignment.

Managing Assignment Submissions

When your students are ready to submit an assignment, they can access the form through the link in the appropriate section in your course. They will see the assignment name, due date, and details. At the bottom of the screen are a text field and two buttons. They will use the Browse… button to find their assignment on their computer. Then they will use the Upload this File button to submit the assignment.

Once they've submitted their assignment, Moodle will show them a block with the date they uploaded the file and the name of the file they uploaded. If you've enabled multiple submissions, they can upload another file, replacing the old one. Each student can submit only one file for each assignment, as shown in Figure 7-2.

> *Warning: Be sure to remind students that if they upload a second file it will delete the file they've already submitted!*

To view your students' submissions, click on the assignment name in the sections list. You'll see the assignment name and details and a link in the upper righthand corner of the page telling you how many assignments have been submitted.

Each assignment will have its own block. The top of the block lists the student's name and the date he last submitted the assignment. Below the student's name is a link to download the assignment. You will need to download the assignment and open it in another application, unless it's in HTML. So if your student submits a Word document, you'll need to save it to your desktop and open it in Word.

Below the download link is your feedback area (see Figure 7-3). Once you've reviewed the student's assignment, pick the grade for the assignment from the dropdown list. You set the scale when you created the assignment. Below the grade scale, you can type feedback regarding his work. When you're done, click "Save all my feedback" at the top or bottom of the screen.

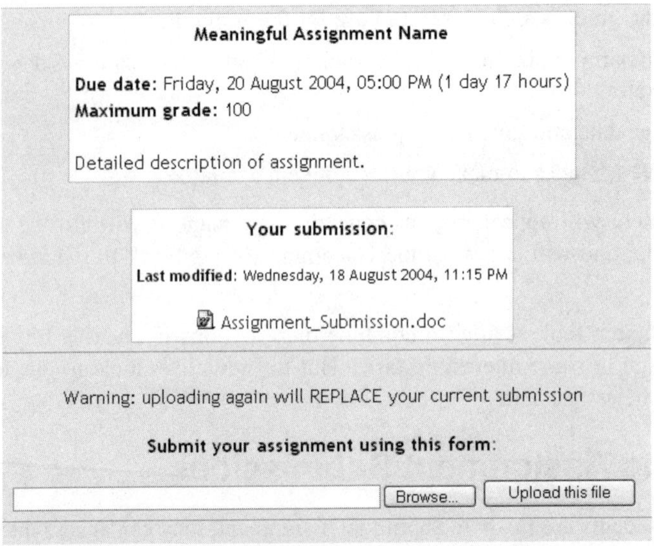

Figure 7-2. Assignment submission

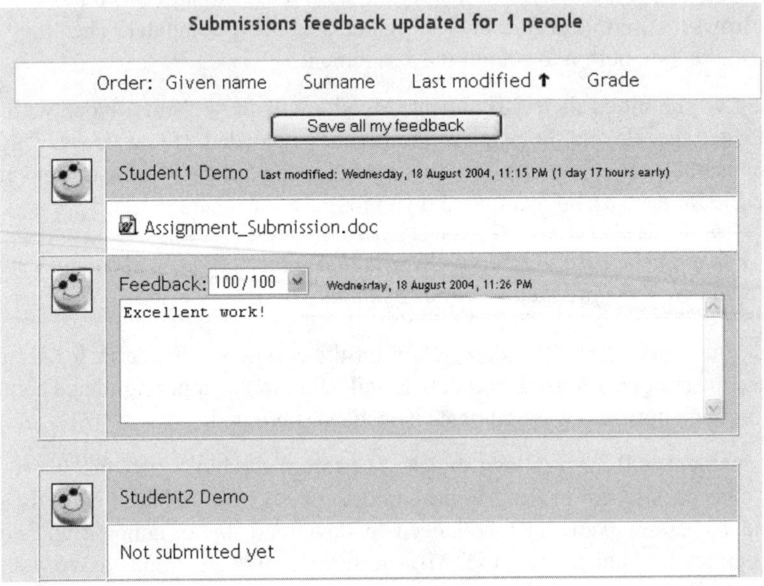

Figure 7-3. Assignment grading

If you've given an offline assignment, you can enter grades the same way. Click on the name of the assignment in the sections list. Then click "View assignment grades and feedback." You'll see a list of all your students with grade menus and feedback boxes for each.

Students can see your grade and comment in two ways. First, they can click on the assignment link again. They will see your grade and comments below the submission block Alternatively, they can click on the grades link. They will see the score for the assignment and can then click on the assignment name to get the written feedback.

Effective Assignment Practices

The two basic assignment types, offline and upload, are so generic you may find it difficult to use them effectively at first. I find it useful to think about them as two separate modules sharing a common interface.

Offline assignments are useful for recording grades for real-world activities. Currently, they are a sort of hack that allows the creation of manual columns in the grades module. If you look at the grades module (which we'll cover in Chapter 12), you'll notice there is no way to add a column so you can add grades not automatically generated by a quiz or other tool. The offline assignment gives you a way around this limitation by adding a column in which you can record any grade at all. Hopefully, the community will address the limitations in the grades area soon.

The offline assignment is more than just a hack, however. You can use this tool to record scores or feedback for student presentations, class participation, performances, sculptures, or any other nondigital performance. You can create a scale to give nonnumeric feedback if you don't want to give a numeric score to a creative performance. Again, I'll cover creating scales in more detail in Chapter 12.

Uploaded assignments are probably what most people expect when they think about assignments. Remember, you can use these assignment types for any sort of digital content. Most instructors use assignments to collect essays and other word-processing assignments. You can also use them to collect other types of student work. Students could upload PowerPoint slides prior to a presentation. You could assign a what-if scenario using a spreadsheet and ask students to submit it. Students could take a digital photograph of a sculpture or mechanical project and submit it for evaluation.

As long as the file is smaller than the upload maximum, you can create assignments for any sort of digital content. Consider the types of work products you want your students to produce during your course. How many of them could be digital files submitted using an assignment?

Creative assignments

Simple, flexible tools can lend themselves to creative problem solving. The uses for the assignment module are limited only by your imagination. Let's take a look at case studies, an advanced use of assignments, to get the creative process started.

Case studies are important learning tools in a number of professional fields. Medical schools, business schools, and others use case studies to convey information in a narrative context and give students a chance to immediately apply their new knowledge.

Designing a good case study does take some time, but I encourage you to try an iterative approach. Start small and build up over time. Eventually, you could follow one case study across an entire semester, or build a set of cases, forming the basis for your students' practice. My wife's engineering capstone course used one case study in several parts over the course of a semester to test her students' ability to apply the engineering concepts they had learned over the previous four years. Each phase of the course introduced new challenges they had to solved using different techniques and concepts.

Case studies have a few basic parts. There's a narrative setup, background data, and a problem statement. The problem statement should be an interesting challenge linked to course goals and solvable by applying concepts and procedures learned in class. The narrative setup is important because it contextualizes the assignment, giving students a feel for the people involved in the problem. You can make the case easier or harder depending on how ambiguous your narrative and data are. In fact, you may want to create a case where there is no clear-cut answer to encourage student discussion.

Most case studies require combining assignments with resources to present the case and give students a way to submit their answers. Add your narrative and data as resources using the files and resources tools discussed in Chapter 4. Then add your problem statement as the description of an assignment.

Students should use the narrative and data to solve the problem posed by the assignment. The response should show how the resolution of the problem is supported by the data.

Exercises

Exercises are a variation on the base assignment tool. Like assignments, students submit a document in response to an assignment prompt. In an exercise, however, they also assess their own work before they turn it in. Students' personal assessments are then compared to your assessment of their submissions. The final grade is a combination of your score and how well the students' assessments match yours.

How to Create an Exercise

Creating an exercise is similar to creating an assignment, with the addition of a scoring guide such as the workshop module. The instructions for the exercise are uploaded as a separate file.

To create an exercise:

1. Click Turn Editing Mode On.
2. Select Exercise from the "Add an activity…" menu.

3.   Give the exercise a name (see Figure 7-4).

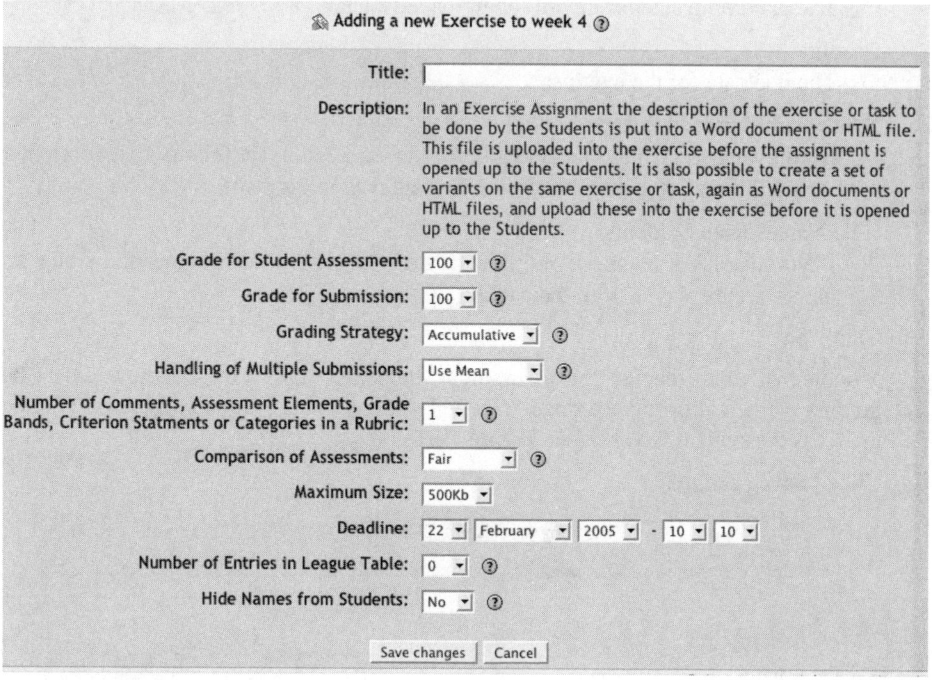

Figure 7-4. Add an exercise

4.   Set the options for your exercise:

Grade for Student Assessment

> The maximum number of points for the comparison of your grade for the submission and the student's self-assessment.

Grade for Submission

> The maximum number of points for your assessment of the student's submission. You can use these two grades to create a relative weight for each component. If you want your grade to be a majority of the final grade, make the student assessment grade less than the submission grade.

Grading Strategy

> The type of scoring guide you and your students will use to assess the submission. For a complete description of each option, see Chapter 6.

Assessment Elements, Grade Elements or Categories in a Rubric

> The number of performance dimensions you wish to evaluate.

Comparison of Assessements

> Determines how the student's self-assessment will be compared to yours. The higher/lower this setting, the more a student will be penalized for not matching your assessment. I encourage you to read the extensive help entry associated with this item.

Maximum Size
>   The maximum size for any of the uploaded files.

Deadline
>   The due date for the exercise.

Number of Entries in League Table
>   If you want to display the students results' in a table, set this to a value greater than 0. The top student entries will be displayed in the table.

Hide Names from Students
>   If you display a league table, this setting will determine whether the students' names are displayed with their work.

5. Click "Save changes."

6. Moodle will then display the assessment elements page. You can now enter the grading elements for this exercise. You and your students will use this scoring guide to assess the students' work. (see Figure 7-5).

7. Click "Save changes."

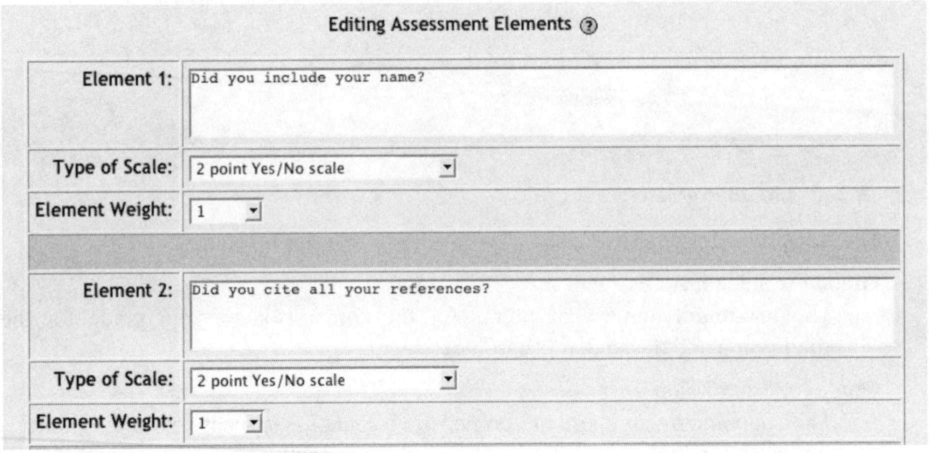

Figure 7-5. Exercise scoring guide

Managing Exercises

Once you've completed the scoring guide, Moodle will take you to the exercise management page (see Figure 7-6). Like the workshop module, the exercise module uses a phased approach to deployment and assessment. Phase 1 is the setup phase, where you can upload the exercise instructions and review the assessment elements. Phase 2 allows students to perform self-assessments and upload their submissions. Phase 3 handles the final grading. These three phases are accessible from the tabs in the exercise management page.

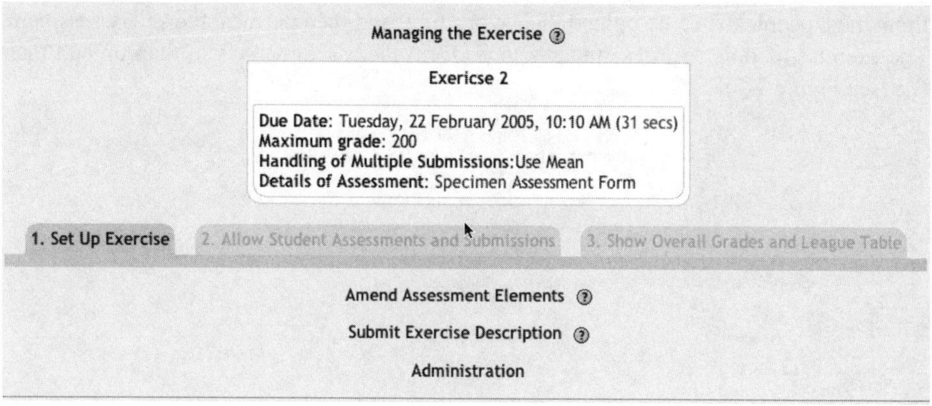

Figure 7-6. Exercise management page

Phase 1: Setup

Once you've entered the assessment elements for the exercise, you'll see the screen for phase 1. At this point, the most important thing to do is upload the exercise description. Unlike most of the other modules, this module requires you to upload a separate document containing the exercise instructions instead of simply typing them into a description field.

> *Warning: Moodle requires you to upload a file for the description before you can move to phase 2.*

To upload an exercise description:

1. From the Managing the Exercise page, click the Phase 1 tab.
2. Click the Submit Exercise Description link.
3. Give the description file a title. You must fill in this field or Moodle will reject the file.
4. Click Browse… and find the file containing the instructions for the exercise.
5. Click "Upload this file."

You can upload multiple files for the description, but I recommend sticking to one file per exercise to avoid confusion. The description file can be any electronic document smaller than the maximum upload size.

Once you've uploaded an instruction file, move to phase 2 to allow students to submit their work and perform self-assessments.

Phase 2: Allow student assessments and submissions

Once you've moved to phase 2, students can perform self-assessments and upload their work for grading. The student interface is a little surprising, so you may want to tell your students what to expect. I know it confused my students when they first encountered it. I think most people expect to upload their work first, and then perform the self-assessment. The exercise module requires students to perform the assessment first, then upload their file (see Figure 7-7).

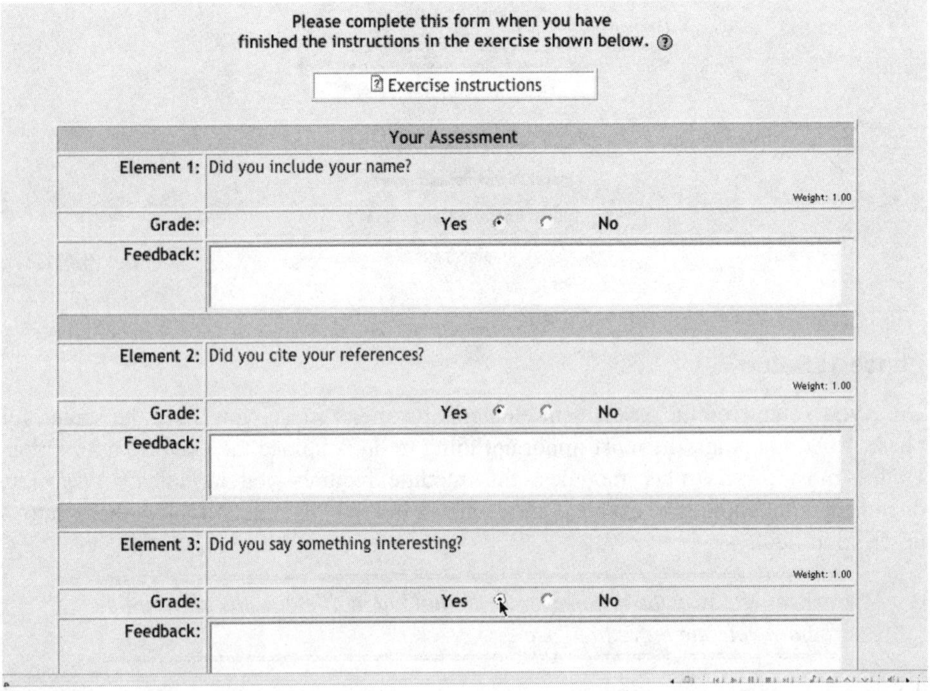

Figure 7-7. Student self-assessment

Once students have uploaded their work, it will be available for you to grade. On the Managing the Exercise page, you'll see the link "X Student Submissions for Assessment." Once students have started to submit their exercises, you can click on this link to download their work and give them a grade. You'll use the same scoring guide the students used.

> *Warning: Like the workshop module, the exercise module updates itself when the periodic script runs on the server. Your system administrator is responsible for setting how often this script is run. Student submissions may not be available for grading for several minutes after they are submitted.*

Once you've scored the students' work, Moodle compares your assessment to the students' assessment and gives a score based on how well the two scores match. This score is the grade for the students' self-assessment, which is added to your score for the submission itself.

Once all students have submitted their work, or the deadline has passed, you can move to phase 3.

Phase 3: Show overall grades and league table

Once the exercise is complete, you can display the results to the students. The overall grades are calculated as weighted averages of the students' self-assessment grades and your grades for their work. The final grades, therefore, depend on the level of comparison and the relative weight of the two scores.

If you have chosen to display a league table, the top scoring submissions will be available for students to review.

Effective Exercise Practices

Exercises can be a valuable tool to help students develop a critical eye for their own work. By performing self-evaluations, students reflect on their own work and practice self-criticism using the same guidelines an expert would use to evaluate their work. Reflecting on their work will help them develop the critical faculties they need to perform at a higher level in the future.

The key to this reflective practice is a good scoring guide. A specific and clear scoring guide is critical to the success of the exercise, from both a cognitive and practical perspective. If students are not clear about exactly what they are evaluating themselves on, they will be unable to gauge future performance. They will also have a difficult time matching your grade. If the scoring guide is too subjective or vauge, the students' self-assessments will never match yours, resulting in poor assessment scores.

Take some time to develop your scoring guide and explain it to your students. I would even recommend sharing the performance dimensions with the students ahead of time, and ask them to discuss what each element means in a forum. This will give them a chance to familiarize themselves with the requirements of the performance and allow them to do a better job on their submissions.

Summary

Assignments are an easy way to gather and track student submissions. Students can submit any type of electronic file to fulfill the requirements. Instead of collecting unwieldy stacks of paper, you can let Moodle track who has turned in a paper and when. The feedback options provide you with an easy way to send grades and/or comments back to the students about their work. Exercises give you the additional capability of requiring students to evaluate their own work as they submit their assignments.

8

Journals

Journaling is a popular educational tool to encourage student self-reflection as they engage in the learning process. Like personal diaries, journaling assignments are meant to encourage reflection by forcing the student to write down his thoughts and reflections about a topic. The act of writing the journal entry encourages deeper reflection and more formal thought.

Moodle's journal tool is an electronic journal where students can record their thoughts and reflections. You can use journals to encourage students to reflect on the course and the content in ways which are difficult to do with other tools. The privacy of the journal and the open-ended nature of the response give students a safe space to explore new knowledge.

Creating Journals

Compared to many of the other tools we've discussed so far, creating a journal is relatively simple.

To add a journal to your course:

1. Click Turn Editing Mode On.

2. Select Journal from the Add Activity… menu in the content block where you want to add a journal.

3. Give the journaling assignment a name and a summary, as shown in Figure 8-1.

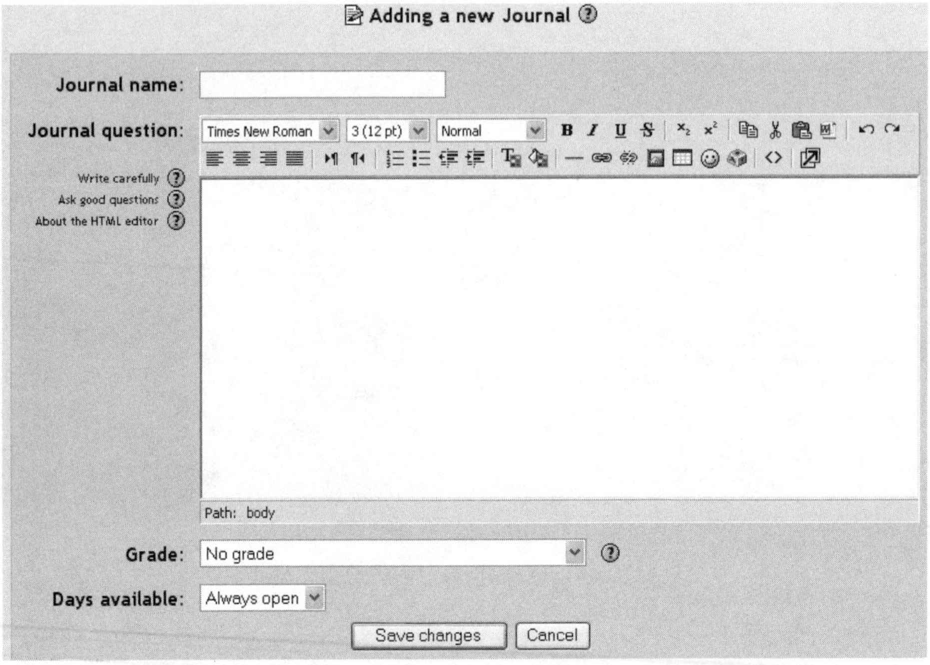

Figure 8-1. Add a new journal

4. If you are going to grade the assignment, select the grading scale you want to use.

5. Select the number of days you want the journal to be available. The timer starts from the day you create the journal.

You can test your journal by clicking on the name of the assignment in the content block. This will display the journal entry page. This is where students will enter their responses to your journal assignment.

To create a journal entry:

1. Click the name of the journal assignment in the content block on the main course screen. You'll see the Journal summary and a button labeled "Start or edit my journal entry."

2. Click the "Start journal entry" button.

3. You'll be presented with a text area (with the HTML toolbar if enabled), such as the one shown in Figure 8-2. Type your entry and click "Save changes." The entry will be visible to the student each time they click on the Journal assignment

4. You can edit your entry by clicking the "Start or edit my journal entry" button again.

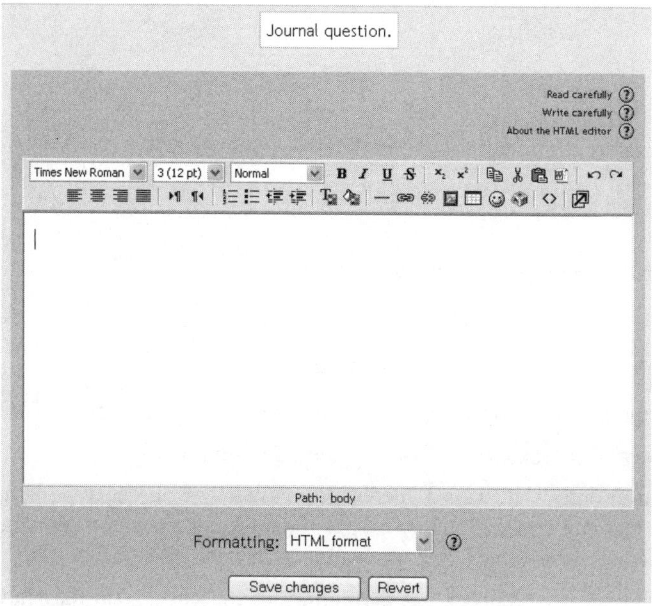

Figure 8-2. Journal entry page

Students can see only one journal entry per journal assignment. If you want students to write multiple journal entries, you'll need to add a journal for each one. For example, if you want students to write one journal entry per week, you'll need to add a journal assignment for every week in the class. Alternatively, you could just add one journal for the entire class, and students could build on it over the entire course. The grading and reading process could get a bit unwieldy, however.

Managing Journals

Journal entries are visible only to the instructor and the student who wrote them. Once students have begun their journals, you will see a link in the upperright hand corner of the journal assignment page, as shown in Figure 8-3.

You'll see a link labeled "View (some number) journal entries." The number in the link is the number of students who have submitted entries.

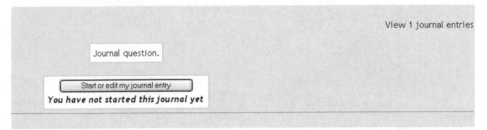

Figure 8-3. Journal page with view entries link

You'll use the link to view the entries and give feedback and grades.

To give feedback and grade journal entries:

1. Click on the journal assignment you want to grade in the content block.

2. Click "View X journal entries" on the journal assignment page.

3. Each journal entry will have a feedback area where you can type your feedback. If you have enabled grading, there will also be a dropdown menu of grade choices (see Figure 8-4). Enter feedback and grades for as many entries as you like.

4. Click "Save all my feedback" at the bottom of the page. You may have to scroll to find the button. Each student will now see their grade and feedback under their entry when they click on the journal assignment in the content block, as shown in Figure 8-5.

If you need to edit your feedback, change the grade, or grade new assignments, you can click on the "View X Journal Entries" link again and simply resave all your feedback.

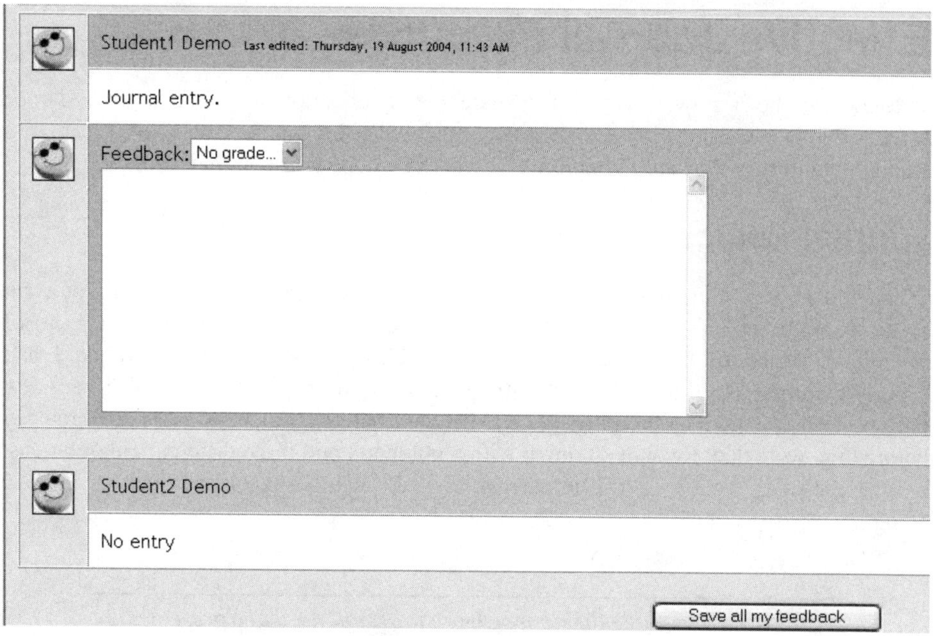

Figure 8-4. Journal feedback page

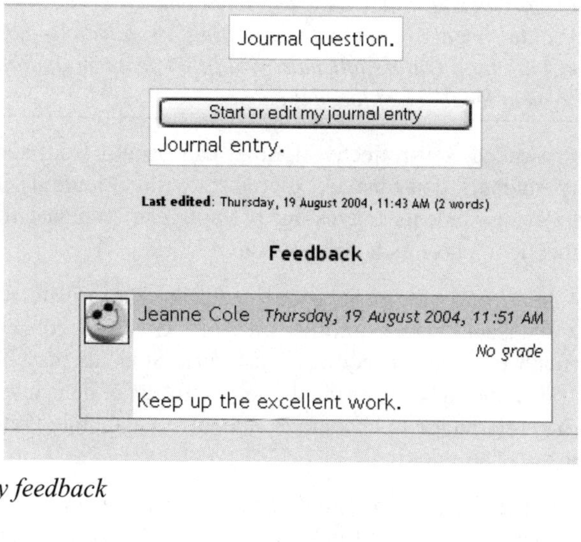

Figure 8-5. Entry feedback

Effective Journal Practices

Journals can be a powerful tool for student self-reflection and engagement. To be effective, however, they have to be integrated with the course goals. Be clear with students about why they are journaling and what you hope to see in their journals.

Journal Basics

When you create a journal assignment for students, be very specific about what you want them to write about. Many academic journal assignments suffer from a lack of specificity. Many of the assignments I received as a student were so vague I had difficulty completing them. They were frequently based on page counts, with very few prompts to help guide my thinking. Many of my journal assignments were written the day before they were due. I would sit down with a notebook and three different colored pens, writing each day's entry in a different pen to make it look like I had been writing all along.

Tip: Take advantage of the opportunity for rapid feedback presented by online journals. I was able to get away with writing my entire journal the night before because they were collected only twice a semester. The instructor didn't want to stop us from writing by collecting our journal notebooks too often. Online journals avoid this problem and allow you to give frequent feedback of journal entries.

Even the most open-ended, self-reflective journal can benefit from some prompting or scaffolding. Many students don't have experience writing journals, especially in an academic setting. Giving students interesting prompts can stimulate their thinking and make your journal assignments much more effective.

Just as important as a good prompt is good feedback. The private nature of journals places all of the feedback responsibilities on you. Giving feedback on a personal reflection is a difficult task, and it requires sensitivity. Students may be trying out new ideas for the first time, and they are probably not confident in their responses. Consider your feedback as a gentle nudge to encourage students to elaborate their ideas further or change the direction of their thinking.

If grades are part of the feedback, you should be clear what you are basing your grade on. Is it grammar and spelling? Length? Evidence of certain kinds of reasoning or support? Giving grades based on content may stifle students into giving rote answers based on the lecture or the textbook. Leave that sort of assessment for a quiz or essay. You'll need to find a balance between giving points for simply completing a journal entry versus making a judgment about quality.

You may want to consider creating a new scale (see Chapter 12) for your journal assignments, incorporating other feedback instead of a grade. You can create a scale indicating what a student has done well and what could be improved, without assigning a traditional letter or number grade to the entry. This may be a way to critique an entry without passing judgment on its personal contents.

Creative Journal Practices

Moodle's journal tool is very simple to learn and can be put to some interesting uses. Journals are a chance for students to reflect on an issue at a deeper and more personal level. They can also provide a private means of backchannel communication between you and the students.

One-minute responses

Effective feedback is important for learning. This is true for both the teacher and the student. One-minute response papers are an easy way to get informal feedback from students about a lesson or activity. Usually, the instructor gives the students a few prompts to get a quick read on the effectiveness of the lesson.

I tend to use three questions when asking for a one-minute response to a lesson:

- What was the muddiest point in the lesson?
- What was the most important point?
- How useful/ interesting was the lesson?

Obviously, there are many more prompts you could use to get the feedback you want from your students. You may want them to reflect on how they feel about the class itself or about a test, or ask other questions about how they perceive various aspects of your course. Or you could ask them for quick answers to more specific, content-related questions you know students frequently have problems with.

> *Tip: One of the most effective geography classes I've seen uses one-minute responses on a daily basis. Every class, the instructor hands out a page asking students what they didn't understand, what the strongest point was, and what they wanted to know more about. The instructor then takes a few minutes at the beginning of every class to address the issues raised in the reflections from the day before.*

To create a one-minute response in a journal assignment, simply place the questions you want your students to answer in the journal question area when you add the assignment to the class.

Reflection on content

Frequently, students don't have a safe place to experiment with the course content and try out new ideas before they are assessed on their understanding or recall. Students need to try out new knowledge before they can truly integrate it into their current understanding. Giving students a journal assignment encouraging them to think specifically about the content, rather than self-reflection or interpretation, can be a valuable tool for promoting deeper learning.

These types of assignments can be effective before, during, or after a given topic or unit is presented. Before a lesson, ask students to record what they already know about the topic, or how earlier course material might tie in with the lesson. During a lesson, ask students to summarize what they are learning, or how they are feeling about their understanding of the material. After a lesson, have them explain how they would tell someone else about the topic in their own words, or what they learned that was different from what they knew before.

Content-reflection assignments require good, specific writing prompts that allow students to engage with the material in new ways. Ask specific questions about controversial or interpretive issues. For example, "If you had been president, would you have ordered the atomic bomb to be dropped on Japan at the end of World War II?" is a better content question than "What is your reaction to the US dropping the atomic bomb on Japan at the end of World War II?"

Brainstorming, drafting, and pre-writing

The best way to learn to write is to write, often. Students faced with academic writing are often apprehensive about the process and the substance of their writing. Writing teachers frequently use journal assignments to get students to start writing in a safe space. You don't have to be a writing teacher to use journals to improve your students' written work. Early in the writing process, students often need to try out ideas, formats, and reasoning before they are ready to address the assignment as a whole. Journal assignments can prompt students to practice their writing skills and get feedback before they attempt to write an essay or research paper.

To use a journal assignment to scaffold the writing process, create a journal students can use well before the final product is due. Give a due date for the assignment to help structure the task. You don't want to be in a position of critiquing thesis statements the day before an essay is due. Ask students to develop a certain aspect of their writing in the journal. They could develop a thesis statement or discuss their research and evidence. You could even ask them to outline a paper directly in the journal entry field.

Once they've completed their pre-writing assignment, be sure to give detailed, constructive feedback. Good feedback will help students develop their ideas before they are overwhelmed by the process of writing the paper itself.

Summary

Journals can be an important tool for allowing students to reflect on their own knowledge and experiment with new ideas in a safe haven. The journal module allows students to write their journals online, so you no longer have to sift through a pile of journal notebooks.

One of the keys to effective journal assignments is your feedback. Be careful when choosing the type of feedback and grading you use in your journal assignment. You want to encourage students to experiment with new knowledge, not just repeat what they've heard for a decent grade.

9

Glossaries

Part of becoming an expert in any field is learning the vocabulary used by practitioners. Experts in an area of study develop new language and word usage to communicate new ideas or subtle variations of old ones. As communities develop within a field and experts communicate with each other over time, a new language emerges. Many experts find it increasingly difficult to communicate with novices as they become more immersed in the language of their field. For example, computer experts have developed an entirely new vocabulary of acronyms, names, and shorthand to help them rapidly communicate complex ideas to each other. As someone with a degree of expertise in computer technology, I know I need to be careful not to confuse others when I explain technical concepts. If you've ever been privy to a discussion among geeks, you know it can be nearly impossible for an outsider to follow the three- and four-letter alphabet soup that passes for geek-speak.

Fortunately, Moodle has a tool to help you and your students develop glossaries and embed them in your course. On the surface, the glossary tool doesn't seem to be more than a fancy word list. In practice, however, it's a powerful tool for learning. The glossary tool has a number of features that make it easy for you and your class to develop shared vocabulary lists add comments to definitions, and even link every appearance of a word in a course to its' glossary entry.

Creating Glossaries

Each Moodle course has its own set of glossaries. The main glossary is editable only by teachers. The secondary glossaries can be configured to allow student entries and comments.

You can create the link to your glossaries anywhere in your course sections. I recommend adding the main glossary to the general section at the top of your course section list. Secondary glossaries can be added to the topic or week where they are relevant, or in a general glossaries section.

To create a glossary:

1. Click Turn Editing Mode On.

2. Select Glossary from the Add Activity menu in the appropriate topic or week section.

3. In the Editing Glossary page, shown in Figure 9-1, give your new glossary a descriptive name.

4. Write a description of the glossary and give directions to your students in the Description area.

5. Select the options you want to use:

    Entries shown per page
        This sets the number of words and definitions your students will see when they view the glossary list.

    Is this glossary global?
        System administrators can make a global glossary accessible to all courses.

    Glossary Type
        You have two options here. The main glossary is editable only by teachers, and you can have only one per course. A secondary glossary can be imported into the main, and you can have multiple secondary glossaries.

    Students can add entries
        This applies only to secondary glossaries. This option gives students the ability to add and edit glossary entries.

    Duplicated entries allowed
        This allows the entry of more than one definition for a given word.

    Allow comments on entries
        Students and teachers can leave comments on glossary definitions. The comments are available through a link at the bottom of the definition.

Automatically link glossary entries

Moodle has a text-filter feature that automatically creates a link from a word in the course to its glossary definition. Linked words are highlighted.

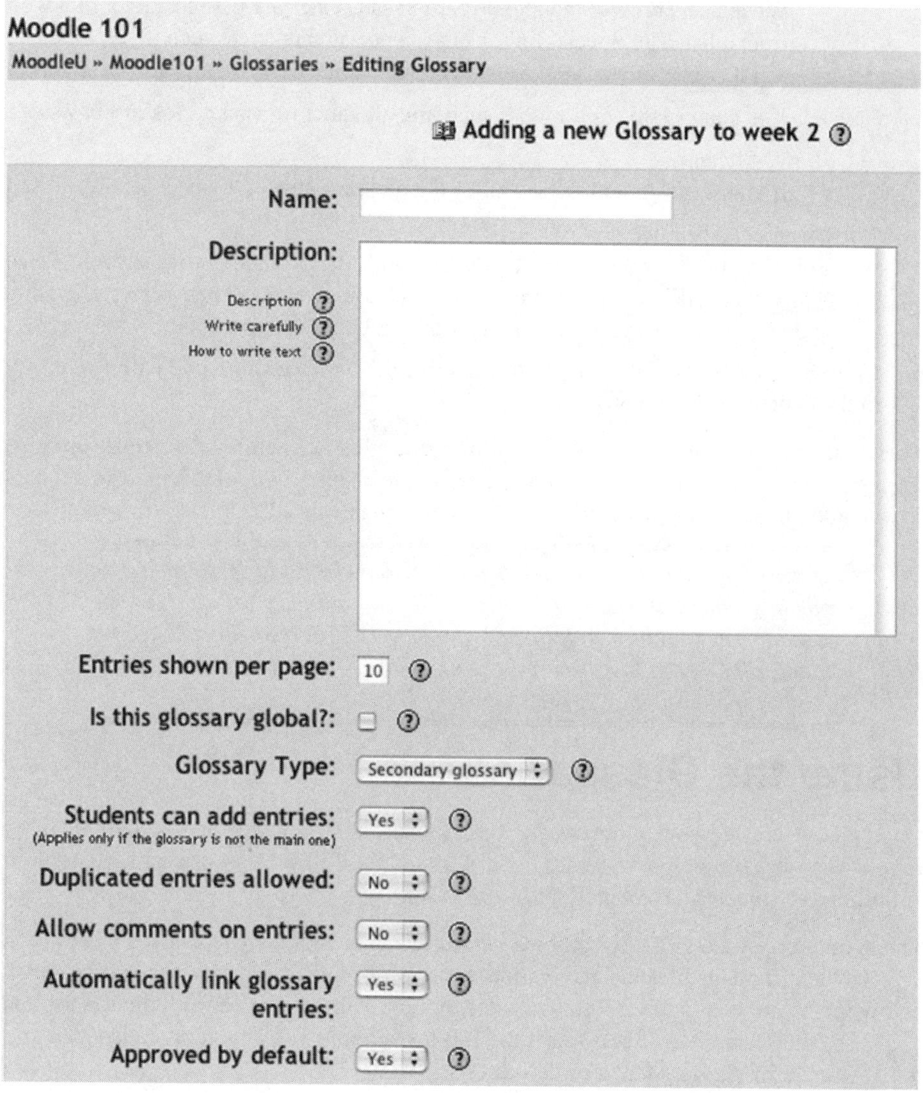

Moodle 101

MoodleU » Moodle101 » Glossaries » Editing Glossary

📖 **Adding a new Glossary to week 2** ⑦

Name: [   ]

Description:

Description ⑦
Write carefully ⑦
How to write text ⑦

Entries shown per page: [10] ⑦

Is this glossary global?: ☐ ⑦

Glossary Type: [Secondary glossary ⬍] ⑦

Students can add entries: [Yes ⬍] ⑦
(Applies only if the glossary is not the main one)

Duplicated entries allowed: [No ⬍] ⑦

Allow comments on entries: [No ⬍] ⑦

Automatically link glossary entries: [Yes ⬍] ⑦

Approved by default: [Yes ⬍] ⑦

Figure 9-1. New glossary page

Approved by default

If students are allowed to add entries, you can allow entries to be automatically approved and added to the glossary, or they can require your approval.

Display format

    You can select how the glossary appears when students list the entries. There are a number of different choices:

Show 'Special' link

    When users browse the glossary, they can select the first character of a word from a list. The Special link displays special characters such as @, #, $, etc.

Show alphabet

    You can use this option to display the alphabet for easier glossary browsing.

Show 'All' link

    If you want students to see all of the glossary entries at once, set this to Yes.

Allow entries to be rated

    You can grade entries yourself or allow students to grade entries as well. Select "Only teachers" or "Everyone" from the users menu. Then select a grading scale. You can also restrict when entries can be graded to a specific date range.

6.   Click Save Changes at the bottom of the screen. Your glossary name will now appear in the course section menu.

There are a lot of options to choose from in the glossary setup. They open up some interesting possibilities that we'll explore later in the chapter. For now, let's take a look at how to add glossary entries and use some of the more advanced features.

> *Warning: The automatic link feature will work only if your system administrator has enabled it in the Filters configuration area of the Administration panel. Autolinking can be very processor-intensive, so if it doesn't seem to be working for you, your sys admin may have turned it off to speed up the system.*

Using the Glossaries

Once you've created your glossary, it's time to start adding words and definitions. Even if you want to have a student-built glossary, it's a good idea to seed it with a couple of definitions so students have a model to work from.

The main view of the glossary can be a bit confusing at first, as you can see from Figure 9-2. Under the main Moodle navigation bar, you'll find the glossary name. Directly below the name, you'll see the glossary description. Almost lost beneath the description, you'll see the search bar. If you select the full-text option, you and your students can use this to search for glossary terms or definitions.

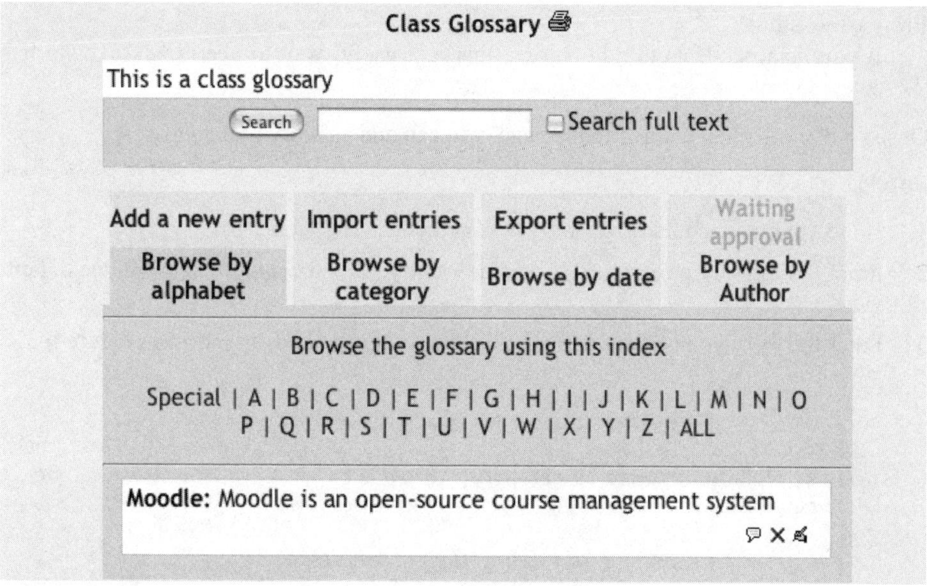

Class Glossary 🖨

This is a class glossary

(Search) [   ] ☐ Search full text

Add a new entry	Import entries	Export entries	Waiting approval
Browse by alphabet	Browse by category	Browse by date	Browse by Author

Browse the glossary using this index

Special | A | B | C | D | E | F | G | H | I | J | K | L | M | N | O
P | Q | R | S | T | U | V | W | X | Y | Z | ALL

Moodle: Moodle is an open-source course management system
                                                              💬 ✕ ✎

Figure 9-2. Main glossary page

Adding Entries

Below the search bar are eight tabs detailing the glossary functions:

Add a new entry
> Clicking this gives you access to the definition entry page.

Import entries
> You can import glossaries from within this course or from other courses.

Export entries
> You can use this to export your course glossary to an export file stored in the course files area. You can then download it to your computer and upload it to another class.

Waiting approval
> If your default approval is set to No, all entries awaiting your approval will be listed under this tab.

Browse by alphabet
> Students can look for glossary entries by the first letter of a word when they select this tab.

Browse by category
> You can create word categories and make them available for students to use when they are searching the glossary

Browse by date
> You can view entries based on the date they were last edited.

Browse by author

If you want students to add entries, this is a useful way to keep track of who has entered what.

Once you've oriented yourself to the page, you can add an entry to the glossary.

To add a glossary entry:

1. Go to your main course page and click on the glossary name.

2. From the glossary page, click "Add a new entry." It's the upper-left tab in the default view.

3. Enter the word you want to define in the Concept text field, as shown in Figure 9-3.

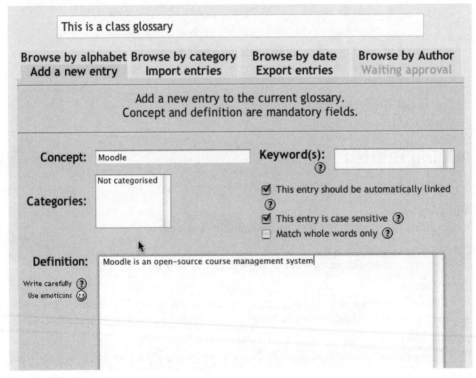

Figure 9-3. New glossary entry

4. If there are synonyms you want to include with the entry, add them to the Keyword(s) text area. Enter one word per line.

5. If you've defined categories in the "Browse by category" tab, you can categorize your entry here. We'll cover how to add a category in the next section.

6. If you want this particular entry to be linked automatically within the course, click the checkbox next to "This entry should be automatically linked" below the Keyword(s) box. If you select automatic linking, the two options below the checkbox determine whether the links are case-sensitive.

7. Add the definition of the word or concept.

8. If you want to add an attachment, such as a picture or an article, you can attach it below the definition.

9. Click Save Changes to add your word to the glossary.

Glossary Categories

You can create categories to help organize your glossary entries. If you've enabled autolinking, the category names can be linked along with individual entries.

To create a glossary category:

1. Click on "Browse by category" in the main page of the glossary.

2. Click "Edit categories" on the left side of the screen.

3. Click the "Add category" button on the resulting Category page.

4. Give the category a name.

5. Choose whether you want the category name autolinked as well.

6. Click Save Changes.

If you autolink the category name, any occurrence of those words will be linked. When a student clicks on the link, she will be taken to the "Browse by category" page of the glossary.

Autolinking

Once you've added an entry to the glossary and enabled autolinking, any instance of a glossary term anywhere in Moodle will have a link to its definition. For example, if you create an entry for the word "Moodle" in the glossary, whenever someone uses the word in a forum, assignment, HTML, or text page, or even in a description field, it will be clickable, as shown in Figure 9-4.

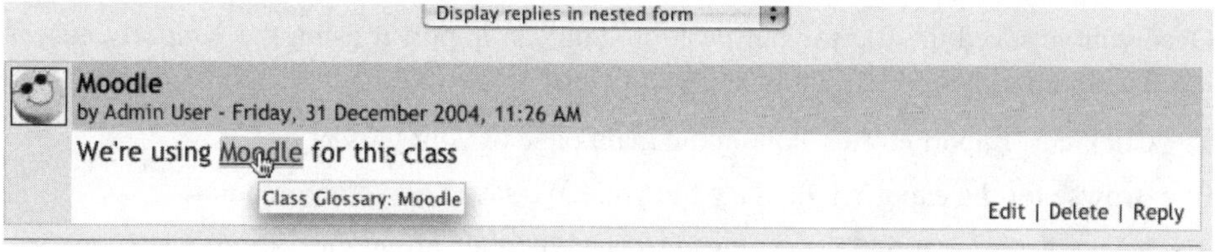

Figure 9-4. An autolinked word in a forum

Once you click on the word, a new window with the glossary entry will pop-up.

Importing and Exporting Glossaries

As you build your glossaries, you may want to share them between classes or with other instructors. Fortunately, there's a way to export and import specific glossaries without needing to share the entire course structure.

Exporting your glossary is easy. When you click the "Export entries" tab, the system automatically generates a file you can save to your computer. At the bottom of the export entries screen, you'll see a link labeled "Exported file" (see Figure 9-5). You'll need to right-click or Control-click on the link and save the file to your desktop. Otherwise, your browser may display the raw XML file, which isn't a pretty sight at all.

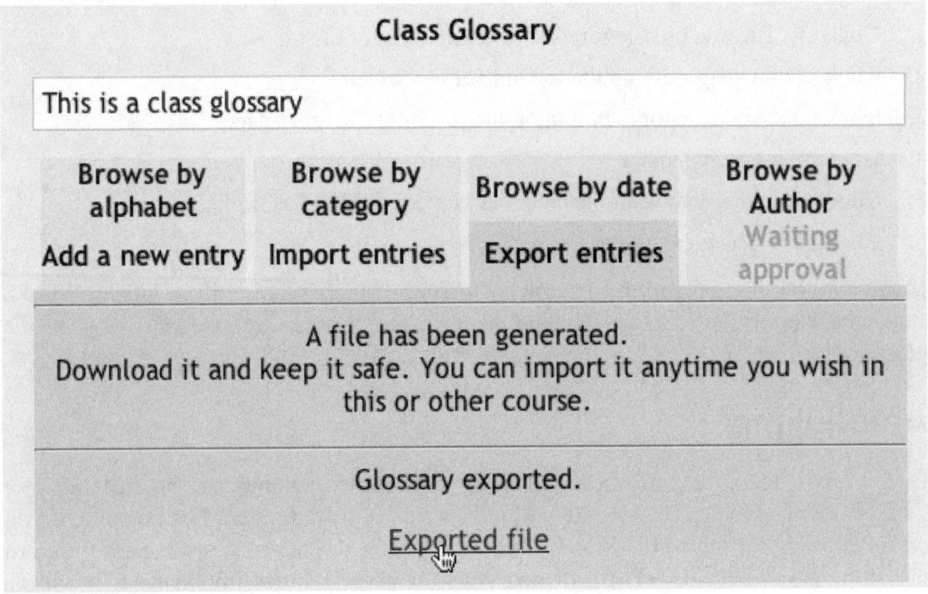

Class Glossary

This is a class glossary

Browse by alphabet	Browse by category	Browse by date	Browse by Author
Add a new entry	Import entries	Export entries	Waiting approval

A file has been generated.
Download it and keep it safe. You can import it anytime you wish in this or other course.

Glossary exported.

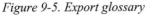

Exported file

Figure 9-5. Export glossary

Once you've saved the file to your desktop, you can import it using the "Import entries" tab. To import glossary definitions into your class:

1. Click the "Import entries" tab on the main page of your glossary.

2. Browse for the exported glossary file you have saved on your computer.

3. Select the destination for the new entries, either the current glossary or a new one.

4. If you want to import category information, select the checkbox.

5. Click Save Changes. You'll then see a report of the entries and categories added to the glossary. If you enabled duplicate entries when you created the glossary, the import process will add all of the new definitions. Otherwise, it will not allow you to import duplicate entries.

Commenting on Entries

If you enabled comments on the glossary entries, users can annotate the definitions in the word list. When you look at a word in the glossary list, you'll see a little cartoon speech balloon in the lower righthand corner of the definition block, as shown in Figure 9-6.

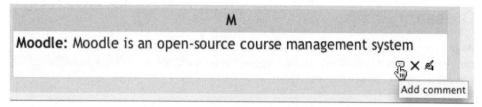

Figure 9-6. Glossary comment link

When you click on the balloon, you'll be taken to the comment entry page. From here, you can add a comment to the definition and then click Save Changes.

Once you've saved your comment, Moodle will display all of the comments for the term. When you return to the main glossary page, you'll see a new message next to the speech balloon telling you how many comments there are for the entry.

Printing a Glossary

There is also an easy tool for printing a glossary. At the top of the glossary list, you'll see a little printer icon. If you click the icon, Moodle will open a new browser window and present all the words and definitions in a printer-friendly format.

To print the glossary:

1. Click the printer icon at the top of the main glossary word list.
2. From the newly opened window, choose Print from the File menu of your browser.
3. Once the word list has printed, close the glossary window.

Effective Glossary Practices

A glossary can be an important part of your course. As we discussed earlier, learning vocabulary in a new field can be one of the biggest challenges to new learners. As an expert in your field, you are comfortable using the important terms and concepts in your area of expertise. Your students, however, are not experts. They may be just starting to learn new words representing new ideas and concepts. More advanced students will need to refine their learned definitions with subtle improvements to make the definitions more useful.

Tip: As an experiment, go to the library and randomly choose a journal article in an area outside your field. As you read the article, does it make sense to you? Notice the number of unfamiliar terms, or familiar terms that seem to be used in a different way than you are used to.

Glossary Basics

At it's most basic, Moodle's glossary can be used like a regular word list for a class. You can develop a list of terms you know students find difficult or confusing and make the list and definitions available for your class.

If you want to get more in-depth, I recommend creating either a weekly or chapter-based word list. Students can use it as they do weekly readings and assignments. A weekly glossary can make it easier for students to organize their learning process.

Creative Glossary Strategies

While a basic glossary is important, creatively applying the glossary can really make an impact on your class.

Collaborative glossaries

Instead of creating a glossary on your own, why not have the students create them as they encounter unfamiliar terms? A collaborative glossary can serve as a focal point for collaboration in a course. Each member of the class could be assigned to contribute a term, a definition, or comments on submitted definitions. Multiple definitions can be rated by you and by the students, with the highest-rated definitions accepted for the final class glossary.

When students are responsible for creating the definitions, they are much more likely to remember the word and the correct definition. Engaging in the process of learning, debating, and refining a glossary can go a long way toward helping students begin using new terms.

You can also structure multiple glossaries over the course of a semester. Break them up by unit, chapter, week, or any other organizational structure.

If you have a large class, assign student teams to come up with definitions and answers. One strategy for managing large courses is to make each team responsible for one week's worth of definitions, while all the other teams must rate and comment. Alternatively, each team could be responsible for one definition per chapter and then rate and comment on the other teams' work.

To set up a collaborative glossary, create a new glossary for each unit with the following options:

* Glossary type: Secondary glossary.
* Students can add entries: Yes.

- Duplicate Entries Allowed: If you want teams to be able to submit multiple definitions for rating, select Yes.

- Allow comments on entries: Yes.

- Default approval status: Yes.

- Allow entries to be rated: Yes – By Everyone.

The other options are up to you. Once you've selected the above options, students can add their own definitions, rate each other's, and add comments.

Credit for word use

This is a combination strategy using the forum and the autolink feature of the glossary. After you and your students have defined the glossary terms, it's important for students to begin practicing using the words in realistic contexts. Students, however, are usually reluctant to experiment with new terms. With the autolinking feature, it's easy to spot when a glossary word has been used in a forum or in a posting on the web site.

To encourage word use, assign a portion of the credit students receive for their forum postings for correct use of glossary terms. As you or other students rate posts, you can quickly scan for highlighted glossary words and award points for usage. You may even want to break the score down further. Perhaps award one point for using the word and two points for using it correctly.

Summary

At first glance, the glossary doesn't seem to be a very interesting tool. You could simply create a word list in a word processor and upload it. The power of the glossary tool in Moodle comes from its ability to automatically create links in your course for every word in the list, and to easily build collaborative glossaries.

Use the glossary tool to help your students learn the vocabulary of your field and encourage them to experiment with new terms. Collaborative glossaries give your students even more practice using the new words and negotiating their meaning.

In the next chapter, we'll take a look at a tool for developing linear lessons that combines multiple resources and little quizzes to help students progress through the course materials.

10

Lessons

When I was growing up, I enjoyed reading a series of books called *Choose Your Own Adventure*. Written in second person, they placed the reader into the story as the main character. Each chapter was a page or two long ended with a choice of actions. I could choose the action I wanted to take and turn to the appropriate page to see what happened. I could then make another choice and turn to that page, and so on until the story ended or my character died, which happened with disturbing regularity.

The Moodle lesson tool is a lot like the *Choose Your Own Adventure* books. Each page in the lesson can have a question at the bottom of the page. The resulting page depends on the answer the student gives. You can create branching paths through the material based on the selections students make at each page.

With branching lessons, you can create programmed learning opportunities in which each correct answer brings up a new piece of information and a new question. You can also easily create flash-card lessons and, with a little creativity, you can use the lesson module to create simulations and case studies to respond to student input which results in a degree of interactivity.

There are two basic page types in the lesson module. The question page presents the student with a question, and the student has to enter a correct answer. After a student submits his answer, he will see the response you've created and will be taken to another page or looped back to the same page. Question pages are scored and added to the student's cumulative grade.

A branc tables page presents the user only with the option to select a branch. There is no correct or incorrect answer for each response, and the student selections do not impact his grade.

The authors of the tool envision branches as tables of contents giving students access to chains of questions. At the end of a chain, the user will return to the branch table, be presented with another branch table, or end the lesson. Of course, you don't have to create a lesson this way. You can use the branch table to create a branch simulation in which the student's choices present him with consequences and new decisions. At the end of the chapter, we'll explore some other creative ways to apply the lesson module.

Creating a lesson isn't complex, but the math of branching lessons means you have to plan carefully how you want to use this capability. Unless you prune your branching lesson, you will end up with huge number of options for students, and a large number of pages to write.

Creating a Lesson

Before you begin creating a lesson, it's a good idea to draw a lesson flowchart. Lessons require more advanced planning than many of the other tools. With the potential for branching on each page, advanced planning is critical before you begin to develop your lesson. Even with two choices per page, if every choice results in a new page, you will quickly need a very large number of pages. The first page will require two additional results pages, and each of these will require two more for a total of seven pages just to two choices. The key to minimizing the number of pages is to reuse as many as possible.

Take a few minutes to draw a flowchart for your lesson. What will the first page display? What are the options? Where will the options take the student? It's important to answer these questions for each page of the lesson to avoid getting lost while you are actually creating the content.

Once you have your flowchart, it's time to start creating a lesson.

To add a lesson to your course:

1. Click Turn Editng Mode On.

2. In the Add an Activity menu, select Lesson. You'll then see the Add a New Lesson page, as shown in Figure 10-1.

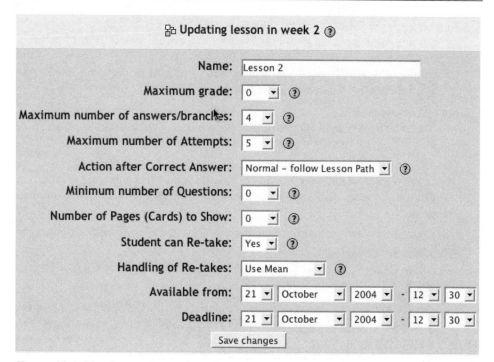

Figure 10-1. New lesson page

3. Give your lesson a descriptive name.

4. Select the maximum grade for completing the lesson (from 0 to 100).

5. Choose the maximum number of answers/branches per page. This is the maximum number of selection options you want per page.

6. Select the options you want to use for this lesson:

    Maximum number of attempts

    This represents the maximum number of attempts a student can make on any question. If a student has difficulty with a short-answer or numerical question type, she can make this number of attempts before being moved to the next page.

    Action after Correct Answer

    This determines how the system responds after a correct answer. Most of the time, you'll want the system to show the page you've selected as a response. You can also elect to have the system randomly display a question the student hasn't seen yet, or one she hasn't answered.

    Minimum number of Questions

    With this option, you can set the number of questions used as a base for calculating the student's grade. If you set a minimum number of questions, the student must answer at least this many questions to receive full credit.

Number of Pages (Cards) to Show

> Set this parameter only if you are creating a flash-card lesson. If this is set to a number greater than 0, students will be shown that number of cards, and the lesson will end. If this is set to a number greater than the number of cards you've created, Moodle will display every card.

Student can Re-take

> You can allow students to retake the lesson or not. You can set this only to Yes or No. You can't set the number of times a student can retake a lesson.

Handling of Re-takes

> If you allow students to retake the lesson, you need to set a grading policy. You can use the mean of the student's grades on the lesson or select the maximum grade.

7. Once you've selected the options you want to use, set the availability date and the deadline.

8. Click Save Changes. You will then be taken to the editing page for the first page of the lesson.

Once you've set up the basic lesson shell, you need to create the first question page of the lesson. Each lesson's question page consists of a title, some content, and the question choices at the bottom of the page. When a student answers a question, he sees the response for his answer and a Continue button. The Continue button takes him to the appropriate branch page.

By default, the first response takes the student to the next page while all other responses return the student to the same page. After you've created a page, you can come back and edit this behavior. The lesson automatically presents the question choices in random order so you don't have to worry about the first response always being the correct one.

To create the first page, fill in the form shown in Figure 10-2:

1. Give the page a name. The name will be visible to the student as he completes the lesson. You can also use it to organize your pages as you build the lesson.

2. Enter the page contents. The contents will need to include the question you want the students to answer as well. If you are creating flash cards, you'll want to enter only the question here.

3. Select the question type. Your options are multiple-choice, true/false, short-answer, numerical, and matching.

4. If you want to use multiple-answer, multiple-choice questions or want case-sensitivity in the short-answer responses, select the question option.

5. Enter the correct answer to the question in the Answer 1 box.

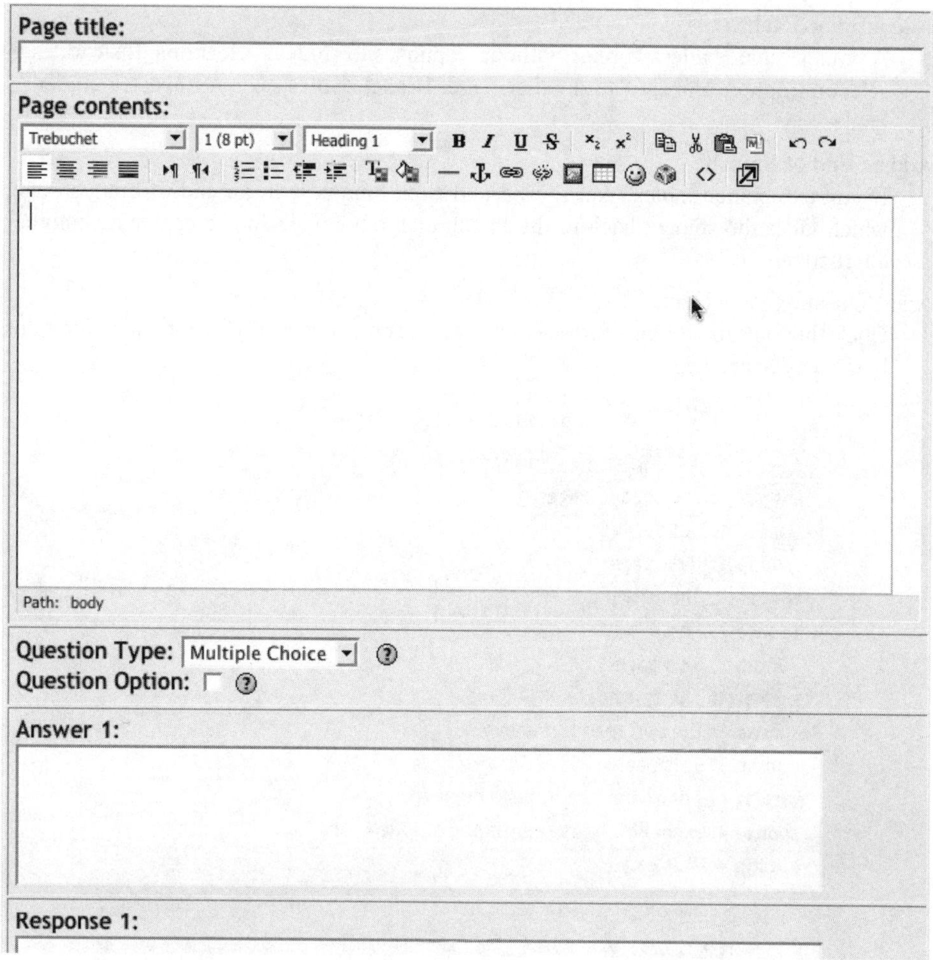

Page title:

Page contents:

| Trebuchet ▾ | 1 (8 pt) ▾ | Heading 1 ▾ | **B** *I* <u>U</u> S̶ | x₂ x² | 🗈 🖋 🖺 🖹 | ↶ ↷ |

≡ ≡ ≡ ≡ | ¶I ¶◀ | ⊟ ⊟ ⊑ ⊒ | 🎨 | — ⚓ 🔗 👁 🖼 🗔 ☺ 🌐 <> 🗗

Path: body

Question Type: Multiple Choice ▾ (?)
Question Option: ☐ (?)

Answer 1:

Response 1:

Figure 10-2. First page in a lesson

6.   Enter the response generated by the answer.

7.   Enter any other answer choices you want to student to consider with responses for each.

8.   Click the Add a Question Page button at the bottom of the page.

You'll then see the lesson construction page, such as the one shown in Figure 10-3. Each page you create will be listed here with a number of options below it:

Import Questions
    You can import questions from a variety of formats. The lesson module will create a page for each question you import.

Add a Branch Table

A branch table is a lesson page without responses to student selections. Instead, each selection option branches to another page. Branch tables do not impact a student's grade.

Add an End of Branch

If you use branch tables, you should end each branch with an end-of-branch page, which takes the student back to the last branch table page so she can select another alternative.

Add a Question Page Here

Click this link to add another question page. You can add a question page above or below any page.

Which page is this?	
Multiple Choice	
Answer 1:	The second page
Response 1:	Not yet
Jump 1:	Next page
Answer 2:	The first page
Response 2:	Yes!
Jump 2:	This page
Answer 3:	The third page
Response 3:	Did you read the above?
Jump 3:	This page
Answer 4:	I don't beleive in page numbers
Response 4:	Hmmmm.. very philosophical, but wrong
Jump 4:	This page
Check Question	

Import Questions | Add a Branch Table | Add an End of Branch | Add a Question Page here

Branch Table ⬆ ✎ ✕

Table of contents	
Branch Table	
Description 1:	Off to the next page
Jump 1:	Next page
Description 2:	Jump to another chapter
Jump 2:	Page 1
Description 3:	Jump to the end of the lesson
Jump 3:	End of lesson
Check Branch Table	

Figure 10-3. Lesson construction page

At the top of each page table, you'll see the icons for moving, editing, or deleting the page. Below the page details, you'll see a button labeled Check Question. Clicking on this button shows the lesson from the student's point of view. You can answer questions, check out branches, and interact with the lesson. The only thing you won't be able to see is the final grade.

You can also test your lesson by clicking the Check Navigation link on the bottom of the page list. This link will take you to the first page in your lesson as a student would see it. You can then start from the beginning of the lesson and work your way through.

Once you've created your first page, you can add a new page, add a branch table, or edit an existing question. You'll need to add each page you want students to be able to view.

Managing Lessons

Once you've created your lesson, there isn't much management involved. Unlike other modules, the lesson module does not give you direct access to a student's performance. Instead, the only way to track a student's progress is through the grades module. As students complete the lesson, their scores will be recorded in the gradebook (see Chapter 12). If you've allowed students to view each lesson multiple times, their scores may change as they repeat the lesson.

Effective Lesson Practices

Lessons can be an interesting change of pace for your students. They may require more upfront development time than many other types of tools, but they do provide some benefits. The two basic lesson types, branching quizzes and flash-cards are relatively easy to set up.

Branching Quizzes

The most basic lesson structure is branching quiz. You use branches to organize sets of questions around different topics or concepts in your course. Each branch of the quiz leads to a linear series of pages and test questions and then returns to the main branch. The main-branch page acts as a table of contents for the lesson, as shown in Figure 10-4.

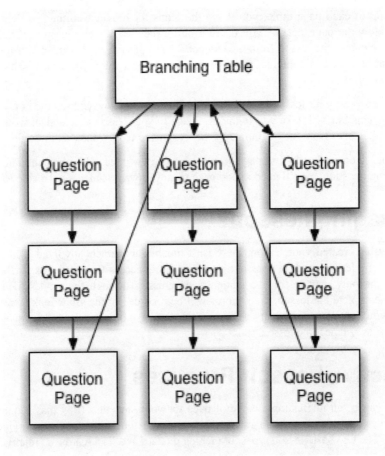

Figure 10-4. Branching quiz schematic

If you decide to build this type of lesson, be sure to include a link to the end of the lesson on the main page. If not, the students will have no way of ending the lesson and recording their score.

If you create a lesson with a branch table and strings of questions, be sure to set a reasonable minimum number of questions. Otherwise, students will be able to visit one branch and receive a maximum score for the lesson, even though they didn't look at any other branches.

To create a branching quiz:

1. Create the lesson and the first question page by following the instructions.

2. Create a question page for the first question in each branch.

3. Create a branch table with a branch for each of the questions you just created.

4. Be sure to make the last branch a link to the end of the lesson.

5. After you've saved the branching table, move it to the top of the pages list.

6. Under the first question for the first branch, create the second question page for the next step in the branch.

7. Fill in the question page for the second question. Put the correct answer in the first answer slot if you are creating a true/false or multiple-choice question.

8. Continue adding questions to the branch until you are finished.

9. Add an end-of-branch after the last question in the branch.

10. Below the first question for the each of the remaining branches, repeat steps 6 through 9.

11. When you have added all your pages, review your lesson by clicking the Check Navigation link.

Flash Cards

Flash cards can be a useful way to practice recalling basic facts and definitions. As we discussed in Chapter 9, learning vocabulary can be one of the most difficult tasks for novices in any field of study. Flash cards allow students to practice rapidly recalling definitions as an initial step toward learning how to communicate in a new field.

The lessons module can act like a deck of flash cards, presenting either the whole deck or a subset of cards to students when they want to study the new terms. Each question page is a separate card, and students can rapidly react to each one in turn. This is a very different structure than the branching quizzes.

Setting up a flash-cards lesson requires specifying options when you first create the lesson. To create a flash-cards lesson:

1. Follow steps 1 through 4 for creating a lesson in the "Creating a Lesson" section.

2. Consider setting a low value for the maximum grade. You want to reward students for using the flash cards but also make them a valuable learning tool.

3. Use the following options:

    Action after Correct Answer
        Set to unseen or unanswered. This tells the lesson module you don't want it to present the next page in order.

    Minimum number of questions
        Keep this at 0. The students shouldn't have a choice about the number of cards they see.

    Maximum number of cards
        If you want to limit the number of questions students see each time they practice with the cards, set this to a nonzero number. Make it large enough to give students enough practice, but not so large they become fatigued by the sheer volume of questions.

Student can Re-Take

> Unless you have a very specific reason for limiting retakes, I recommend setting this to yes. Flash cards are used to practice recalling information rapidly. Save the assessment of students' recall skills for a quiz.

Handling of Re-Takes

> I recommend setting this to the maximum to encourage students to reuse the flash cards to attempt to get the maximum score.

4. Once you save the lesson options, simply create question pages. The order doesn't matter. You're basically creating a deck of questions to draw from.

Once you've created the deck of flash cards, you can release it to your students so they can practice answering the questions you've created.

Creative Lesson Uses

While branching quizzes and flash cards are interesting applications, there is a hidden potential in the lessons module that makes it much more interesting than it at first appears. If we take advantage of the ability of each answer in a question page to link to any other page, we can create branching *Choose Your Own Adventure* -style simulations or case studies.

Simulations and case studies

A branching simulation can be a great learning tool. On each page, the student reads some information or looks at a picture (or both) and makes a decision about what to do next. For example, a medical simulation may start out by presenting a patient's complaint and then asking what should be done next. Possible choices could be to order a test or to do nothing. If the student orders a test, each branch would present the results of the test and asks the student what should be done next. Each page could include an option to switch from diagnosis to treatment, which would branch the student to a different set of options.

To successfully create a branching simulation, you will definitely have to map out each page in advance. The first page should introduce the situation. You'll need to include enough details in the first page to get the students started. If you have other materials you want them to use in the simulation, you may want to create a resource link the students can access before they start the lesson.

If you just want students to engage in the decision-making process and not receive a grade, simply create a series of branch tables. Otherwise, you can create a combination of branching tables and questions.

To create a simulation:

1. Create a lesson as you would a branching quiz lesson. If you're just using branch tables, assign a point value of 0 to the lesson.

2. Create the first question page. If the first question page will be the first page in the simulation, be sure to provide enough details about the case so the students can start making decisions.

3. Create the first set of decision-result pages from the first page.

4. Go back and edit the first page and assign each answer a link to a resulting page. Be sure the first answer is the best choice since students will receive a point it.

5. Create the decision-result pages for each of the other decision pages.

6. You'll need to create all of the pages in advance or, after you create each iteration of decision-result pages, go back and add the links to those pages in the decision page.

7. After you've completed adding all of the pages and links, test your simulation with the Check Navigation link.

11

Wikis

A wiki is a collection of collaboratively authored web documents. Basically, a wiki page is a web page everyone in your class can create together, right in the browser, without needing to know HTML. A wiki starts with one front page. Each author can add other pages to the wiki by simply creating a link to a page that doesn't exist yet.

Wikis get their name from the Hawaiian term "wiki wiki," which means "very fast." A wiki is indeed a fast method for creating content as a group. It's a hugely popular format on the Web for creating documents as a group. There is usually no central editor of a wiki, no single person who has final editorial control. Instead, the community edits and develops it's own content. Consensus views emerge from the work of many people on a document.

Moodle's wiki is built on top of an older wiki system called Erfurt wiki (*http://erfurtwiki. sourceforge.net/?id=ErfurtWiki*). If you want more information about wikis other than the Moodle version, check out the Erfurt web site.

In Moodle, wikis can be a powerful tool for collaborative work in education. The entire class can edit a document together, creating a class product, or each student can have their own wiki and work on it with you and their classmates.

161

Creating Wikis

Creating a wiki is relatively simple. Compared to the lesson module, you'll find there are far fewer steps to creating a wiki. Most of the work involved with using wikis becomes easier once you start using them.

To create a wiki:

1. Click Turn Editing Mode On.

2. Select Wiki from the Add an Activity menu in the course section where you want to place the wiki link.

3. From the Adding a new Wiki page, give your wiki a descriptive name, as shown in Figure 11-1.

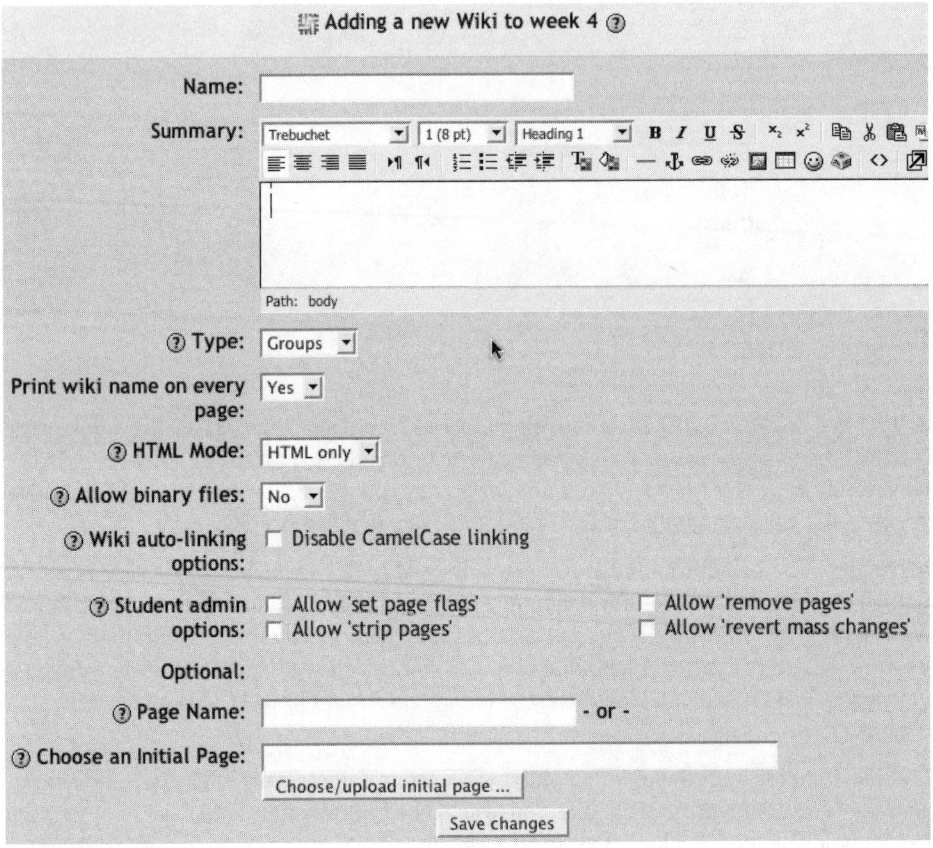

Figure 11-1. Create a new wiki

4. In the summary field, describe the purpose of the wiki and what you hope students will contribute.

5. Set up your wiki by selecting the appropriate options:

    Type

    There are three types of wiki: teacher, groups, and student. These types interact with the groups setting for your course, resulting in 9 options, as shown in Table 11-1.

Table 11-1. Wiki group permissions

	No Groups	**Separate Groups**	**Visible Groups**
Teacher	Creates a single wiki that only the teacher can edit. Students can view the wiki, but not make changes.	Each group has a wiki that only the teacher can edit. Other groups can't view the page.	Each group has a wiki that only the teacher can edit. Other groups can view the page.
Groups	There is one wiki for the class. All students can edit the wiki.	There is one wiki per group. Students in that group can edit the wiki. Other students can't view the page.	There is one wiki per group that group members can edit. Other groups can view the page.
Student	Each student has their own wiki that only the teacher and student can edit.	Each student has their own wiki that they can edit. Students in the same group can view the wiki as well.	Each student has their own wiki that they can edit. All the other students in the course can view page as well.

Print wiki name of every page

If you select this option, the top of each page will have the name of the wiki.

HTML Mode

There are three options here as well. No HTML will display all HTML tags as tags (a bold tag will look like a <b> instead of making the word bold). Formatting is done with WikiWords instead. Save HTML will allow some tags to be displayed. "HTML only" uses HTML, not WikiWords, but you can use the HTML editor.

Allow binary files

Binary files are graphics, audio, video, and other non-text resources. If you want students to be able to attach pictures to the wiki, be sure to set this to Yes.

Wiki auto-linking options

When someone wants to create a new page to a wiki, they type in a word using CamelCase. CamelCase combines all the words for the link into one word. Each word in the link is capitalized. Once someone has added a word in CamelCase, the wiki automatically creates a new page and makes the word a link. You can disable this feature if you wish.

Student admin options

When students can edit a page, you can allow them certain administrative privileges in the wiki. We'll cover each of these options in more detail in the "Managing Wikis" section.

6. Seed the wiki with a page name for the first page or upload an initial page. If you created a first page in another HTML editor, you can use this option to upload it to seed the wiki.

7. Click Save Changes. You will then be taken to the editing view of the wiki page you just created.

Once your wiki is up and running, you and your students can begin collaborating on creating content.

Managing Wikis

After you've created your wiki, it's available for editing. You and your students can create wiki pages, link them together, and collaboratively create a collection of web pages.

Creating Wiki Pages

After you create the wiki itself, Moodle will take you to the editing screen for the first page, as shown in Figure 11-2.

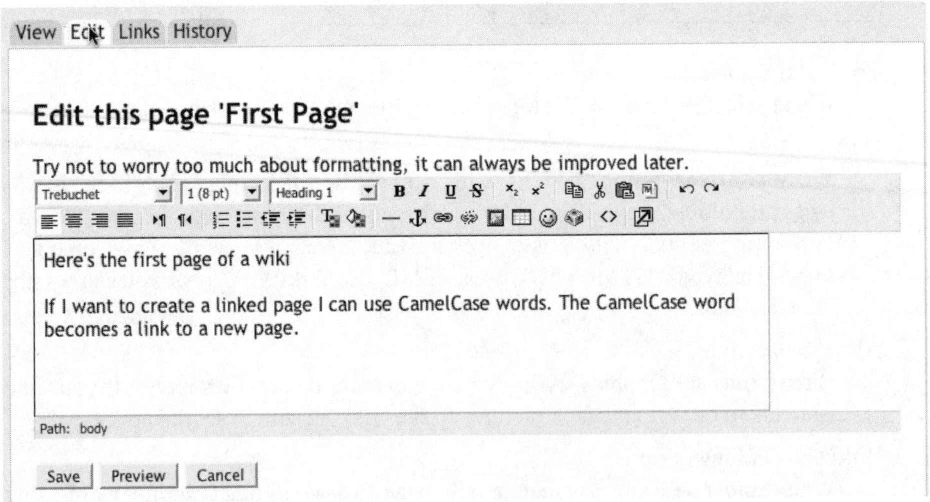

Figure 11-2. Wiki editing page

In the center of the screen, you'll see the editing area for your wiki page. You can use the HTML editor as you would for any other document. You can add images, tables, and any formatting you need.

To add other pages to your wiki, simply type a word with a capital letter at the beginning and a capital letter somewhere else in the word. This is called CamelCase, as the two capital letters resemble a two-humped camel. Whenever you type a CamelCase word, Moodle will recognize it and look in the database for a page with that name. If you haven't created a page with that name, Moodle will put a question mark next to the word. When you click on the question mark, you will be taken to another editing screen for the new page.

For example, if I create a new wiki and type the word "CamelCase" in the page, Moodle will look to see if a page with the name "CamelCase" has already been created. If it hasn't, I'll see a blue question mark next to the words when I view the page, as shown in Figure 11-3.

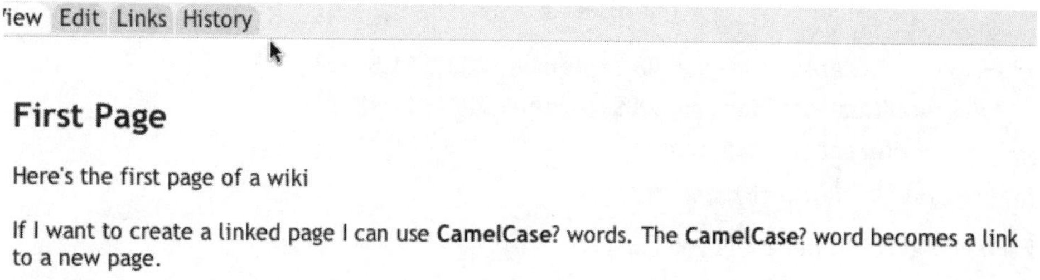

'iew **Edit Links History**

First Page

Here's the first page of a wiki

If I want to create a linked page I can use **CamelCase?** words. The **CamelCase?** word becomes a link to a new page.

Figure 11-3. CamelCase words without link pages

Once I click on the question mark, I'll see an editing screen for the page about CamelCase words. Once I add some content and save the page, it becomes active. Whenever I type the word "CamelCase" using the same capitalization, Moodle will automatically create a link to the CamelCase page and highlight it..

There are four tabs above the editing area: view, edit, links, and history. When you browse a wiki, every page is displayed in view mode. If you want to edit a page, click the edit tab and you'll see the editing area for that page. The links tab will display the pages that have links pointing to the page you are viewing. You can use this to backtrack and see where this page is referenced elsewhere in the wiki.

The history tab gives you access to the version history of the page. Whenever someone clicks the Save button, they create a new version of the wiki page. Moodle tracks all these versions until you strip them out (see the strip tool in the administration menu in the next section). Figure 11-4 shows the history page for our wiki's first page.

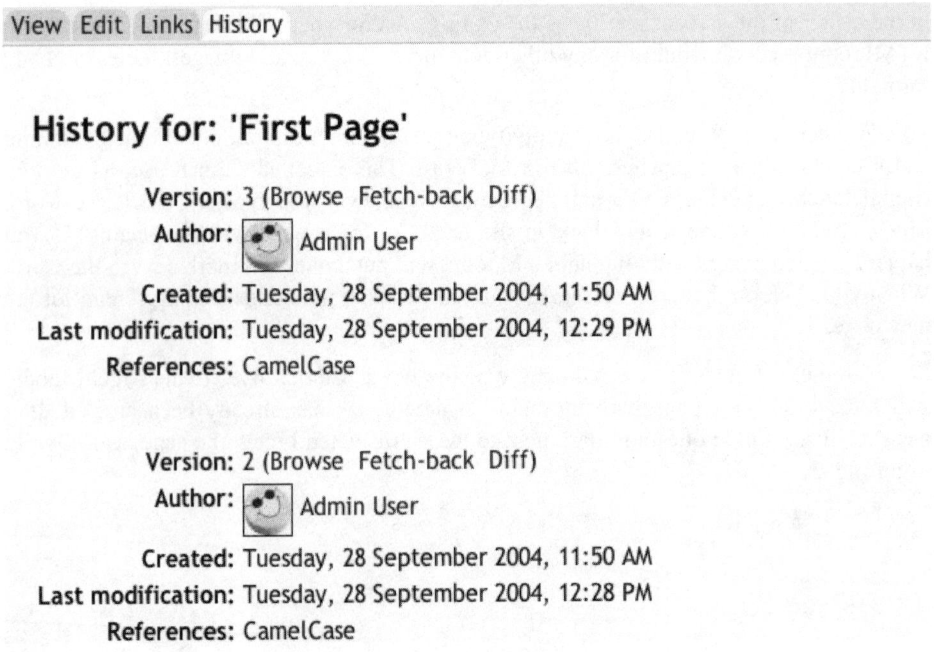

View Edit Links History

History for: 'First Page'

Version: 3 (Browse Fetch-back Diff)
Author: Admin User
Created: Tuesday, 28 September 2004, 11:50 AM
Last modification: Tuesday, 28 September 2004, 12:29 PM
References: CamelCase

Version: 2 (Browse Fetch-back Diff)
Author: Admin User
Created: Tuesday, 28 September 2004, 11:50 AM
Last modification: Tuesday, 28 September 2004, 12:28 PM
References: CamelCase

Figure 11-4. Wiki history page

Each version has three tools you can use:

Browse
> You can view every version of a page.

Fetch-back
> Brings back an old version of the page for editing. Once you save your changes, it becomes the newest version of the page.

Diff
> Highlights the differences between two consecutive versions of a page. Additions have a + symbol next to them. Deletions have a – symbol next to them. A simple diff page is shown in Figure 11-5.

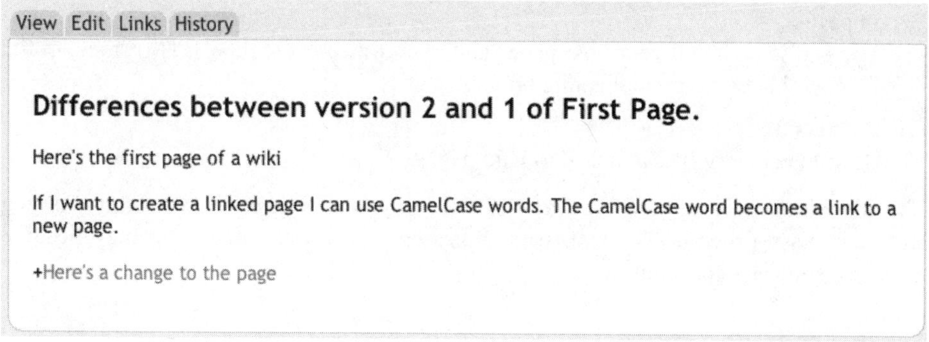

View Edit Links History

Differences between version 2 and 1 of First Page.

Here's the first page of a wiki

If I want to create a linked page I can use CamelCase words. The CamelCase word becomes a link to a new page.

+Here's a change to the page

Figure 11-5. Version diff with an addition

As you build your wiki, you and your students can use these very simple tools to create a very sophisticated information space.

Administering a Wiki

Under the Moodle navigation bar, there are three tools: search, links, and administration. The Search Wiki button allows you to search the wiki for key terms. Moodle will return all the pages containing your search term.

The Wiki Links button provides you with tools to view your wiki in different ways. The tools include:

Site map
> A hierarchical view of the pages and links in the wiki, starting with the first page.

Page index
> An alphabetical list of all the pages in the wiki.

Newest pages
> A list of the most recently created pages.

Most visited pages
> A list of pages with the most views.

Most often changed pages
> A list of most frequently edited pages.

Updated pages
> Lists all the pages in the wiki by date and time of last edit.

Orphaned pages
> A list of pages that were created and had all the links to them deleted.

Wanted pages
> A wiki page where people can list pages they want to see in the collection.

Export pages
> You can wrap up all your wiki pages and export them as regular HTML to a zip file for download or to a Moodle directory.

File Download
> Download binary files attached to wiki pages.

The administration area gives you tools that keep your wiki running smoothly. As you and your class generate the wiki, pages may become orphaned or you may need to manage a student's contributions.

Set Page Flags
> Page flags are properties you can set on a per-page basis. Every page can be set with different permissions:

> TXT
>> Indicates whether the page can contain text.

> BIN
>> Flag for allowing binary (graphics) content.

> OFF
>> Stands for "offline." The page is still there; it just can't be read by someone who doesn't have editing permissions.

> HTM
>> Allows HTML content instead of wiki text.

> RO
>> Stands for "read-only." You and your students can only read the file, not make changes.

> WR
>> The writeable flag allows anyone in the course to make changes to the document.

Remove Pages
> The wiki engine automatically tracks pages that aren't linked from anywhere else (they were created and then the link was deleted) and empty pages. This tool allows you to remove these orphaned wiki pages, which can't be reached through the ordinary wiki interface.

Strip Pages
> While the wiki engine tracks changes, it stores old versions in the database. To declutter the data, you may occasionally want to delete all the old versions and just keep the new one.

Revert Mass Changes
> Use this tool to roll back changes to all pages if a particular author makes a mess of many pages in the wiki.

Effective Wiki Practices

Wikis are gaining popularity as a collaborative tool in many environments. There are now several commercial vendors offering wikis for group collaboration in corporate settings. Many social web sites also have wikis to allow their members to collaborate on documents. Effective management practices are the key to a wiki's success. You'll need to think about your wiki's editorial policy, as well as its educational objectives.

Wiki Basics

Wikis are a simple, flexible tool for collaboration. They can be used for everything from simple lists of web links to building entire encyclopedias. Wikipedia (*http://www.wikipedia.org*) is the largest wiki in the world. As of September 2004, Wikipedia contained 358,000 articles on everything from general topology to split infinitives. The entire Wikipedia is written by volunteers from around the world. An article is started by someone with an interest in the subject, and then anyone in the community can add content, edit other people's work, or add another page elaborating on a sub-topic. It has become so large and so frequently used that there is a lively debate about how authoritative a collaborative work without a central editor can be.

Of course, wikis in your own class probably won't be that extensive. But it's important to have a plan for your wiki before you release it to the class. Students need to know the purpose of the wiki and how it fits in with the class. If it's a personal wiki, will they be graded? Is it simply a staging area for group work that will be submitted later? Students need to know so they can submit appropriate work. A brainstorming wiki is very different from one that will be submitted for a grade.

You'll also need to decide on an editing policy. Will you be a central editor? Or will you let the students be completely responsible for the work? How will you deal with offensive content?

In most circumstances, you'll find that you can trust students. But on the rare occasion a student does do something offensive to others, you will need to have a policy to deal with it. Will you roll back the changes by that author? Or will you create a new version by deleting his content? Creating a new version leaves a trail you can use for evidence later, but it also makes it easier for the perpetrator to restore his comments.

Creative Wiki Practices

The free-form, collaborative nature of wiks makes them easy to apply in creative ways. Any sort of group process can be facilitated using a wiki.

Group lecture notes

Usually, lecture notes are a solitary activity. But one person can easily miss an important point during a lecture either through daydreaming or trying to understand a prior point.

Students also have difficulty deciding what information is important and what is elaboration or example. Creating a wiki for group lecture notes after a lecture gives students a chance to combine all their notes. Those that missed information can get it from their peers. The group can also decide what information is critical and give it proper emphasis.

Group lecture notes could be done with the entire class, if it is small enough, or with small working groups. Groups can also compare notes for further discussion and refinement.

Brainstorming

Brainstorming is a creative process in which ideas are elicited from a group of people. In a face-to-face meeting, a brainstorming facilitator will usually stand in front of a big piece of paper and elicit ideas from the participants in the room. You can use a wiki to create an online version of this process. Set up a wiki for the entire class, or for student groups, and ask people to submit ideas around a brainstorming topic. People can add ideas as they occur to them and link to other pages for elaboration.

Contribute to other wikis

Consider assigning your class the task of contributing to Wikipedia, or to another wiki on the Web, on a topic in your class. Assign your students to groups (or make it a class project if the class is small enough and the topic broad enough) and challenge them to collaboratively create an article they would feel confident posting to a public-information space. Your students will use the course wiki to create drafts of the article they will publish to the community at the end of the semester.

This type of assignment has a number of benefits.

- It gives students additional motivation to do their best since they know their work will be viewed and critiqued by the public instead of just their instructor.

- It can act as a summarizing activity for an entire semester's worth of material.

- Students will know their work will be used by other people, not just graded and filed away.

12

Grades and Scales

Grades are a necessary evil in modern education. They take a complex task-learning a new subject-and reduce it to a single measure. They can function as both carrot and stick in motivating students, and are the primary measure of success in a course. Tracking and calculating grades are serious and tedious tasks. Fortunately, Moodel has a tool to help.

The Moodle gades area is a simple tool for tracking student scores in your course. Currently, gradebook functions as an automated tool for tracking scores in Moodle activities. It doesn't do a lot of fancy calculation, but you can download your scores to a spreadsheet or other tool for additional analysis.

Grades aren't the only way to give feedback to students. With Moodle's scales, you can create lists of non-numeric feedback options for assessing student work. Moodle comes with one scale by default, "Connected and Separate Ways of Knowing," which we'll discuss later in this chapter. You can easily create your own additional scales for feedback options that are meaningful to you and your students.

Using Grades

There isn't much to do with the current grades area. You can access the grades area by clicking the Grades link in the administration area on the left side of the main page of your course.

After you click the link, you will be taken to the Grades display, as shown in Figure 12-1. The students in the course are listed in the lefthand column. Across the top, you'll see all of the activities you have added to your course with the possible points for each. The far-right column records the students' total points and the total possible points.

		Meaningful Assignment Name Max: 100	Journal Assignment Name	Descriptive Forum Name	Chapter 1 Max: 10	Here's a forum Max: 10
First name	Surname					
Student1 Demo		100	Interesting			
Student2 Demo						

Figure 12-1. Grades area

Once grades have been recorded in the grades area, students can check their grades by clicking on the grades link in the administration area. They can see only their own grades, not the other students', as shown in Figure 12-2.

MoodleU » Mdl101 » Grades		
Grades		
Activity	Maximum grade	Grade
Meaningful Assignment Name	100	100
Journal Assignment Name		Interesting
Descriptive Forum Name		
Chapter 1	10	
Here's a forum	10	
Workshop	100	
Lesson 1	100	
Total	320	100
Continue		

Figure 12-2. Student grade view

Adding Manual Assignments

One of the chief complaints with the current gradebook in Moodle is the difficulty of adding a manually scored assignment. Scores for activities you've added to your course are automatically added to the gradebook, but what if you want to record a grade for something that isn't a Moodle activity?

Currently, the only way to add a manually scored column to the gradebook is to create an offline assignment. When you add the offline assignment to your course, it will create a column in the grades area. After you enter grades for the new assignment, they will appear in the grades table.

Downloading Grades to a Spreadsheet

Most instructors want to be able to do more advanced calculations on their grades than a simple point average. Currently, the Moodle gradebook does not support curving, weighting, or dropping grades. The only way to perform these calculations is to download the gradebook to a spreadsheet and perform your calculations there.

Fortunately, it's easy to download and manipulate the grades into a spreadsheet:

1. Click on Grades in the administration area
2. From the Grades table, select "Download in Excel format."
3. Save the file to your local hard drive, as shown in Figure 12-3.

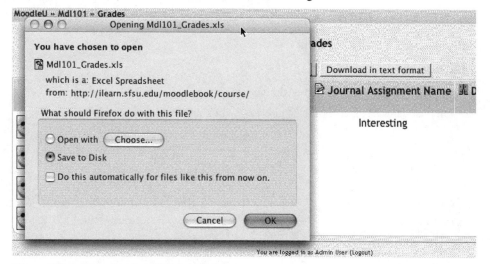

Figure 12-3. Download grades in excel format

4. Open the file you just downloaded with Excel or another spreadsheet. It will appear like the example in Figure 12-4.

	First name	Surname	ID number	Institution	Department	Email address	Assignment:	Journal: Jour	Forum: Descr	Quiz:
1	First name	Surname	ID number	Institution	Department	Email address	Assignment:	Journal: Jour	Forum: Descr	Quiz:
2	Student1	Demo				student_dem	100	Interesting		
3	Student2	Demo				student_dem				
4										

Figure 12-4. Moodle grades in Excel

5. Add additional columns and calculations as necessary.

Once you have manipulated the grades in Excel, you will need to communicate the new scores or final grades to students. While there is currently no way to upload a spreadsheet into Moodle, you can share the new scores with students. Simply create a new offline assignment and enter the results from the Excel spreadsheet.

Creating Scales

Scales are a non-numeric way of evaluating students' performance. Instead of giving an assignment a number from 1 to 100 as a grade, you can give the student a word or a small phrase as standard feedback.

Moodle's default scale–"Separate and Connected was of knowing"-gives you three options: Mostly Separate Knowing, Separate and Connected, and Mostly Connected Knowing. These phrases relate to a theory about how people approach the world. Separate knowers try to remain objective and avoid personalizing knowledge. They like to debate and critique new ideas. Connected knowers learn in a socially connected, empathetic way. They try to find consensus instead of confrontation.

This scale comes with Moodle as a default. Some people use it, but many create their own. You can create a scale using any rating system you choose. You can even create a different scale for each assignment.

To create a new scale:

1. Click on the Scales link in the Administration panel.

2. On the Scales page, shown in Figure 12-5, click the "Add a new scale" button.

Scale	Activities	Group	Action
Journal Scale Insightful, Funny, Interesting, Too Short, Tell me what you really feel	1	Custom scales	
Separate and Connected ways of knowing Mostly Separate Knowing, Separate and Connected, Mostly Connected Knowing	1	Standard scales	

Figure 12-5. Scales page

3. On the next page, shown in Figure 12-6, give your scale a name.

4. In the Scale box, create your scale. Each item in the scale should be separated by a comma. For example, a good–bad scale would be very good, good, fair, poor, very poor.

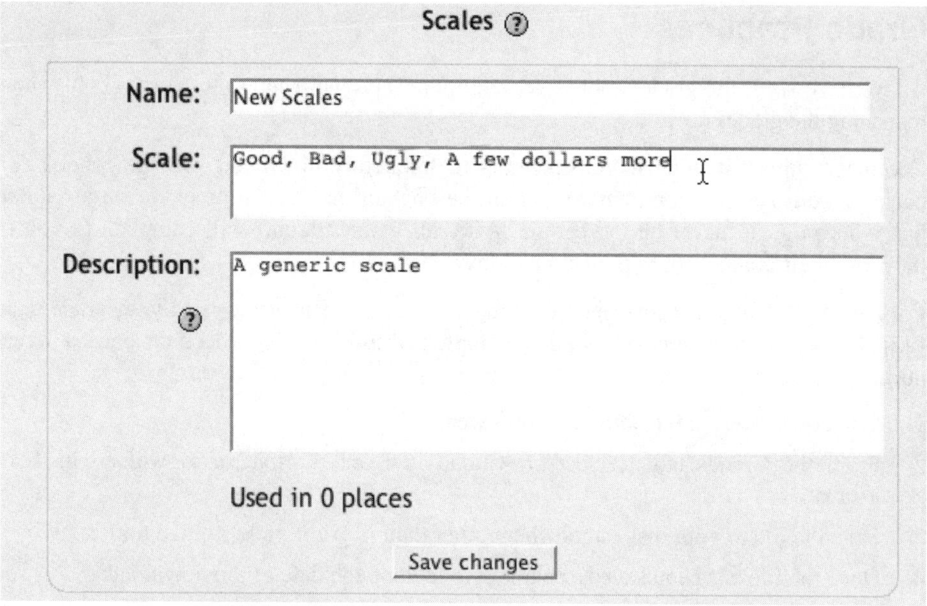

Scales (?)

Name: New Scales

Scale: Good, Bad, Ugly, A few dollars more

Description: A generic scale

(?)

Used in 0 places

Save changes

Figure 12-6. Adding a new scale

5. Write a detailed description for your scale. Your students will have access to the description, and you can use this to give them additional feedback. The more details you put in the description, the more students will understand what each scale item means.

Once you've created your scale, you can use it in any activity where you would give a grade, except of quizzes. Quizzes are the only tool where you have to use a numeric grade so Moodle can compute a score.

When you give feedback using a non-numeric scale, the activity does not appear in the total grade column. Instead, the word you select for the feedback appears in the grades list, as shown in Figure 12-7.

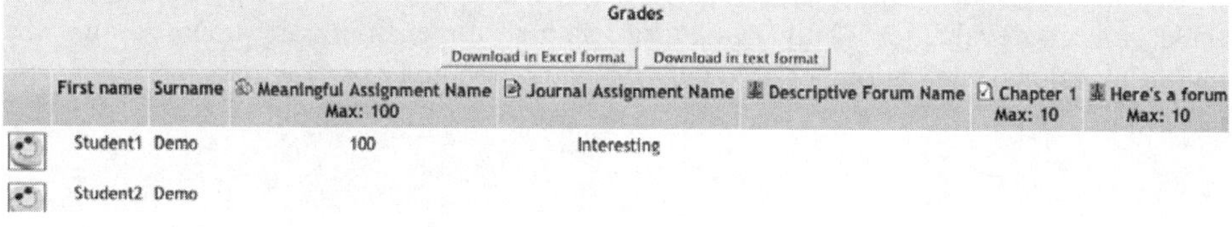

Grades

Download in Excel format | Download in text format

First name	Surname	Meaningful Assignment Name Max: 100	Journal Assignment Name	Descriptive Forum Name	Chapter 1 Max: 10	Here's a forum Max: 10
Student1	Demo	100	Interesting			
Student2	Demo					

Figure 12-7. Scales in the grades area

Effective Grade and Scale Practices

Grades and scales are important tools for providing feedback to your students. Using these tools effectively can help you create a more powerful learning environment.

Grade Practices

As we have seen, the grades tool is very simple. There isn't much to worry about when managing the grades area.

The most important thing to remember is to frequently download your gradebook for backup. Your system administrator should be backing up the entire server on a regular basis, but you can never be too certain. After all, your students will complain to you if they lose their grades, not to the system admin.

For regular backups, I recommend creating a folder specifically to hold your grade data files. Once you've created the folder, complete the following procedure once a week during your course:

1. Click on Grades in the administration area.
2. From the Grades table, select Download in Excel Format or Download in Text Format.
3. Save the file to your disk, somewhere other than in your grade storage folder.
4. Once the file has been saved, rename it to include the date of the download.
5. Copy the renamed file into your grades storage folder.

If you follow the backup procedure on a regular basis, you will have a record of student grades if there is a catastrophic loss of data on the server. You can always recover students' grades up to that point in the semester if you have a regular backup.

Scale Practices

Scales give you the ability to provide qualitative, instead of quantitative, feedback, but they require careful wording. When creating scales, ensure your word choices are meaningful to the students and provide information they can use to improve their performance in the future. For example, the good-bad scale I used as an example in the "Creating Scales" section is actually a poor choice. A scale that includes some indication of why the assignment was poorly done would be useful. This is a difficult task because a scale allows evaluation only along a single dimension, as opposed to the multidimensional evaluation possible with the workshop and exercise tools.

13

Managing Your Class

Now that we've covered all the learning tools in Moodle, we'll look at some of the administrative functions that are necessary to keep your course and students organized. This chapter will detail the interfaces for adding and deleting users, creating user groups, creating backups, and managing other course settings. Most of these functions can be accessed from the Administration block. Student groups and the student roster are the only exceptions, and you can manage these from the People block at the top left of the screen.

Before we can create student groups, we need to make sure the right students are enrolled in the course.

Managing Users

There are only a few things you need to do to effectively manage your students. Adding and deleting student enrollments are the primary functions. Later, you may want to edit student profiles or log in as a student to help them troubleshoot a problem with the course.

Adding Students and Teachers

Most of the time, students will enroll themselves or be added automatically by your university's enrollment system. So there shouldn't be much need for you to manually enroll students. However, if you need to add a TA, an outside guest, or a student who is having a problem with financial aid, you'll need to manually enroll them in your Moodle course.

To add a student:

1. Click Students in the administration area.

2. On the Enroll Students page, shown in Figure 13-1, you'll see two columns. The lefthand column lists the students currently enrolled in the class. The righthand column lists all the user accounts on the system, minus the students already enrolled.

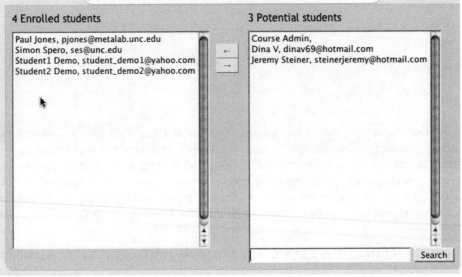

Figure 13-1. Enroll students

> *Warning: A student must have an account on your Moodle server before you can enroll them in your course.*

3. Find the student you want to add to your course in the righthand column. You can limit the list by searching for the student's name or email in the Search box below the righthand column.

4. Select the student's name from the list and click the arrow between the two columns pointing toward the "Enrolled students" column.

5. You can add multiple students by holding down the Shift key to select a number of students in a row. If you want to select multiple students who aren't listed next to each other, hold down the Control key (Apple key on a Mac) and click each name you want to add.

Students will have access to your course as soon as you enroll them. They won't need an enrollment key or to confirm the enrollment.

Removing Students

If a student drops your class, you'll want to remove her from the Moodle enrollment as well. Leaving a student enrolled in your Moodle section when she is not on the official roster makes grading and class management much more difficult. When you record grades, or look for student assignments, having extra students on the roll gets confusing. The student will also have access to your discussion boards and other potentially sensitive information.

Fortunately, removing students is easy. Simply reverse the above procedure.

To remove students:

1. Click Students in the administration area.

2. On the Enroll Students page, you'll see two columns. The lefthand column lists the students currently enrolled in the class. The righthand column lists all of the user accounts on the system, minus the students already enrolled.

3. Find the student you want to remove from your course in the lefthand column.

4. Select the student's name from the list and click the arrow in between the two columns pointing toward the "Potential students" column. The student's name will be moved out of the "Enrolled students" column to the "Potential students" column.

5. You can remove multiple students by holding down the Shift key to select a number of students in a row. If you want to select multiple students who aren't listed next to each other, hold down the Control key (Apple key on a Mac) and click each name you want to add.

Managing Enrollment

Ensuring that only students who are officially enrolled in your course have access to your Moodle site can be tricky. At my university, students can drop and add courses at will for the first three weeks of the semester. Many instructors find it difficult to track the constant movement in the roster. To minimize the amount of work you need to invest in this administrative detail, I recommend a three-pronged strategy.

First, use the course enrollment settings to limit who can enroll in the course and when. Set an enrollment period for the length of your drop/add time. Be sure to set an enrollment key as well. Only students who know the key will be able to enroll in your course, so you won't need to worry about students enrolling in your course without permission. For more information on these settings, see Chapter 2.

Second, closely monitor your official course roster during the drop/add period. Be consistent about dropping and adding students on a regular basis so you don't have a big mess at the end of registration.

Third, encourage students who are enrolled to create an account and join the Moodle course as quickly as possible. Many instructors make logging in and joining the Moodle course a small, mandatory assignment. This helps students by forcing them to access your online resources early in the semester, and makes enrollment management easier for you since you won't have to add as many students by hand.

Student Groups

Moodle has an unusual, but effective, way of managing small student workgroups. You define your groups then set the group mode for the class or for each tool. The group mode you choose also determines the behavior of each.

There are three group mode options:

No groups
>   Everyone participates as part of the class. Groups are not used.

Separate groups
>   Each group can see only their own work. They can't see the work of other groups.

Visible groups
>   Each group does their own work, but they can see the work of the other groups as well, as shown in Figure 13-2.

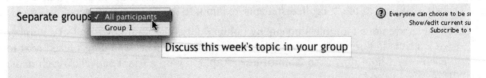

Figure 13-2. Visible groups

Once the group mode is set for the course or for the tool, students will interact with your Moodle course as they normally would. The only difference will be the people they meet in the forums, workshops, assignments and other tools. For example, if you set the group mode of a forum to separate groups, Moodle will create a forum for each group. Each student will see the same link to the forum, but they will be able to access only the discussions for their particular group. You need to create the forum only once; Moodle takes care of creating the individual group forums.

To utilize the group mode, you first need to create the student groups:

1. Click Groups on the People block.

2. Click Turn Editing Mode On. You will then see the Groups editing page with three columns, as shown in Figure 13-3. The left-most column lists the people who are not in a group. Teachers will have a # next to their name. The middle column lists the groups. The right-most column lists the people in a particular group once they have been assigned.

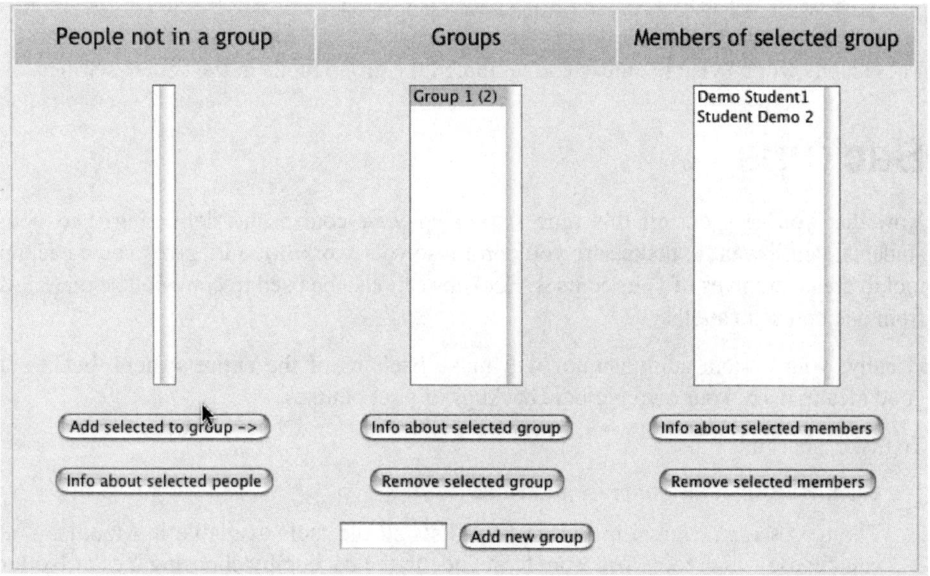

People not in a group	Groups	Members of selected group
	Group 1 (2)	Demo Student1 Student Demo 2
Add selected to group -> Info about selected people	Info about selected group Remove selected group Add new group	Info about selected members Remove selected members

Figure 13-3. Groups editing page

3. At the bottom of the Groups editing page, type the name of a new group and click "Add new group."

4. The name of the group will now appear in the groups list. Select the group you just created.

5. Select the students from the lefthand column you want to add to the group. Then click "Add selected to group ->."

6. Repeat steps 3 through 5 for each student group you need.

Once you've set up your groups, you can set the group mode for each tool. Once you've added a tool to your course, such as a forum, you can set the group mode on the course's main page. When you look at the page in editing mode, the right-most icon next to each tool toggles between the three possible group modes shown in Table 13-1.

Table 13-1. Group mode icons

♟	No groups mode
♟♟	Visible groups mode
♟♟	Separate groups mode

These icons will be visible unless you've forced the group mode in the course settings.

Backups

Now that you've spent all this time setting up your course and delivering it to your students, you'll want to make sure you don't lose your work. Moodle gives you a backup tool to create archives of your courses. Backups can also be used to copy course materials from one course to another.

Usually, your system administrator will make backups of the entire system, but it's a good idea to make your own periodic backups of your courses.

To make a backup:

1.   Click Backup in the administration area.

2.   The next screen, shown in Figure 13-4, lists all the tools available in Moodle. You can choose which tools you want to include in the backup by choosing Yes or No for each tool.

3.   You can also choose to backup user data individually for each tool. User data consists of all student files, submissions, and other activities:

     Users
         Backups the user accounts for everyone in the course. If you select None here, no user data will be backed up.

     Logs
         Backs up all course activity logs.

     User Files
         Backs up all student submissions for assignments and other file uploads.

     Course Files
         Backs up any file stored in the Files area for the course

4.   When you have selected your options, click Continue.

5.   The next screen previews the files Moodle will include in the backup and give you the name of the backup file. Click Continue at the bottom of the page.

6.   The next screen will report the results of the backup. You should see Backup Completed Successfully at the bottom of the page. Click Continue.

7. You will then be taken to the backupdata directory in your files area. The backup file will have a name like "backup-COURSESHORTNAME-DATE-TIME.zip." Click on the filename of the backup file to download it to your desktop.

Course backup: Moodle 101 (Mdl101)

Include Choices:	Yes ▾	with user data ▾
Include Glossaries:	Yes ▾	with user data ▾
Include Labels:	Yes ▾	with user data ▾
Include Lessons:	Yes ▾	with user data ▾
Include Quizzes:	Yes ▾	with user data ▾
Include Resources:	Yes ▾	with user data ▾
Include Scorms:	Yes ▾	with user data ▾
Include Surveys:	Yes ▾	with user data ▾
Include Wikis:	Yes ▾	with user data ▾
Include Attendance Rolls:	Yes ▾	with user data ▾
Include Assignments:	Yes ▾	with user data ▾
Include Chats:	Yes ▾	with user data ▾

Figure 13-4. Course backup selection

> *Tip: Some browsers or operating systems will automatically try to decompress a zip archive. If the browser or operating system unpacks the archive, you can simply delete the decompressed file. If you need to upload a backup to restore or copy a course, be sure to use the zip archive file.*

Restoring and Copying Courses

Once you've created a backup, you can use it to restore your course if there is catastrophic data loss on the server. Alternatively, you can use it to create a copy of your course without student data to create a new course or section.

To restore or load a new shell:

1. If the backup zip file is not in the files area for your course, upload the archive file from your desktop. See Chapter 3 for details on uploading files.

2. Find the backup file in the files area, as shown in Figure 13-5. If you didn't upload the file manually, it will be located in the backup folder of the course you backed up.

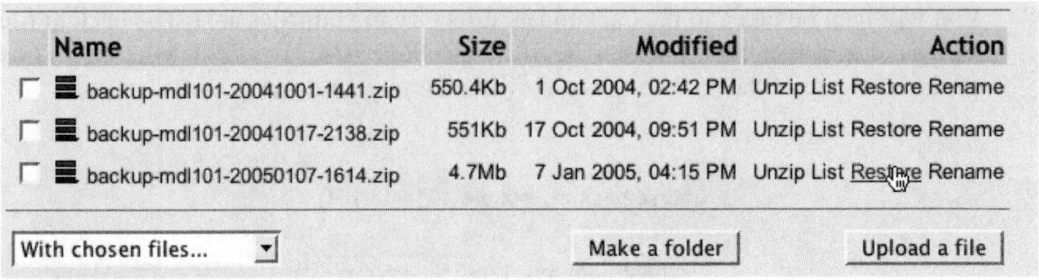

Name	Size	Modified	Action
☐ 🖿 backup-mdl101-20041001-1441.zip	550.4Kb	1 Oct 2004, 02:42 PM	Unzip List Restore Rename
☐ 🖿 backup-mdl101-20041017-2138.zip	551Kb	17 Oct 2004, 09:51 PM	Unzip List Restore Rename
☐ 🖿 backup-mdl101-20050107-1614.zip	4.7Mb	7 Jan 2005, 04:15 PM	Unzip List Restore Rename

With chosen files... ▼		Make a folder	Upload a file

Figure 13-5. Backup file

3. Click the Restore option next to the file you want to back up.

4. Click Yes under "Do you want to continue?".

5. The next screen will detail everything in the backup you have selected. Click Continue.

6. On the next screen, shown in Figure 13-6, first select whether you want to delete the data in the target course before you copy the backup or simply add the data in the backup to the target.

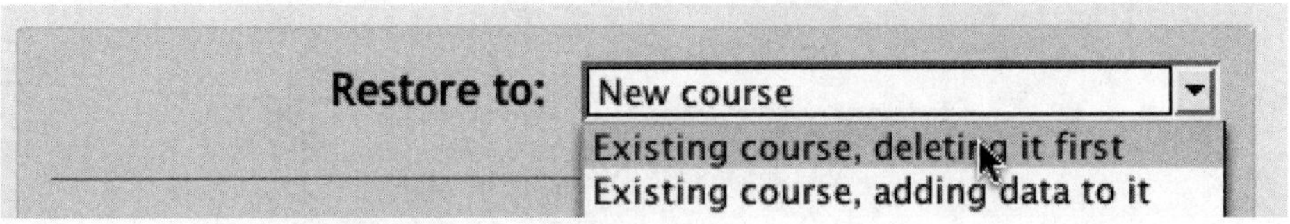

Restore to: `New course ▼`
`Existing course, deleting it first`
`Existing course, adding data to it`

Figure 13-6. Restore a course

7. On the same page, select whether you want to restore each tool and whether you want to add user data.

> *Tip: Most people have two main reasons for restoring course data from a backup: restoring lost data and copying a course shell. If you are trying to restore lost data, you'll want to include all the user data and delete the target course. If you are copying a course shell for another semester or course section, don't copy any user data. If you have data in the target course, be sure not to delete the target course data.*

8. At the bottom of the page, select whether you want to include users with the course.

9. Choose whether you want to include user files.

10. Click Continue.

11. Next, select the target course for the backup.

12. Click "Restore this course now!". The course data will be moved into the new course.

Once you've restored your course, all the data will be available. If you're copying your course to a new course shell, be sure to check the course start date and the due dates of all your assignments.

Logs

Once your course is up and students are working, Moodle provides you with detailed logs of student activity. When you click Logs in the administration area, you'll be taken to the log-selection panel. Here you can select how you want to view course activity. You can view logs by course, person, date, or activity.

You can see what page the student accessed, the time and date they accessed it, and the IP address they came from, as shown in Figure 13-7.

Displaying 25 records

Fri 31 December 2004, 11:53 AM	127.0.0.1	**Admin User**	course view		Moodle 101
Fri 31 December 2004, 11:52 AM	127.0.0.1	**Admin User**	user view all		
Fri 31 December 2004, 11:52 AM	127.0.0.1	**Admin User**	course view		Moodle 101
Fri 31 December 2004, 11:51 AM	127.0.0.1	**Admin User**	forum view forum		Group Forum
Fri 31 December 2004, 11:51 AM	127.0.0.1	**Admin User**	forum add		Group Forum
Fri 31 December 2004, 11:51 AM	127.0.0.1	**Admin User**	course add mod		forum 18
Fri 31 December 2004, 11:50 AM	127.0.0.1	**Admin User**	course view		Moodle 101
Fri 31 December 2004, 11:50 AM	127.0.0.1	**Admin User**	course update		
Fri 31 December 2004, 11:49 AM	127.0.0.1	**Admin User**	course view		Moodle 101
Fri 31 December 2004, 11:47 AM	127.0.0.1	**Admin User**	course view		Moodle 101
Fri 31 December 2004, 11:33 AM	127.0.0.1	**Admin User**	glossary view		Class Glossary
Fri 31 December 2004, 11:27 AM	127.0.0.1	**Admin User**	glossary view		Class Glossary
Fri 31 December 2004, 11:26 AM	127.0.0.1	**Admin User**	course view		Moodle 101
Fri 31 December 2004, 11:26 AM	127.0.0.1	**Admin User**	forum view discussion	Moodle
Fri 31 December 2004, 11:26 AM	127.0.0.1	**Admin User**	forum view forum		News forum
Fri 31 December 2004, 11:26 AM	127.0.0.1	**Admin User**	forum add discussion	Moodle
Fri 31 December 2004, 11:25 AM	127.0.0.1	**Admin User**	forum view forum		News forum

Figure 13-7. User log

The logs are useful for tracking students' activity in a class. If a student doesn't spend time with the material, he will have difficulty succeeding in the course. Frequently, students who don't do well simply haven't spent the time working with the material.

If you analyze your class logs on a regular basis, you can monitor when your students engage with the course material. You won't be able to tell exactly how long they spent with a certain activity or resource because the logs report only the time of access. Of course, you can guess how long a student spent with a resource by noting the time the student began the next activity.

Logs can also tell you which resources and activities students find most valuable. For example, if you upload all your Powerpoint slides for student to take notes on in class, but no one accesses them, then you might want to find out why.

14

Surveys and Choices

Moodle has two tools specifically designed for collecting ungraded feedback from your students: surveys and choices. Surveys are a set of predetermined questions already developed by the Moodle developers. Currently, there is no way to create your own survey questions in a survey. This option is planned, but it isn't yet ready. The current surveys focus on getting feedback from students about the nature of the course.

Choices are little, one-question surveys. They act as small web polls that you may have seen on other web sites. You can use a choice to get rapid feedback from your students about any topic you wish, as long as it's only once question long and has a maximum of six answers.

Creating Surveys

The limited nature of the surveys tool makes surveys very easy to create. Basically, you select the set of prewritten questions you'd like to give, edit the introductory text, and you're done.

There are three types of surveys you can give:

COLLES (Constructivist On-Line Learning Environment Survey)
This is a set of 24 statements that asks students about the relevance of the course, provides opportunities for reflection and interactivity, provides peer and tutor support, and facilitates interpretation. These factors are based on social constructivist theory, as discussed in Chapter 1. Variations on the survey ask students to discuss their preferred learning environment or the actual learning environment. Moodle offers three types of COLLES surveys: preferred, actual, a combination of the two. The preferred COLLES survey asks students to discuss how they think they want to interact with a course, while the actual COLLES survey asks them how they are interacting currently.

ATTLS (Attitudes to Thinking and Learning Survey)
ATTLS seeks to measure the quality of interaction within a course. It builds on the "separate and connected ways of knowing" scale, which we discussed in Chapter 12.

Critical Incidents
The Critical Incidents survey asks students to consider recent events and answer questions about their relationship to those events. It is similar to the one-minute response paper we discussed in Chapter 8.

Once you've determined the type of survey you'd like to conduct, create the survey to make it available to your students.

To create a survey:

1. Click Turn Editing Mode On.

2. Select Survey from the Activities menu in the appropriate section in your course.

3. From the survey-creation page, shown in Figure 14-1, give the survey a name.

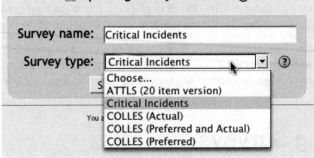

Figure 14-1. Survey creation page

4. Select the type of survey you want to give from the dropdown list.

5. Click Continue.

6. On the following screen, edit the introductory text if necessary.

7. Click OK.

8. The next screen displays the question set you have chosen. Click Check and Continue at the bottom of the page.

Administering Surveys

Once you've created the survey, students can begin to give their feedback. They simply click on the survey name in the course section and answer the questions. Once students have begun to answer the survey questions, you can track the survey results by clicking on the name of the survey in the section.

The results section in each survey allows you to view the data by course, by student, or by question. You can also download the data to a spreadsheet.

> *Warning: Moodle surveys are* not *anonymous. While students cannot see each other's results, you can view each student's survey. There is no way to assure anonymity. If you are using these results for research, you must develop a scheme to download the data and assign participant numbers. You should also inform students of this limitation.*

The COLLES and ATTLS questions are five-point scales that range in responses from Almost Always to Almost Never. These results are reported in graphical form when you view them, as illustrated in Figure 14-2.

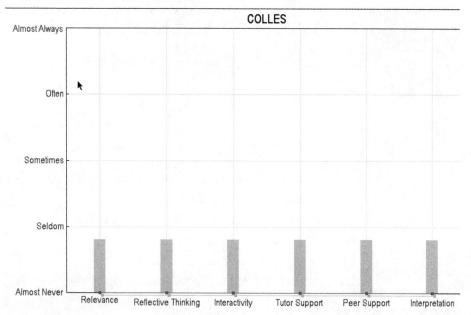

Figure 14-2. Survey results

The Critical Incidents survey is a free-response survey where students must type their answers. You can see what students have typed for each answer.

Later in this chapter, we'll discuss how to apply the data you gather. Now we'll move on to choices.

Creating Choices

Unlike Surveys, the choice tool allows you to ask any question you'd like, as long as it's multiple-choice. Once you've set up your choice, it acts as a rapid poll in your course. Students click on the choice and select their answer. You can choose when they see the results of the poll and even let them change their mind.

To create a choice:

1. Click Turn Editing Mode On.
2. Select Choice from the Activity menu.
3. Give your question a name, then enter the question text in the Choice text area, as shown in Figure 14-3. You can give students a choice between one of six responses to your question.

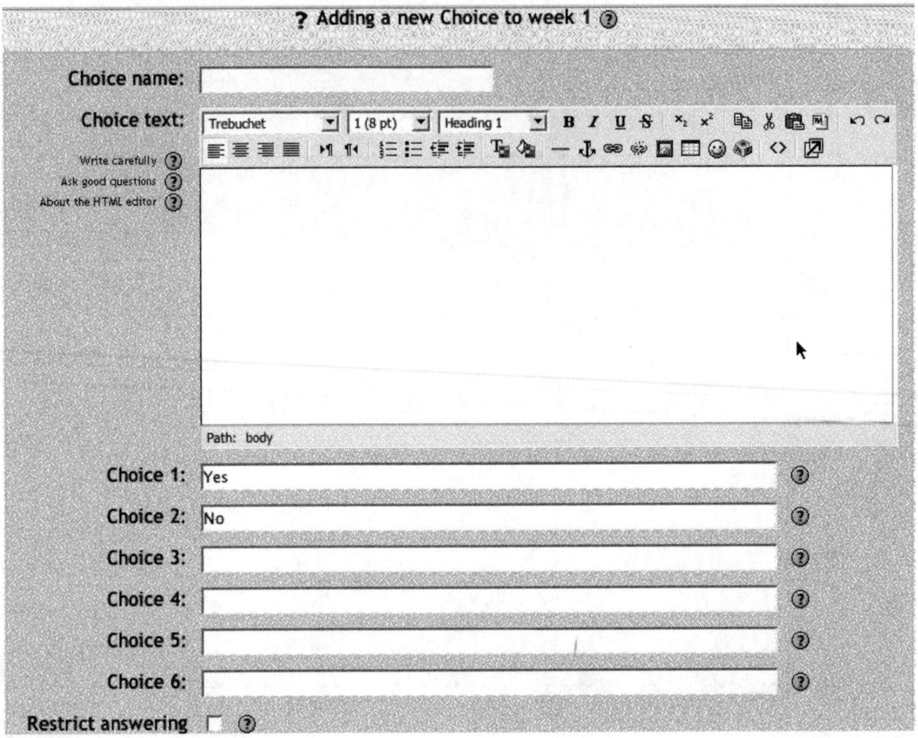

Figure 14-3. Choice creation page

4.   Set the options for your choice

Restrict answering to this time period
> If you want the question to be available for a limited time, set a starting and ending time for the choice.

Publish results
> You have four options for revealing the results of the poll to students:
>
> *   Never display the results
> *   Display the results only after the ending time for the poll (if you've set one above)
> *   Display the results only after they've answered
> *   Always display the results

Privacy of Results
> Here you can choose whether to display the students' names with their response in the poll results.

Allow choice to be updated
> If you want to allow students to change their minds after they've answered, set this to Yes. Otherwise, students will be able to answer the question only once.

Show column for unanswered
> This option determines whether students will see the number of people who haven't answered the question when they see the poll results.

5.   Click Save Changes.

Once you've created the choice it will be available to students after the starting time, if you've set one.

Administering Choices

After students have answered the poll, you can see the results by clicking on the choice name in the course section. You'll see the choice question and a link to view the students' responses. Unlike the students' view of the results, you'll see a column for each response with the student's picture and name, as shown in Figure 14-4.

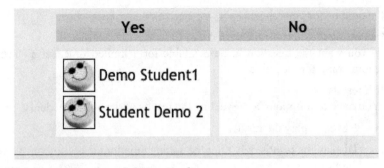

Figure 14-4. Teacher's view of choice results

Using Surveys and Choices

Surveys and choices represent two different tools for gathering feedback data from students. Moodle surveys are formal and based in theory. Choices are quick and simple for both you and your students. They can both provide useful data about your course and your students' success.

Moodle surveys are a bit too long to be used frequently. They provide useful feedback if you want to revise your course to meet student needs, but answering a set of 24 questions on a regular basis can become tedious for your students. I recommend using the ATTLS or COLLES survey three times per semester (or twice a quarter if you're on the quarter system). You may want to deliver the first survey after the first few weeks to get some early feedback on student perceptions of the course, once at the mid-term to make adjustments for the second half, and once at the end of the course to get summative feedback to include in the next semester's course design.

Of the available surveys, the COLLES and Critical Incidents are the most useful for making decisions about your course design. In the COLLES survey, pay close attention to the relevance scores. Student perception of course relevance is very important in determining student satisfaction and learning. If a student believes a course isn't relevant to his life, he will have difficulty spending the time required to be successful. His performance will suffer, and his perception of the value of the course will diminish.

The Critical Incidents survey can provide useful feedback at the end of a topic or week. If you're trying something new, use this survey to get student feedback on the success of the topic. Because it's only five questions long, you can use it more frequently than the other two surveys.

Choices can be offered much more frequently. Many web sites use quick polls to inform or entertain their readers. Local and national news outlets run informal, nonscientific polls through their sites to gauge public opinion. You can use your choices to do the same. Choices could be about anything from course content to current school events. They can be a great way to keep students engaged in the class.

15

Putting It All Together

Now that we've taken a look at all the tools available in Moodle, I want to take a step back and look at the big picture. Moodle has a lot of nifty capabilities, but they are only useful if they are applied in the service of effective course design.

If you are a professor in higher education, you are an expert in your field. You know more about your discipline than 99% of the rest of humanity. Universities do a great job helping people become domain experts and resarchers. They do a poor job of teaching those experts how to teach. The assumption is that teaching comes naturally, that since we've all been to school, we know how to teach. Unfortunately, this isn't the case. Creating effective learning environments requires training and careful preparation.

In this chapter, I hope to give you some ideas and background from which you can develop your courses. We'll spend a little while talking about learning environments in general, then we'll talk about how to apply everything you've learned so far to your courses. I'll provide some design patterns for different types of courses that research and experience have shown to be successful.

What Is a Learning Environment?

Since we're developing an instructional environment, it would be a good idea to have a definition of what we're hoping to develop. What makes a web-based learning environment different from a web site?

There are two important features of a learning environment that are different from other types of web sites: goals and feedback.

Learning environments have very specific goals for students. Most other web environments are there for the user to achieve her own goals. They provide information, a way to buy things, or a way to connect with other people. People come to these environments of their own volition and can participate at whatever level they choose.

Learning environments are unique because they provide goals for students to achieve, goals they are currently unable to meet on their own. Your course objectives define a set of goals for students, goals they would not normally set for themselves. These goals define how students will interact with the material, other students, and you.

For example, if you are teaching a large survey course, the course goal will be to introduce the main concepts of the field to your students. In an advanced theory course, you will want students to demonstrate the ability to reason critically about advanced topics, and possibly synthesize their own ideas.

The second defining feature of learning environments is feedback. Feedback is critical for students to monitor their progress as they pursue the course goals. Goal-oriented feedback is one of the critical defining aspects of a learning environment. If a student doesn't receive feedback, he has no way of knowing if he is closer to achieving the goals of the class or not. Other types of information environments don't can't provide feedback to their users because the users' goals are defined by them, not by the environment. The only exception is an online game, which defines external goals and measures the player's progress toward them.

Feedback in a learning environment can take many forms. Tests and quizzes are a frequently used tool for measuring student progress. They can provide feedback to students in the form of right and wrong answers or a percentage score. Homework can also provide feedback to students about their understanding of the materials. Less formal feedback might include interaction with students in class, conversations with experts, or applying new knowledge in a work setting.

These two features make learning environments unique. Moodle provides you with tools to implement these ideas in unique ways. Moodle's educational philosophy guides how those tools are designed and can influence how you structure your learning environment.

Course Design Patterns

Design patterns are abstract solutions to recurring design problems. The term was originally used in architecture, but it has been applied more recently to software design. In architecture, the placement of doors and gates, windows, and other elements are design patterns that recur in many buildings. The idea of a lobby in a large office building is a design pattern. Over time, these patterns become almost invisible to us as we are continually exposed to them. Changing a pattern can lead to the discovery of an entirely new way of interacting with a space.

Instructional design patterns are similar. There are abstract solutions to the design challenges that occur in many courses. We can abstract four basic course types in higher education:

Introductory survey course
> These tend to be large lecture courses designed to expose students to basic concepts, vocabulary, and foundational ideas.

Skills development course
> These courses are designed to apply the ideas introduced in the beginning courses. Labs, recitations, workshops, and second-level courses tend to fall into this category. While there is discussion of theory, applying the theory to problems is the core of the course.

Theory/discussion course
> In more advanced courses, students are expected to think critically about research and theory. Application is typically secondary to the discussion of the theory itself.

Capstone course
> Many programs have some sort of summative experience that enables students to demonstrate what they have learned in their course of study.

While there are variations and combinations of these course archetypes, these categories cover most of the courses taught in most universities.

Understanding the abstract problem types is the first step toward designing a solution pattern. We also need principles of quality that will help us decide which solutions will be more likely to result in a better solution. Every professor develops a response to the course archetypes. The question is, which solutions are more likely to result in a quality course?

Fortunately, the American Association for Higher Education has come up with some recommendations for high-quality university courses. The AAHE has published 12 recommendations in three categories:

Culture:

- High expectations
- Respect for diverse talents and learning styles

- Emphasis on early undergraduate years

Curriculum:

- Coherence in learning
- Synthesizing experience
- Ongoing practice of learned skills
- Integration of education with experience

Instruction:

- Active learning
- Assessment and prompt feedback
- Collaboration
- Adequate time on task
- Out-of-class contact with faculty

It would be impossible to apply all 12 of these principles in every class. But a course that integrates as many of these principles as possible will likely be of higher quality than one that doesn't.

Fortunately, many of the tools in Moodle lend themselves well to realizing these quality principles. Let's take a look at how to apply the tools in Moodle to meeting these quality principles in the four class types.

Introductory Survey Course

The introductory survey course tends to be a large lecture course. The primary goal is to expose students to the basic concepts and vocabulary of a field of study. In the best case, this course helps students develop a basic conceptual structure that serves as the foundation for more advanced courses.

There tend to be two primary, related problems to address in these courses. First, their large size makes it difficult to assess open-ended assignments such as projects and reports. Second, student motivation is difficult to maintain due to the course's large size and its nature. Students who are required to take the course may find it difficult to engage in the subject matter, and long lectures are hard for anyone to get excited about. So how can we use the Moodle tools and the above principles to create a successful survey course?

Groups

    The key to success in a large class is the strategic use of groups. To promote active learning, create a group project that students must complete by the end of the semester. Such a project cuts the number of submissions you need to grade and provides students with opportunities for collaboration.

Resources

Posting your lecture notes before each lecture will help students stay engaged by giving them a structure for taking notes. Before each lecture, post an outline of the upcoming class to help students plan ahead for that class.

Quizzes

Use the quiz tool to provide a small quiz for each reading assignment. This will reward students for completing the reading and allow them to test their understanding of the material. Each quiz should be relatively low-stakes, but all of them taken together could add up to a significant part of the student's score. These small quizzes will provide assessment, prompt feedback, and help students spend adequate time on task.

Forums

A mix of class forums and group forums can be an effective tool for collaboration, active learning, and out-of-class contact with faculty. Forums for questions to the instructors and for general course discussion are great for class discussions. Each group should also have a discussion area for reading groups and lectures. Be sure to seed the discussion each week with a good question that will require students to apply the concepts learned during that week. Bring the best questions and discussions to the attention of the whole class to help motivate students. Create a class forum for the submission of final group projects. Everyone can see the projects, and each group needs to post the project only once.

Glossaries

A good glossary is critical when students are learning a new vocabulary. You can use the glossary to promote active learning by assigning a different group to create definitions for each week or topic. You and the other students can rate their submissions based on their usefulness. Be sure to turn on autolinking to get the most benefit.

Wikis

Each group should have a group wiki for their course project that they can submit at the end of the semester. Using a wiki this way promotes active learning and collaboration.

Lessons

Learning vocabulary is difficult without a lot of practice. To provide another opportunity for assessment and feedback, create a series of vocabulary flash cards in the lesson module to help students drill themselves on the new concepts.

Combine these tools to create an effective learning environment. Each week or topic should have lecture notes, a glossary, a quiz or quizzes, and a forum. At the beginning of the course, post the course glossary, the course forum, and your syllabus. At the end of the course, post the final-project forum.

Skills Development Course

The skills development course is generally the second-level class in a course of study. The aim of this course is to give students the opportunity to apply the basic concepts learned in the survey course and explore one aspect of the field in more detail. These are usually workshop or lab courses that focus on a project or the repetitive application of important skills.

Skills development courses require continuous feedback and assessment. Engaged students need feedback so they can know if they are performing the skills correctly. They also need resources to help them troubleshoot when they cannot solve a problem on their own. You can create an effective practice environment for skills development with the following tools in Moodle:

Resources
> As students practice on their own, they will need information resources to help them diagnose their mistakes. If you can post demonstrations, step-by-step instructions, or other aids for students as they practice on their own, you'll make it easier for students to succeed and eliminate a lot of repetitive questions.

Forum
> Forums provide valuable opportunities for your students to help each other. Set up a forum for each topic or week and have students ask each other for assistance with course assignments. Allow post ratings in these forums to reward students who provide assistance to their classmates. This encourages collaboration and gives students an important out-of-class communication channel for support.

Quizzes
> If your class is focused on math skills, you can use the new calculated-question type to provide your students with unlimited practice opportunities. Create a library of questions for each topic and let students take the quiz as many times as they'd like. Each time, they will see a different set of questions. Writing or other project-based skills don't lend themselves to the quiz tool very well.

Workshops
> For project- or writing-based skills courses, the workshop is a great tool for active learning. Students learn from creating the work for submission and from evaluating the work of others. The scoring guides also give you an important tool for reminding students about the important dimensions of their performance. Remember that you don't need to use the workshop just for electronic submissions. If each student uploads a placeholder file, you can use the workshop to evaluate speeches, paintings, sculptures, and any other performance you may require of students.

Exercise
> As a summative experience at the end of the class, make the final-project submission an exercise rather than an assignment. The self-assessment piece of the exercise tool

creates an opportunity for self-reflection. The scoring guide also helps you eliminate ambiguity in the students' final grade.

Theory/Discussion Course

A discussion course focuses on readings and the discussion of ideas. These are usually senior- or graduate-level courses that focus on discussions of theory and research. There is little practical application. Instead, ideas are discussed, debated, and critiqued. Emphasis is on reasoning, presenting evidence from the research literature, and critical thinking.

Student motivation is typically not a problem in these courses. They are advanced courses taken by students who are usually interested in the subject. The problems come from creating opportunities for active learning, and providing prompt feedback. Fortunately, there are a few Moodle tools that can help you overcome these issues:

Journal

Critical thinking and analysis of theory typically requires periods of private reflection along with public discussion. Encourage students to actively engage in these activities by providing them with a space to privately journal about the course topics. Having students keep a journal in Moodle rather than on paper allows you to give them feedback on their entries without interrupting the writing process.

Assignment

One of the hallmarks of most theory courses is a large amount of reading, usually as original research. To help your students keep on top of the reading, create a weekly assignment asking them to submit a short summary or abstract of the papers they read. This strategy will reward them for keeping up with the reading and encourage them to actively engage with the reading.

Choice

As a stimulation for conversation, include a choice each week. Poll the class about a controversial point in the reading or discussion. Combine this with a forum asking students to explain their responses.

Forums

Forums are one of the keys to a successful discussion course. As we discussed in Chapter 4, forums allow students to compose their thoughts and focus on the content of their responses. Encourage careful, well-reasoned postings in the forum by scoring posts. Encourage more active engagement by assigning groups of students as moderators for different topics.

Wiki

A class wiki can be used to create a shared understanding of the ideas under discussion. At the end of the semester, the students will have a synopsis of the entire class to take with them.

Workshop
> A workshop for papers is a good way to provide rapid feedback and additional learning opportunities for students. Give students an opportunity to give each other feedback on early drafts of research papers or essays as well as a summative evaluation of the final product.

Capstone Course

Capstone courses are usually focused around a final project that requires students to demonstrate what they have learned during their course of study. In graduate school, these courses are focused around a thesis or dissertation. In undergraduate study, students are expected to produce a paper or another artifact. These project-based courses present challenges for both the instructor and students.

Assignment
> You can help students structure the task by assigning a set of deliverables over the course of the semester. Each deliverable should be a one- or two-week project you collect with an assignment. For example, if students are writing a paper, you could collect an annotated bibliography, a subject proposal, an outline, a couple of early drafts, and a final draft.

Dialogue
> Set up a dialogue as private feedback channels so students can discuss their work. As they work on each section of the project, they will need to ask questions about the assignment and their performance. The dialogue tool is an organizational tool that allows you to track multiple simultaneous conversations.

Journal
> Part of a student's capstone experience is reflecting on what a he has learned over the course of study. Journals can act as a tool for reflection and as a project notebook. Encourage students to use the journal for both activities.

Exercise
> Use the exercise tool for the final submission. The self-assessment and scoring guides make for a good summative experience.

These design patterns are abstract starting points for designing a solution that works in your class. I've tried to recommend patterns that I have seen work, or that other researchers have reported to be successful. They are not the final word on effective course design by any means.

16

Moodle Administration

If you are the site administrator for your Moodle installation, there are a lot of options at your fingertips. Most of the time, the default settings that come with your Moodle installation will work well. But there are a lot of options for customization and performance that can make your version of Moodle work exactly as you'd like.

The role of system administrator can be challenging, even if you're just administering your own site. You are responsible for keeping the system up and running.

Configuration

The configuration settings in Moodle affect the basic functionality of the site. There are eight areas in the configuration menu: variables, settings, themes, module settings, blocks, filters, backup, and editor settings. Each of these areas affects the functioning of your Moodle site in different ways.

Site Variables

Site variables are settings that determine how your entire Moodle site functions. The site variables are the most technical settings.

The variables fall into seven clusters.

Language/location variables

Lang
> Sets the default language for the site. This setting can be overridden by users using the language menu or the setting in their personal profile.

Langmenu
> Sets whether the language menu is displayed on the login page and the home page. If this is turned off, the only places where a user can change the language setting is in her user profile or in the course settings if she is a teacher.

Langlist
> If you want to limit the number of languages students and teachers can select from, enter that list here.

Locale
> Determines date format and language. You need to have the locale set on your operating system for this to work.

Timezone
> Sets the default time zone for date display. This can be overridden by the user's profile setting.

Country
> Sets a default country for user profiles.

Mail settings

SMTPhosts
> SMTP stands for Simple Mail Transfer Protocol. The SMTP host is an email relay that will take the email from Moodle and send it to users. You will need to set this only if your server does not allow mail relay. Otherwise, PHP will send out the mail using its built-in mail server. All the email sent by forums and other modules will be sent through this host.

SMTPuser
> If you set an SMTP server and it requires authentication, enter the username for the account that will be relaying the email from Moodle.

SMTPpass
> Enter the password for the SMTP user you set earlier.

Noreplyaddress

> Email sent from Moodle needs to have a return address or many servers will reject it as spam. Some users also want to keep their email private, so Moodle sends all of its email using the noreply address you set here.

Graphics library

Gdversion

> GD is a graphics library that manipulates graphics. It's used to create thumbnail images from uploaded files and other graphics on the fly. If you don't know what version is installed, leave this on the original setting.

Timing settings

Maxeditingtime

> Sets the editing time for the forums and other feedback. The editing time is the amount of time users have to change forum postings before they are mailed to subscribers.

Longtimenosee

> To help keep course rosters organized, you can tell Moodle to unenroll any student who hasn't logged in for a certain amount of time. Be sure to keep this time long enough so students aren't unenrolled accidentally while they still need access to the course.

Deleteunconfirmed

> If you're using email account confirmation (see the section "User management"), users must confirm their account within a certain timeframe. Once the time set here has passed, any account that hasn't been confirmed will be deleted.

Loglifetime

> Moodle keeps extensive logs of user activity. Eventually, however, the logs will become so large that they begin to clog your server. Although the instructions on the screen suggest that you don't delete the logs, I recommend keeping the logs only as long as you need them. Usually, a year is enough time.

Security and login settings

Displayloginfailures

> The logs display login failures. This is probably necessary only if people are attempting to steal student or teacher logins.

Notifyloginfailures

> If you're concerned about login failures, you can also have email sent to system administrators.

Notifyloginthreshold

> Sets the number of failed logins for a given user from a single computer that will trigger notification.

Sessiontimeout

    Once someone logs in to your Moodle server, the server starts a session. The session data allows the server to track users as they access different pages. If users don't load a new page during the amount of time set here, Moodle will end their session and log them out. Be sure this time frame is long enough to cover the longest test your teachers may offer. If a student is logged out while he is are taking a test, his responses to the test questions may be lost.

Sessioncookie

    Most of the time, you can leave this blank, unless you are running more than one copy of Moodle on the same server. In this case, you will want to customize the name of the cookie each copy of Moodle uses to track the session. That way, if you're logged in to one copy of Moodle, you won't also be logged in to the other copy.

File and picture handling

Zip and unzip

    If you are running Moodle on a Unix or Unix-like server (Linux, Solaris, BSD, Mac OS X), you may need to specify where the zip program is located. Zip and unzip are used to compress and decompress zip archives such as the backup folder.

Slasharguments

    You will need to change this setting only if you are having trouble viewing files or images. Most of the time, Moodle will display files and pictures with no problem using the slash arguments. If you get errors when you try to view pictures or files from within Moodle, your PHP server doesn't allow the slash argument method and you will need to use the file argument method instead.

Proxyhost and proxyport

    Your Moodle server may need to access the Internet through a proxy server, depending on your network configuration. If you're not sure about whether you need a proxy server, contact your network administrator or ISP.

Debug

    Setting debug to Yes turns on PHP warnings and messages to help developers debug new modules. Unless you are actively writing new code, leave this turned off.

Framename

    If you've developed a web wrapper for Moodle and you want to include Moodle in a larger frame, set the name for the Moodle frame here.

Secureforms

    Whenever a user sends form data to Moodle, the browser also sends a piece of data called HTTP_REFERER. This data contains the sending computer's IP address. If you turn on this setting, the referrer data will be compared to the IP address of the machine sending the request. If they match, then the data is being sent from the machine that originated the request. If they don't match, someone may be trying to spoof the user's IP address and initiate a man-in-the-middle attack to compromise her Moodle data. This security check may cause problems with some firewalls. IP spoofing is rare, so you'll need to choose between locking out people with their firewalls on or risking an IP spoof attack.

Loginhttps

HTTPS encrypts the user's login data, so it's difficult to sniff out a user's username and password on the network. You will need to enable HTTPS on your server before you turn on this setting, or else you will be locked out of your site. Every web server has a different method for enabling HTTPS, so you should check the documentation for your web server. Most versions of Moodle won't let you set this to Yes unless HTTPS is enabled on the server.

Teacherassignteachers

If you want teachers to be able to assign other teachers to their courses, set this to Yes.

Allusersaresitestudents

The front page of your Moodle site is actually a Moodle course. If you want everyone who has an account on the server to be able to participate in the front page forum and news, set this to Yes. If the users should be associated with another class before they can participate, set this to No.

User management

Showsiteparticipantlist

Determines who can view the site participants list. For privacy reasons, you will probably want to set this to Site Teachers.

Allowunenroll

Students may need to be able to unenroll themselves from courses, especially old versions of courses that are still visible.

Maxbytes

Determines the site-wide absolute maximum for file uploads. Any file upload sizes in the modules must be set lower than this number.

Fullnamedisplay

Determines how full names will be displayed.

Extenededusernamechars

Leaving this set to No restricts students' login names to alphanumeric characters. If you enable this setting, they can use extended characters such as (!@#$%^&*) in their username. This does not limit their first or surname settings.

Autologinguests

If a visitor goes to a course that allows guest access without first logging in as a guest, this setting will log them in automatically.

Forcelogin

By default, anyone who visits your Moodle site can see the front-page news and course listings. If you want users to log in before they see this page, set this to Yes.

Forceloginforprofiles

> Forces users to log in before they can view other users' profiles. I usually leave this enabled for privacy reasons.

Opentogoogle

> Enabling this setting allows Google's search spiders guest access to your site. Any part of the site that allows guest access will then be searchable on Google.

Enablerssfeeds

> Individual modules can send RSS feeds to users' news readers. RSS feeds are headlines that let a user know when there is new content on the Moodle site. If you enable RSS here, you will also need to enable RSS in each RSS-enabled module.

Digestmailtime

> Moodle now allows mail digests from the forums, so users get only one email per day instead of an individual message for every posting. This setting specifies when digests are emailed to users.

Site Settings

Site settings determine how the site's front page looks. Compared to the site variables, these are simpler to work with.

The site settings include:

Full site name

> The name for your entire site, which appears at the top of every screen above the breadcrumbs navigation.

Short name for site

> The short name appears at the beginning of the breadcrumb navigation as a link back to the main site page.

Front page description

> A short message to your users on the right side of the front page.

Front page format

> The central block on the front page can display one of three things: news items, a list of the users' courses, or a list of course categories. This setting determines which of the three your site displays.

Include a topic section

> Adds a full-course topic section with an Add Resource menu or activity menu. The topic section appears at the top of the central block.

Name for administrator and teachers

> You can customize the label for people with administrator and teacher roles. The teacher-name setting can be overridden in the course settings.

Themes

Themes set the background color, font types, and font color for your entire Moodle site. Moodle comes with a number of prepackaged themes. To select a new theme for your site:

1. Click on Themes in the administration area.

2. Click on a theme.

3. Once you have a theme you like, click Save Changes. If you don't click Save Changes, the theme will revert to the last saved theme when you leave the Themes page.

Module Settings

The modules settings area allows you to control access to the Moodle modules.

Each activity module can be made available for teachers or turned off. If the modules are turned off, instructors won't be able to add them to their courses.

In addition to adjusting the site settings, you can adjust settings in many of the modules. Fortunately, the Moodle developers have done an excellent job documenting each of the variables you can adjust for each of the modules.

To change any of the module settings, select Modules from the administration area. Then select the settings for the module you want to adjust.

Blocks

The settings for administration blocks determine which blocks available to all Moodle users. Just like the module settings, you can show, hide, and delete blocks. Two blocks have settings that can be changed: the courses block and the online users block.

Filters

Moodle filters are text filters that help Moodle analyze the text in a course. Each of the 10 filters has a specific function.

Glossary Auto-linking
    Enables the Glossary module to highlight glossary entries in the forums and resources.

Resource Names Auto-linking
    Works a bit like the glossary text filter. If you use the name of a resource (text files, uploaded file, or other resource) anywhere in a Moodle course, the word will be linked to back to the definition.

Wiki Page Auto-linking
    Links the names of wiki pages back to the original wiki page.

Activity Names Auto-linking
If you use the name of an activity elsewhere in the Moodle course, it will be linked back to the activity.

Algebra Notation
Converts text mathematics notation into mathematics notation. See *http://moodle.org/mod/forum/discuss.php?d=5402* for some good examples.

Word Censorship
Automatically deletes profanity in forum postings or other data from users.

Email Protection
Scrambles user emails in user profiles. Once the emails are scrambled, outside search engines and guests won't be able to see users' email addresses. This will protect your users from spammers and other attackers.

Multimedia Plugins
Associates uploaded multimedia files with the correct media players.

Multi-Language Content
Allows you to print characters in different languages. It recognizes different character sets and displays them appropriately.

TeX Notation
Another mathematics markup tool that allows you to use export TeX notation and display it correctly in Moodle.

The text filters also have two settings that will affect how the filters and your server work:

Text cache lifetime
Text filters can take a lot of processor power to analyze. If you have a large number of courses, the filters may slow your system. The text cache lifetime determines how often the filters run. If you set them to run too frequently, your system may slow down. If you set them to run too infrequently, analyzing new content will take too long and users will notice. You should experiment to find the correct amount of time for your server.

Filter uploaded files
Moodle can also apply filters to uploaded HTML and text files as, well as content entered directly into Moodle itself. Again, you will need to balance the increased load imposed by filtering more files against the added usefulness of applying filters more widely.

Backup

There's a saying in the computer industry: "There are two types of users, those who have lost data, and those that will." Eventually, a hard drive will fail or your database will collapse on your Moodle server and you will lose data. Fortunately, Moodle has an automated backup system that you can run on a nightly basis to export all the course materials for the entire site.

The backup tool in Moodle actually runs the same functions as an individual course backup. It simply runs automatically on all of the courses on the site at a designated time. It's a good idea to schedule backups for when your server isn't usually busy. Running the backup tool over all the courses can be processor-intensive, so you shouldn't run it when there are a lot of students trying to access the server.

There are two steps to setting up the backup. When you access the backup screen, the top section lets you set the types of material to be backed up. Again, the Moodle developers have done a good job of describing each setting. If you are running a nightly full-server backup (which I heartily recommend), I suggest you use the following settings:

Include Modules
> Set this to "Yes with user data" to preserve all student work for each course.

Users
> Set this to All. If you need to restore your Moodle server from a backup, you don't want to lose any accounts, even if they aren't associated with a current course.

User Files
> Set this to Yes as well. You want the restored server to look as much like the original as possible, so all user files should be restored as well.

Course Files
> Again, set this to Yes. You'll need to deal with a lot of angry teachers if they have to restore all of their course files after you restore the server.

Keep X Files
> This setting determines how many old backups will be saved. Set this as high as you can without taking up too much space on your server. If you need to restore a course a few days after you run the backup (as I've had to a few times), you'll be glad you have a few weeks' worth of data.

Once you've set the backup settings, you'll need to set a backup schedule at the bottom of the screen. To set the backup schedule:

1. Set Active to Yes. This turns on the automated backup system.

2. Click the days of the week to run the backup. I recommend backing up every day.

3. Set the execution time for the backup process. For most servers, early morning will be the best time.

4. Set the "Save to..." path. If you can, choose a backup path on another machine or on a different drive than the one Moodle is on. You don't want to lose your backups at the same time you lose your Moodle site if the drive fails.

5. Click Save Changes.

Once you've set up your backup sessions, Moodle will automatically create archives of all the courses on the server at the time you specified. Once the backup is complete, Moodle will send you an email describing the status of the backup.

Editor Settings

In this area, you can enable and customize the HTML editor. If users on your site cannot see the HTML editor when they use a supported browser, check this page to make sure the editor is enabled on your site. As of this writing, the HTML editor is *not* enabled by default.

Users

User management can be one of the most time-consuming jobs for a system administrator. As your system grows, the number of users who lose their password or have difficulty creating a new account grows as well. Fortunately, there are a few tools to help make the job of user management easier.

Authentication

In Chapter 2, we covered how to create a user account using email authentication. You created the account and Moodle sent you an email with a link to confirm your address. While this is an effective and efficient way to create new accounts, Moodle provides a number of other account-authentication methods as well. If you are in a university environment and have access to a university email or directory server, you can tell Moodle to use them to authenticate new user accounts instead.

External servers prevent users from creating multiple accounts and prevent people from outside the university accessing your server when they shouldn't.

Moodle provides the following account-authentication methods:

Email-based
> Email authentication is the default account-authentication method. With this method, users can create their own accounts. They then receive an email at the address they specified in their account profile to confirm their account.

Manual
> This method requires the administrator to manually create all user accounts. If you are using Moodle with a limited number of people or are synchronizing your database with a student-information system, use this method.

No authentication
> Users can create accounts with no external validation. Avoid using this option if you can.

Use FirstClass/POP/IMAP/LDAP/NNTP server
> These methods use an external server to check a user's username and password. If the name and password match the data on the mail server, an account with the same username and password is created on your Moodle site. Unfortunately, to avoid a performance bottleneck, Moodle doesn't check the password every time a user logs in. This means that if a user changes his email password on the external server, he will also need to change it in Moodle as well.

Use an external database
> This functions much like the other external account-authentication methods. The difference is that it uses a database of user data, such as the one in a student-information system. Once the username and password stored in the external database have been validated, you can tell Moodle to copy additional data. This is done by mapping fields at the bottom of the database-authentication screen. Each data field in the user profile has a text field next to it. Enter the name of the column in the external database that maps to the profile data field.

Add and Edit User Accounts

Once you've configured authentication, you'll want to be able to maintain users' accounts. Below the authentication link are three other tools: edit user accounts, add a new user, and upload users.

Edit user accounts
> Allows you to edit the user profile of anyone on the system. Most frequently, you will use this to reset user passwords if users are unable to log in.

Add a new user
> Allows you to create a new user account. You must use this if you've set authentication to manual and need to add a new user. The form to add a new user looks just like the new user profile page in Chapter 2 you used to create your own account.

Batch upload users
> Allows you to add a number of users at once using a text file. If you have a student-information system at your institution but are unable to connect directly to the database, you may be able to export user data from the database as a text file and upload it into Moodle.

The user data text file must follow a certain format. The first line contains the names of the column headers, such as username and password. Below the first line, each user record must be on one line and each column must be separated by commas.

The user text file must have the following columns: username, password, firstname, lastname, and email. These columns are optional: institution, department, city, country, lang, timezone, idnumber, icq, phone1, phone2, address, url, description, mailformat, maildisplay, htmleditor, and autosubscribe.

You can also enroll students in courses using the text file. In the column headings folder, list course1, course2, etc. Then in the data file, put the courses' short names in the appropriate columns.

So a properly formatted course-enrollment text file would look like:

```
username, password, firstname, lastname, email, course1
student1, abc123, Jane, Student, jstudent@mail.com, mdl101
student2, abc124, Joe, Student, joe@university.edu, mdl101
```

The course-enrollment feature can be a handy way to enroll students in a university-wide course on how to use Moodle and other university resources. I wouldn't use the user upload feature to enroll students in their regular courses, however. It's useful to keep the user data and the enrollment data separate so you don't have to constantly reload students to change their enrollments. In the next section, we'll explore some other ways to make sure students have access to their courses.

User Roles

Once users have accounts on the server, they need access to the courses they are taking. The first step is to enroll the user in a course. By default, students must enroll themselves in their courses. Fortunately, Moodle now includes some tools to automatically enroll students in the proper courses.

But users also need to have the proper permissions once they are enrolled. Teachers need to have teacher permissions so they can build their courses. This next section explores the tools you will use to manage user enrollment and roles.

Enrollments

The enrollment settings are similar to the authentication settings. You can choose between four methods of associating user data with the correct courses:

Internal Enrollment
　　The default enrollment method. It requires students to find their courses and enroll manually. They can enroll in any course unless it has an enrollment key (see Chapter 2 for details on setting a course-enrollment key). This is an easy method to use, but it isn't very secure.

External Databases
　　This method looks up enrollments in another database. You'll need to configure the login settings so Moodle can access the remote server. You'll then need to map the fields in Moodle to the fields in the remote database.

Flat File
　　Like the upload users tool, this method checks for an enrollment file at the specified location. If it finds a new file, it will process the data. The file should be structured

with the action, role, student number, and course's short name. There is a good example of a flat file in the flat-file instructions.

Paypal

The latest enrollment addition, PayPal enrollment allows you to set up an e-commerce system so students can pay to enroll in a course. If you are running a business selling Moodle-based courses, this is an easy way to enable students to use a credit card.

Enroll students

Enrolling students by hand is a tedious task. If you can, I recommend using one of the above methods to avoid this chore. But occasionally, a student or teacher will need access to a class that is not part of their regular schedule.

To enroll students in a course:

1.   Click the Enroll Students link.

2.   Find the course to which you want to add students. Click the link for that course.

3.   Once in the course, click on the Students link in the course Administration panel.

4.   Find the name of the student you want to add to the course and select it.

5.   Click the left arrow to move the name to the course-enrollment box.

Of course, unless there is a good reason for you as system administrator to enroll students in a course, it's usually better to give leave the responsibility of maintaining their course rolls to the teachers.

Assign Teachers, Creators, and Admins

As the system administrator, you are also responsible for adding teachers, course creators, and other system administrators. Assigning teachers to their courses is critical (unless you are using an alternative enrollment method). Otherwise, teachers will never be able to access their courses. Course creators can create courses they teach themselves, which is one way to overcome this limitation.

To add a teacher to a course:

1.   Click Assign Teacher in the course Administration panel.

2.   You will then see the course category list. Click on the category that includes the course you need.

3.   Find the course that needs a teacher. Click on the teacher icon to the right of the course name.

4.   Find the course teacher in the list of system users and click Add Teacher.

The only tricky step to adding teachers is identifying the correct icon. As of this writing, the face icon is second from the left.

The "assign course creators" link allows you to identify specific users as being authorized to create and teach their own courses. If you are managing a small Moodle system, this is not a bad way to go. If you are administering a small Moodle installation for your department, then enabling your colleagues to create their own courses removes you as a potential bottleneck. If the other teachers are enabled to create their own courses, they may also take more ownership in the system as a whole.

If you are running a university-wide server, however, I do not recommend using this extensively. On a large installation, it can become difficult to track who is creating legitimate courses and who is abusing the system. A large number of bogus courses will clutter your system and could lead to performance slowdowns.

To enable course creators:

1. Click on the Assign Creators link in the Site Administration panel.
2. In the right column, select the names of the new creators.
3. Click the left arrow to add them to the creators column.

Once someone has been designated as a course creator, they can add their own courses and create new courses using the restore procedure.

System administrators have unlimited authority on their Moodle server. You should limit the number of people with administrator privileges to a bare minimum. A lot of people with administrator access is a recipe for disaster since they can add accounts and courses and change site variables at will.

To assign system admins:

1. Click on the Assign Admins link in the Site Administration panel.
2. In the right column, select the names of the new administrators.
3. Click the left arrow to add them to the admin column.

Courses

The system administrator and course creators are also responsible for adding courses to Moodle. Currently, there isn't yet a way to automatically create courses, though I suspect this will be added soon. So for the time being, you will need to manually create courses for your teachers.

Courses can be organized by course category, and each course can be listed in only one category. It's up to you to define the categories.

Creating Course Categories

By default, there is only one Moodle category: Miscellaneous. While you are certainly free to put all your classes in the miscellaneous category, your users will find it easier to find their classes if they are organized in descriptive categories.

Most people organize their courses by department and college or by topic. Be sure to test your organizational scheme with a few users before entering a large number of courses.

Fortunately, adding categories is very simple:

1. From the administration area, click Courses.

2. You will then see the course categories page. At the top of the page is a text area and an "Add new category" button. Type the name of your new category in the text area and click the button.

You now have a new course category.

Creating Courses

Once you set up a few course categories, you are ready to create a course.

To create a course:

1. From the administration area, click Courses.

2. In the course category page, select the category for the new course.

3. In the courses list for the category, click "Add a new course" at the bottom of the page.

4. You will then see the course settings page for the new course. Consult Chapter 2 for details on the course settings. Once you've entered the course settings, select Save Changes at the bottom of the page.

5. You will then see the Add Teacher page. Find the teacher for the course and click the Add Teacher link.

Once you've added the course, the teacher will be able to add content and students will be able to enroll.

Logs

Finally, as the administrator, you have access to user activity logs for the entire site. You can select to view logs based on course, user, date, and activity. Unfortunately, there currently isn't a way to see aggregate logs.

One of the nicest tools in the logs area is the View Live Logs. This is a continually refreshed page that displays all user activity for the past hour. I use it to gauge server load and to get a snapshot of how students and teachers are using the system. Obviously, I could use the regular logs to do this as well, but I like the excitement of live viewing.

Index

About the Author

Jason Cole is a product development manager at The Open University in the UK, where he works on the development of the OU's course management system. Prior to joining the OU, he was the academic technology manager at San Francisco State University, where he initiated the process of upgrading the university from Blackboard to Moodle.

A member of the Moodle community, he has developed a student data integration tool for the system and contributed to discussions regarding a document management system and object model for Version 2.0. Jason earned a Ph.D. in educational technology from the University of Northern Colorado.

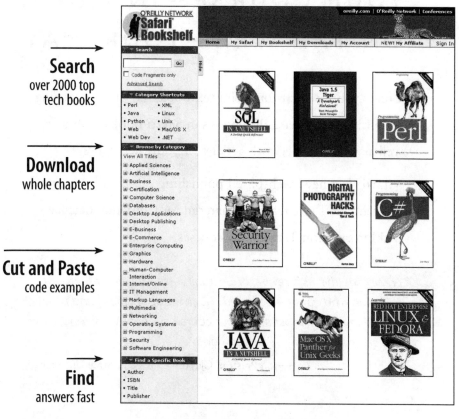